...guidance from friends
...e book is no exception.
...be made of the effects of
... Hyde Park-Kenwood came
...d both provided continuing and
...a critical stage Paula O'Neill Bourne
... the dint of unstinting hard work. As raw
mat... ...nto working papers, reactions, evaluations
and s... ...rom Basil Zimmer, William N. Kinnard, Jr.,
Stephen ... ...er, John C. Melaniphy, Jr., Robert B. McKersie,
George S. ...ey, Robert Venning, John H. Makin, Muriel Beadle,
Howard Cayton, Don Patch, James E. Victory, E. Lally, O. Badal, Dean
Swartzel and Walter Kloetzli. Gerald F. Pyle drew the maps.

And throughout the process, Leona Cochran typed, cut, pasted and
retyped. Katherine Smith read proof and prepared the index. To each
we are indebted.

None of their help and guidance would have led to productive research
without the ultimate contribution of the businessmen of Hyde Park-
Kenwood, however. Their experiences with renewal — happy and otherwise — stimulated this study and their willingness to talk with us at
length and respond to sensitive and often personal questions provided
the raw materials. In particular, Walker Sandbach and Everett Ramsey
were most helpful. The other businessmen we worked with are too
numerous to name individually, but to each we express our profound
gratitude.

The manuscript of which this book is the final version was completed
in August, 1967.

BJLB, August, 1968.

iii

CONTENTS

LIST OF TABLES

LIST OF FIGURES

LIST OF PLATES

. . . nothing amuses more harmlessly
than computation, and nothing
is more often applicable to . . .
speculative inquiries. A
thousand stories which the
ignorant tell, and believe,
die away at once when the
computist takes them in his grip.

Samuel Johnson

SUMMARY

The primary objective of this study was to evaluate the assertion that the liquidation rate of small businesses dislocated by urban renewal is excessive. The principal analytic conclusion is that, in the aggregate, the liquidation rate is **not,** but that displacement followed by liquidation affects individual businesses differentially, with benefits to some and to the disadvantage of others.

These findings are based upon detailed analysis undertaken in the Hyde Park-Kenwood community of the City of Chicago, where three renewal projects sought to combat encroaching blight perceived to be penetrating the community along its commercial strips. Six hundred and forty-one businesses were displaced by these projects. Of these 207 liquidated upon dislocation, 201 have since gone out of business, and 233 are still in operation. Of the 233 only 83 remain in Hyde Park-Kenwood; of 61 businesses operating in three new business centers constructed in the clearance areas (The New Hyde Park Shopping Center, Kimbark Plaza and Harper Court) only 23 are displacees. Altogether, during the renewal period, the number of commercial premises and offices available in the community decreased from 2200 to 700, and the number of operating businesses from 1490 to approximately 700. In all, in this period, 3361 businesses operated for some time in the community, many only very briefly — 56 per cent for three years or less.

The first two projects, "Hyde Park A and B," in which clearance extended from 1955 through 1959, provided little or no compensation to the displaced businesses. In fact, it was the plight of many of these displacees that led to new federal legislation providing minimum types of compensation, as a result of the actions of Hyde Park's Senator and Congressman. Many of the early displacees originally were among the strongest supporters of the renewal projects, but support turned into disillusionment when it was found that no compensation was available, access to a new shopping center was very unlikely, a staging plan for clearance and redevelopment was not to be executed, and time-delays and uncertainties mounted. When a developer was chosen to construct the New Hyde Park Shopping Center in the Hyde Park clearance area, he preferred AAA tenants to ensure his own financing, and only determined community pressure and special financial arrangements enabled the Hyde Park Coop to be included in the center. Other displacees fared poorly, and only three other neighborhood businesses ultimately found new locations in the center.

The disappointed expectations of merchants seeking access to the original center led the most solvent of the 55th Street displacees to develop Kimbark Plaza on land cleared by the later Hyde Park-Kenwood renewal program. This center broke new ground in that it was created entirely by a redevelopment corporation of displacees, aided by special disposition provisions attached to the land, and specially arranged loans both on the market and from the Small Business Administration. However, this type of redevelopment and relocation is only possible for the most solvent, capable and enterprising businessmen, with the greatest potentiality for raising the necessary capital, with good organization and careful, independent pre-planning.

For the marginal low-volume merchant, especially one offering old-fashioned services and products or involved in the arts and crafts, survival is the paramount issue, for there is no prospect of access to new centers like the New Hyde Park Center or Kimbark Plaza. The loss of neighborhood businesses of this type became quite apparent in Hyde Park by the early 1960s, and the community responded by building Harper Court. Again, special disposition provisions had to be attached to the sale of the land. Members of the community and The University of Chicago subscribed to low-yield debentures, and along with arranging low-interest SBA loans, it was possible to develop a center in which rents were 22 per cent less than would have been charged if conventional financing had been used. Thus it became feasible for small merchants to enter the center. Harper Court now houses 25 small businesses, many dealing in the arts and crafts. However, only six of the original tenants were displacees. The project has contributed to the revitalization of adjacent blocks along the community's remaining shopping street, but like the other new centers, is facing substantial problems of increased vandalism, and unlike the others (but as probably befits the kinds of businesses occupying it) has experienced substantial turnover of tenants already.

The 56.8 per cent decline in numbers of businesses operating in Hyde Park-Kenwood in the period 1953-1966 compares with 55.6 per cent in the adjacent low-income community of Oakland, 28.8 per cent in Woodlawn, which experienced transition from middle- to low-income status in the period, and 16.2 per cent in what was at that time the "stable" middle-income community of South Shore. But in each case, these changes were almost exactly what might have been expected to happen on the basis of population and income shifts that altered the community markets in the face of ongoing technological change in retailing. In Hyde Park, of course, the renewal projects were responsible for the substantial changes in market conditions that faced the community's businessmen.

Significantly, the liquidation rate of businesses in Hyde Park-Kenwood only rose to the level of that in the adjacent low-income Woodlawn and Oakland communities at the height of renewal clearance, with low compensatory lags between the two main phases of clearance. Life-spans of businesses, in effect, were no different than might have been predicted from the socio-economic status of Hyde Park, except in the case of business types occupying the commercial ribbons which it was the goal of the renewal project to eliminate.

In the aggregate one of the principal conclusions of the analytic parts of this study is therefore that the liquidation rate in Hyde Park-Kenwood was not excessive. Firstly, it was not as high as it might have become if renewal had not taken place and Hyde Park had experienced the same transition as Woodlawn. Secondly, the substantial decline in the number of businesses operating in the community was accomplished by clearance of land that effectively reduced the entry-rate of new businesses rather than the exit-rate of old. Viewed dispassionately, dislocation at worst hastened the inevitable for a few.

But regardless of the issue of survival, displacement had two ancillary effects on individual businesses, within the aggregate: (a) it increased "natural" inequities among businesses in the same line, and (b) by shortening the life-spans of those kinds of businesses that only find the space they need at rentals they can afford in commercial ribbons, it created inequities between businesses in different lines. Thus, *from the viewpoint of the individual businessmen, renewal did introduce certain costs, even if the change in costs did not alter liquidation experience in the aggregate. And regardless of whether or not they were adversely affected, most businessmen believed that they would have been better off if renewal had not taken place—that they had incurred costs which were inadequately compensated.* For in contrast to chain store executives, who articulated the alternatives more dispassionately, none of the small businessmen considered that if renewal had not taken place there would still have been changes in the market and that they most likely would, as a result, have experienced serious and continuing competitive pressures. These "natural" changes in the market would have operated, of course, on businesses within lines, but would have been unlikely to create the same inequities between lines.

Most displacees felt that the aid received was inadequate, the compensation insufficient, and that when payments were made they were often too late to help. Along with neighborhood merchants not displaced, but with markets and incomes affected by clearance, they felt the most serious problem to be the uncompensated loss of patronage.

These findings are quite consistent with other studies in other parts of the U.S. All show negative impacts to be greatest on smaller firms with elderly owner-managers, having or requiring small capitalization, in which business operations require few specialized skills, and the offerings are ubiquitous goods and services. Many of the firms liquidating are marginal, even sub-marginal, surviving by paying less-than-going rentals in the substandard properties generally cleared. But among the liquidations are individual businesses which might have been salvable by alternative redevelopment concepts, better information, more or better assistance, and proper compensation. It is in these cases that changed administrative procedures, new legislative provision, or changed renewal concepts will be required.

The cluster of new provisions emerging from legislation in 1964 and 1965 signaled the beginning of a new period of needed experiment and innovation in meeting the problems of commercial relocation. The threshold of this new era was the Housing Act of 1964, lauded as "a significant advance in the development of this nation's programs to eliminate blight and to intelligently renew our cities . . ."[1] Perhaps its primary claim to significance lies in its unprecedented efforts to protect "little people,"[2] especially the small businessman. Two important instruments of relocation assistance, displacement payments and counselling services, originated in the 1964 Act. Another device, the SBA loan, was significantly expanded to include new construction.

---

1 Melvin Stein, "The Housing Act of 1964: Urban Renewal," *New York Law Forum,* Vol. 11 (Spring, 1965), p. 1.
2 *Ibid.*

Much of the changed concept of "just compensation" evidenced by this new legislation stemmed from experience in Hyde Park. The opportunity now exists to make additional progress, based upon other aspects of the Hyde Park-Kenwood experience.

In particular, we recommend on the basis of the study:

(1) Extension of the Small Business Displacement Payment concept of remuneration for loss of patronage and goodwill to *all* businesses located in a designated *project impact area,* whether displaced or not, according to an equitable compensation schedule for income lost as a result of clearance of markets and/or a period out of business due to dislocation.

(2) Speeding of claim processing and of payments so that monies due a displaced firm are available at the greatest time of need, *before* and *during* dislocation, rather than months afterwards.

(3) More attention to be paid to providing every businessman with complete information on what will happen to him, when, what he must do, and what compensation will be available to him and at what time. Similar information, with *guarantees* where necessary, should be provided to the private lending institutions to which the businessman may also turn.

(4) Rethinking of the development criteria that prevent many kinds of businesses from gaining access to a renewal area after redevelopment. Evidently, HUD needs to provide Local Public Agencies with a set of *standards and guidelines for commercial redevelopment* that are compatible with the array of retail and service needs of the redeveloped community.

Above all, the community contemplating urban renewal should consider the welfare of displaced merchants to be just as important as the relocation of displaced families. While this obviously cannot extend to a guarantee of profitable operations in the future, it should certainly include just compensation of losses and inequities directly attributable to the renewal project. Such is the requirement of socially-responsible public intervention.

INTRODUCTION

. . . the problem posed

Plate 1

LAKE PARK AVENUE LOOKING SOUTHEAST FROM THE ILLINOIS
CENTRAL TRACKS IN MARCH, 1951. *Photo provided by Department of
Urban Renewal, City of Chicago.*

CHAPTER ONE

Background to The Liquidation Problem

In the past decade and a half, over 60,000 small businesses have been dislocated by over 1,000 urban renewal projects in more than 500 cities. Of the businesses dislocated, close to 20,000 went out of business upon displacement, a liquidation rate of thirty-three per cent.[1] A growing literature holds that this rate is excessive.[2] In this book we evaluate this assertion.

INCIDENCE AND MAGNITUDE OF BUSINESS DISPLACEMENT BY URBAN RENEWAL

The earliest urban renewal projects displacing small business followed the 1949 Housing Act, but it was particularly after the enactments of 1954 that projects involving business displacement spread across the country. The latter act was the first to authorize expenditures for projects not primarily residential in intent, and it also introduced community-wide approaches to urban renewal that contrasted with the earlier projects involving total clearance of primarily residential areas.

---

1 The source of this information is a special tabulation, through mid-1966, provided by the Department of Housing and Urban Development.
By "small business" we mean enterprises that
    (1) are businesses in that they involve all or most of the business functions and decisions concerning marketing, financing and management; and
    (2) do not exceed a size which permits personalized management in the hands of one or a few executives, as opposed to institutionalized management characteristic of larger enterprises.
Small business, thus defined, is self-initiated, largely self-financed, and self-managed. See Edward D. Hollander and others, *The Future of Small Business.* New York: Frederick A. Praeger, Publishers, 1967, pp. 4-5.
"Liquidation" is used in the study to refer to formal actions to liquidate, and other discontinuances including those firms which simply disappear.
The figure of 20,000 displacees liquidating includes 12,000 known liquidations for projects with adequate record-keeping, and an estimate using the mean liquidation rate for known projects applied to the workload of the projects which completed their displacements before 1960.
2 For example, in 1964 William N. Kinnard, Jr., one of the first professionals to undertake a serious study of the liquidation problem, made the following statement to the Select Sub-Committee on Real Property Acquisition, Committee on Public Works, U.S. House of Representatives: ". . . the evidence is irrefutable that forced dislocation is associated with greatly increased discontinuance rates among affected businesses."

1

By 1963, 39,000 businesses had been displaced. In 1964 the number had risen to 49,000,[1] and by mid-1966 it was 60,000. By 1972 the figure is expected to be between 100,000 and 120,000.[2]

Many of the first projects developed were located in the largest central cities of the northeastern and midwestern industrial belt states. Only later did urban renewal take place in the southern border states, the southeast and the northern plains. The west and the southwest lagged far behind.

In each region, the largest cities developed renewal projects first, followed in order by successively smaller places. However small cities located close to larger centers which had already initiated renewal activity tended to develop projects at an earlier date than more isolated cities of comparable size. By the end of 1966 most cities with populations exceeding 50,000 had at least one renewal project involving small business displacement, but below that size the proportion of urban centers participating in the program declined very rapidly.

The incidence of projects and the relative expenditures of funds parallel the diffusion process. The regions that adopted renewal programs earliest now have the great proportion of participating communities. Cities with populations exceeding 250,000 account for less than ten per cent of participating communities, but more than twenty-five per cent of all projects, whereas communities with populations of less than 25,000 represent almost one-half of the participating localities, one-quarter of the projects, but only one-tenth of the federal funds.[3]

Displacement of small merchants in large cities of the industrial belt is especially high. Eight cities account for one-third of

---

1 U.S. Housing and Home Finance Agency, Urban Renewal Administration, *Urban Renewal Relocation of Business Concerns and Nonprofit Associations; a fact sheet.* Washington, August 1965, p.2. Cited hereafter as U.R.A. Fact Sheet.

2 W. Kinnard and Z. Malinowski, *The Impact of Dislocation from Urban Renewal Areas on Small Business.* Connecticut: The University of Connecticut, 1960 p. 86. Also U.S. Advisory Commission on Intergovernmental Relations, *Relocation: Unequal Treatment of People and Businesses Displaced by Governments,* Report A-26. Washington, D.C.: Government Printing Office, 1964 (Cited hereafter as *U.S. Advisory Commission*).

3 The figures refer to all renewal projects, not simply those communities with projects involving small business displacement, where there is even more marked concentration in larger urban places. Harriet Saperstein, "The Dislocation of Small Business: Elmwood 1," *Studies in Change and Renewal in an Urban Community,* ed. Charles Lebeaux and Eleanor Wolf. Detroit: Wayne State University, 1965, Vol. 1, Part IV, p. 4. Basil G. Zimmer, *Rebuilding Cities.* Chicago: Quadrangle Books, 1964, p. 10.

all displacees (19,878), but involve only sixteen per cent of the projects (158), as follows: New York City, 6,772 displacees from 39 projects; Chicago, 2,866–30; Philadelphia, 2,492–36; Boston, 2,094–9; Pittsburgh, 1,890–6; Detroit, 1,441–15; Baltimore, 1,291–16; Washington, D.C., 1,032–7.[1] These are, of course, among the nation's oldest cities, and they each have large deteriorating inner city areas badly in need of renewal.

VARIATIONS IN LIQUIDATION RATES

Individual projects vary substantially in the number of businesses they displace[2] and in the number of displacees who liquidate upon dislocation. If these two figures are used to plot each urban renewal project in the United States involving displacement of small businesses in a graph, Figure 1.1 results. The number of businesses discontinuing operations is scaled on the ordinate, and the number of businesses displaced on the abscissa. Each project appears as a dot. To the left of the ordinate, a frequency polygon shows the distribution of projects by numbers of displacees liquidating. Beneath the abscissa, a second polygon shows the distribution of projects by numbers of businesses displaced. Because many of the earliest projects were not required to keep records of liquidations, a special box along the abscissa simply records the project size.

Both axes in the graph are arranged logarithmically. This permits the liquidation rates for projects to be read off along parallel lines extending upwards to the right at an angle of 45°.[3] Additionally, another frequency polygon can be drawn showing distribution of projects by their liquidation rate. The polygon is approximately log-normal in shape, with a mode of 25 per cent, a median of 29 per cent, and a mean of 33 per cent. *On the average, one in every three businesses displaced by an urban*

---

1 This information comes from special tabulations provided by HUD. For earlier data, see U.S. Congress, Subcommittee Number Five of the Select Committee on Small Business, *Hearing, Small Business Problems in Urban Areas*, Vol. 11, 89th Cong., 1st. Sess., 1965, pp. A116-A129. (Cited hereafter as *Hearings, Chicago*).
2 "Project workload" in federalese.
3 Each such line on double-logarithmic paper shows a constant rate, so for example the line representing 10 per cent liquidation rate joins up projects with 1 liquidation among 10 displacees, 2 among 20, 5 among 50, 10 among 100, etc.

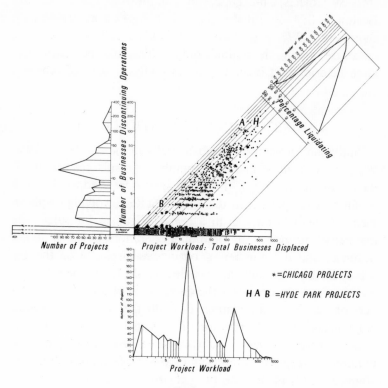

Figure 1.1
BUSINESSES DISPLACED BY URBAN RENEWAL
PROJECTS IN THE U.S. COMPARED
WITH LIQUIDATION RATES OF DISPLACEES.

renewal project in the United States liquidates upon displacement.

THE PROBLEM POSED

The magnitude of the liquidation rate has provided a base for
criticism by the opponents of urban renewal. ". . . we have
allowed the urban renewal law to be used in such a way that it
literally destroys thousands of small businesses yearly" says one

outspoken critic.[1] Is the rate excessive? This is the problem addressed in Part I of this study by trying to determine in several case studies (a) whether the rate differs significantly from what it might have been under the business conditions likely to have prevailed in the study areas if urban renewal had not been undertaken, and (b) whether the relative competitive position of individual businesses was changed by the renewal process.[2] Can the rate be reduced? In part, an answer to this question resides in renewal policy, which is the focus of Part II of the book.

THE HYDE PARK-KENWOOD CASE

Thirty Chicago projects, shown by stars and the letters A, B and H in Figure 1.1 had much the same range of liquidation experience as other projects in the nation. In all, they displaced 2,866 businesses, of which 900 discontinued operations (Table 1.1 and Figure 1.2, which come from a special tabulation provided by HUD). The 900 liquidations represent in turn, ten per cent of the decline in numbers of retail and service businesses in Chicago in the same period (see Chapter 3).

Three projects in Chicago's Hyde Park-Kenwood community, Hyde Park A and B, and the Hyde Park-Kenwood project (A, B and H in Figure 1.1) accounted for almost a quarter of these displacements and liquidations in Chicago. In all, the three projects, the particular concern of this study, displaced 641 businesses, 207 of which liquidated. The three projects therefore represent one per cent of the nation's displacement and liquidation experience to date.

The projects are of interest for several reasons. According to one of the authors of the projects, Julian H. Levi, Executive-Director of the South East Chicago Commission, "The loss [along 55th Street] is just as widespread as if a tornado were to

---

1 Testimony of Mrs. Florence Scala. *Hearings, Chicago*, p. 169.
2 Kinnard has pointed out the need for dispassionate research between the extremes of those who cry that the city's economic base is being decimated unnecessarily, to those who say that the public good is being saved by eliminating undesirable, unproductive businesses. William N. Kinnard, Jr., *The Mythology of Business Displacement in Urban Renewal—and in Other Public Improvement Programs*, Institute of Urban Research, University of Connecticut, 1964.

TABLE 1.1 STATUS OF CHICAGO RENEWAL PROJECTS INVOLVING BUSINESS DISPLACEMENT AT THE END OF 1966

Project	Total Workload[a]	Discontinued Operations[b]	Remaining on Site	Business Begun[c]	Relocation Completed	Relocation Payments Completed
Lake Meadows	180	*		4911	5412	
West Central Industry	57	*		5209	5803	5803
Project Area 6A	36	8		5506		
Michael Reese	58	*		5507	5803	5906
Hyde Park A	190	*		5601	5910	6002
Hyde Park B	4	*		5512	5801	5801
Hyde Park-Kenwood	447	156		5912		
Harrison-Halsted	197	46		5901		
Near West Side	131	12	32	6403		
13th and Blue Island	9	*		5906	5906	5906
Washington-Hermitage	16	4		5907	6108	6303
Roosevelt-Clinton	119	22		5901	6402	6503
Segment 6-D	32	6		5904	6301	
State-Pershing	10	*		6103	6201	6201
State-51st Street	11	*		6001	6201	6201
69th and Stewart	29	6		5910	6603	
North-LaSalle	235	117		5812		
Englewood	124	16	21	6403		
25th-South Parkway	48	5	2	6110		
Pershing-Cottage Grove	42	5	19			
Noble-Division	62	15	5	6406		
Project 6B-South Central	48	*		5804	5908	6204
Lincoln Park No. 1	36	2	31	6604		
Roosevelt-Blue Island	277	51		6209	6512	
Congress-Racine	153	19	57	6311		
Project 6C	77	13		6105		
Illinois Institute of Technology	51	*		5803	6001	6204
Lake Street-California Avenue	14	3		5810	6603	6001
Lake-Maplewood	69	13	2	5901	6303	6303
37th-Cottage Grove	104	28	1	6006	6212	6303
TOTAL	2866					

* Record not kept, or unreported

a Number of businesses formally displaced

b 539 known discontinuances, plus 360 estimated for the projects without reporting, make up the 900 number used elsewhere in this study

c By year and month, e.g., 4911 is 1949, 11th month (November)

Figure 1.2

BUSINESS DISPLACEMENT BY URBAN RENEWAL PROJECTS IN CHICAGO.

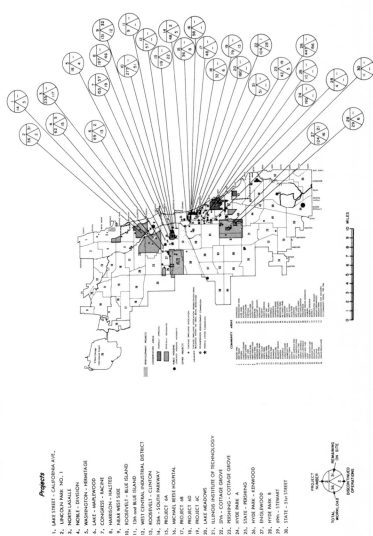

have devastated a half mile of street,"[1] an impression reiterated by other studies in other communities, so that an examination as to whether or not the liquidation rate was excessive is not inappropriate. In many ways, the Hyde Park projects broke new ground. Experience in them played a major role in changing compensation provisions for displacees. Commercial redevelopment included pioneering ventures with new kinds of business centers, Kimbark Plaza and Harper Court. Yet there are more lessons to be learned from what happened in Hyde Park-Kenwood, and these are the basis of further changes in public policy recommended in the last chapter.

---

1 Testimony of Julian H. Levi, Hearings of Select Committee on Small Business, House of Representatives, *Urban Renewal Projects and Slum Clearance*. Washington, D.C.: U.S. Government Printing Office, 1956, p. 15. The statement was made in the context of an appeal for federal assistance to the displaced merchants.

PART I

THE HYDE PARK – KENWOOD CASE

. . . history of commercial redevelopment
. . . effects of displacement
. . . comparative analysis of mortality
  experience
. . . businessmen's feelings about the
  renewal process

Plate 2

AERIAL VIEW OF HYDE PARK LOOKING NORTHEAST IN JUNE,
1964. *Photo taken by Chicago Aerial Survey, and courtesy The University of Chicago.*

CHAPTER TWO

History of Commercial Renewal
In Hyde Park-Kenwood

Hyde Park and Kenwood, middle-aged communities within the city of Chicago, began to show a pattern of disrepair and disuse in the postwar era. They also experienced considerable racial change in the decade from 1945 to 1955. The possibility that the powerful forces of age and disrepair and increasing rates of crime and delinquency would lead to complete racial succession and to irreparable deterioration of the physical and social qualities of the communities' environment led to determined efforts at counteraction. Unlike most other communities in similar circumstances, Hyde Park is the location of a large private university, The University of Chicago, which has a strong attachment to the community and which was willing to marshal its resources of talent and money for the protection of itself and its community.

The University of Chicago and its surrounding community of educated people, faced with the threat of disturbances by accelerating population change and consequent transformation of their neighborhood, reacted to the problem with a program of urban renewal and conservation which had three major objectives:

(1) To provide an environment suitable to a person who works at the University or who wants to live in a pleasant community near a university; (2) to obtain a community which is open to residents on the basis of free choice, meaning the freedom for anyone who can afford the cost of accommodations to move in; (3) to obtain an integrated community.[1]

Among the features of the program were substantial clearance of the community's older commercial ribbons and the construction of three new shopping centers.

---

[1] Interview with Jack Meltzer, former Director of Planning, University of Chicago Planning Unit, August, 1966.

11

THE THREAT PERCEIVED: CREEPING BLIGHT

Fears for the future of the community were first articulated in a 1951 *Report to the Community* by the Hyde Park-Kenwood Community Conference.[1] The report concluded:

". . . the Hyde Park-Kenwood community is becoming an island surrounded by blighted and near-blighted areas; its very foundation as a desirable residential community is being threatened . . . What, exactly, is blight?

Condition of Buildings

Defective design and character of building
Faulty interior arrangement
Over-age buildings, buildings in need of major repair or unfit for use
Significant degree of fire hazard
Obsolescence because of poor location, design, or mixed use

Conditions Relative to the People

High density of population
Overcrowding of dwelling units, inadequate sanitary facilities
Inadequate recreation facilities
Excessive juvenile delinquency and crime rates
Higher incidence of infant mortality, tuberculosis, other diseases
Poor mental health — suicide, prejudice

Conditions Relative to Land and Public Utilities

Uneconomic land shapes and sizes
Inadequate public utility services
Disproportionate expenditure for police and fire protection and other
    public services
Lack of building and maintenance of utilities

Conditions Relative to Value

Impairment of tax structure due to depreciated property values
Inadequate tax receipts in relation to service costs
Disproportionate number of tax foreclosures
    Some people believe blight is the result of the movement of minority groups into a community; the facts are otherwise . . . it is the eastern section of Hyde Park-Kenwood — where neither Negroes nor Orientals have ever lived in large numbers—in which three is the greatest concentration of deteriorated structures. One important reason: this is the area which was settled first and which has, therefore, the largest number of old buildings.
    A number of factors are contributing to incipient blight in Hyde Park-Kenwood:
    1. There are feelings of insecurity about the future, because of fear

---

1 Table 7.1 summarizes the renewal chronology in Hyde Park-Kenwood.

that property values will decline. This fear is based largely on the false theory that any movement of Negroes into an area leads to the creation of a slum.

2. In both Hyde Park and Kenwood there are some aged tenement buildings, conspicuous because of their overcrowding, dirt and disorder. Unless these conditions are remedied, they will hasten the spread of blight.

3. Automobile ownership has risen so rapidly that lack of parking space and general street congestion have become major problems.

4. The area is now crowded, and its facilities are beginning to be overtaxed. City services are not keeping pace with the growing population. There is inadequate school plant, garbage collection, police and fire protection, and street cleaning, repair and lighting. Though a few buildings are now under construction, continued overtaxing of facilities will tend to discourage investment in new buildings."[1]

A series of neighborhood crimes, following on the heels of this report, sparked community action. On March 17, 1952 nearly 2,000 local residents gathered at a University of Chicago lecture hall to join together for the first time the forces of University power and community interest for the purpose of fighting community decline. Although the Hyde Park-Kenwood Community Conference had been established in 1949 and faculty members of the University had recommended to the administration of the University action preventing decline of the neighborhood, the meeting in 1952 was a clear point of beginning for urban renewal in Hyde Park.

At the general community meeting of March, 1952, a committee of five community leaders was selected to study the question of community improvement and to submit recommendations to the residents. Lawrence Kimpton, who had been appointed Chancellor of the University of Chicago in 1951, was chairman of the Committee of Five. Kimpton was prepared to act quickly against the increased number of local crimes, with the public support created by unification of community interests.

Another community meeting was held in May, at which time the Committee of Five presented their recommendation calling for concerted community effort to fight against the increase of crime and to check the growing number of illegal conversions in old houses and apartment buildings. These two objectives, reduction in crime and prevention of illegal conversions, were

---

1 Quoted directly from the *Report to the Community*, 1951.

strong points of general community sentiment; there were virtually no individual interests opposed to the objectives. The Committee of Five recommended that a commission, to be known as the South East Chicago Commission (SECC), be established for the specific purpose of aiding the community in achieving its objectives, through the employment of a full time staff financed by the University of Chicago. In addition, the Committee recommended that the SECC consider action along certain other routes, including urban renewal.

In the fall of 1952, Julian Levi, a corporation lawyer whose brother was a University faculty member and administrator,[1] and who had a long family connection with the University, was appointed Executive Director of SECC. Under Levi's direction, the SECC used the power of University influence in mortgage and insurance operations to control undesirable real estate operations. Through its financial influence, such as hints of withdrawal of deposits or replacement of insurance by the University, the SECC was able to persuade mortgage and insurance companies to restrain undesirable activities in the community. In a typical case against an undesirable bar or tavern, locus of criminal residents, or case of residential crowding, the cancellation of insurance coverage would lead to a foreclosure of mortgage and the substitution of more desirable ownership.

A second stage in the urban renewal process came in 1953-1954. A successful request to the Field Foundation for funds made $100,000 available to the University for planning the changes desired in the community. Jack Meltzer was appointed chief planner of the University Planning Unit established with the Field Foundation grant. The unit moved quickly. By July 1954, under the newly amended Federal Housing Act of 1954, the first two renewal projects, called "Hyde Park A and B," had been fully approved. Demolition began in 1955. Further planning continued, and resulted in approval of the Hyde Park-Kenwood Urban Renewal Plan for the complete community in 1958.

---

1 Edward H. Levi was recently appointed President of the University to succeed George Wells Beadle in 1968.

COMMERCIAL BLIGHT: PRELUDE TO RENEWAL

There was a clear association in the community's mind between its commercial ribbons and incipient blight, although the deleterious features were as often associated with the walk-up apartments, boarding houses and hotels, and with increasing industrial usage, as they were with retail occupants and service establishments found in them:

". . . At present, Lake Park Avenue, parts of Harper Avenue, Cottage Grove Avenue and 47th Street form a band around our area from which blight may spread inward. Pockets of deterioration dot the area, particularly in Hyde Park, and 55th Street shows the effects of overcrowding and inadequate maintenance. A number of conversions into rooming houses and cramped light-housekeeping quarters, together with the encroachment of small factories, are taking place in this relatively narrow band of blight.

There is also evidence of an inward movement of near-blight along certain parts of Drexel, Ingleside and Maryland, the streets closest to Cottage Grove, and along Blackstone and Dorchester, adjacent to Lake Park and Harper. Here a number of large apartments and single family homes have been converted into small, overcrowded kitchenettes, share-bath units. Because of the excessive wear and tear now put on them, these will be our tenements of 10 to 20 years hence."[1]

". . . The main commercial and shopping facilities of the community are located in "string" fashion on seven through streets.

East-West Streets
47th Street — The whole length
51st Street — Only within 3 blocks of the I.C.
53rd Street — Nine blocks
55th Street — The whole length
57th Street — Only four blocks

North-South Streets
Lake Park — Between 51st and 57th Streets
Cottage Grove — Near 51st and 55th Intersections

The major part of the structures on these streets are mixed commercial and residential in use. Usually the ground floor fronting the street is used as a shop while the second and third floors contain apartments.

This "string" layout has several disadvantages . . ."[2]

In contrast to the predominantly residential use of the community, ranging from the mansions of South Kenwood to the

1 *Report to Community, op. cit.*
2 *Ibid.*

Plate 3
5200 BLOCK OF LAKE PARK AVENUE PRIOR TO CLEARANCE.
Photo provided by Department of Urban Renewal, City of Chicago.

comfortable old apartments and frame houses of central Hyde
Park to the slums of the western edge, the principal thoroughfares were lined solidly with street-level commercial space,
usually with cheap walk-up flats or offices above (Figure 2.1).
Eighty-five per cent of the property strung along these "strips"
had been built before 1905.[1] Indeed nearly all of the structures
along Lake Park Avenue and the eastern six blocks of 55th
Street dated either from the Columbian Exposition of 1893 or
earlier (Figure 2.2). And, like all older commercial areas in the
central city, there was a progressive accumulation of surplus
commercial property and store and office vacancies.[2]

A picture of the state of business along these streets is provided by a 1956 study conducted by the Real Estate Research
Corporation under contract with the University of Chicago.

1 Computed from map contained in "Proposed Ordinance to the City Council" (Committee on Planning and Housing Pamphlet No. 21, City of Chicago, October 22, 1958)
p. 44. Computation and all subsequent discussion refers to both sides of 55th Street and
Lake Park Avenue, the *east* side of Cottage Grove, and the *south* side of 47th Street.
2 Brian J. L. Berry, *Commercial Structure and Commercial Blight. Retail Patterns and
Processes in the City of Chicago.* Department of Geography Research Paper No. 85,
University of Chicago, 1963.

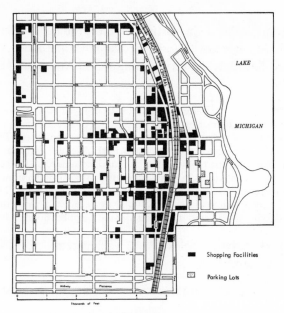

Figure 2.1
COMMERCIAL PATTERN OF
HYDE PARK-KENWOOD IN 1951.

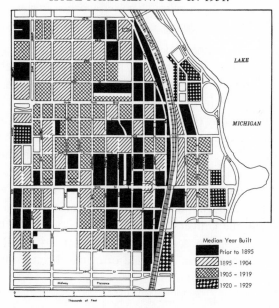

Figure 2.2
YEAR OF CONSTRUCTION OF
STRUCTURES IN HYDE PARK BEFORE RENEWAL.

This report isolated, in particular, the problems of the "commercial rectangle" of Cottage Grove and Lake Park Avenues, 47th and 55th Streets, surrounding the square mile of the "village core:"

". . . In general, the pattern of retail uses in Hyde Park-Kenwood is to concentrate on certain streets and stretches of streets, leaving sizeable portions to be taken over by typically lower rent uses. Thus 47th Street, Cottage Grove Avenue, Lake Park Avenue, and most of 55th Street have declined noticeably as good commercial streets. There are many vacant stores in this community, indicating an unmistakable trend to fewer and larger stores in concentrated districts. Those districts being abandoned by the better stores are fast turning into slums and affecting their surrounding residential neighborhoods adversely."[1]

The RERC survey disclosed 112 vacant retail stores in Hyde Park-Kenwood.[2]

Another contemporary account portrays the same street as:

". . . Characterized by the frequency of vacant stores available for rent, the number of stores utilized not for the retailing for which they were designed but for storage, manufacturing, wholesaling, and distributing, and by the marginal character apparent in numerous retail establishments."[3]

Some types of commercial use created more immediate problems. Twenty-three bars, lounges, and cafes clustered along five blocks of 55th Street alone. (Altogether urban renewal removed 43 taverns from the Hyde Park-Kenwood area.)[4] Moreover the ubiquitous rooms for rent above the taverns attracted drifters and prostitutes. In the community's mind, the streets could fittingly be characterized as "skid rows," with effects that were perceived in diverse ways. The commercial thoroughfares formed barriers which impeded pedestrian transit between the residential neighborhood within, the the great parks to the east and west and the University campus to the south. The denizens of the strip not only posed a hazard to passers-by but also could be blamed in part for a high rate of crime throughout the en-

1 Real Estate Research Corporation, *Analysis of Commerical Land Requirements in the Hyde Park-Kenwood Area*. Chicago: 1956, p. 5.
2 *Ibid.*, p. 12. There are difficulties in defining the base because of the nature of the RERC study, but the vacancy rate is approximately 15 per cent.
3 *Hyde Park Herald*, August 22, 1956, p. 1.
4 Interview with Mr. Herbert Erfurth, Department of Urban Renewal, October, 1966.

closed area. According to South East Chicago Commission figures, offenses (excluding homicide and rape) were committed at the following levels between 1953 and 1957:[1]

	1953	1954	1955	1956	1957
TOTAL	2298	1983	1712	2013	1632
Square mile N. of 55th, W. of Ill. Central	1317	1253	1122	1353	1053

It was felt in the early 1950s that the problems associated with the commercial ribbons were destined to increase rather than decrease. A survey conducted by the Chicago Community Inventory in 1954 compared retailing trends in Hyde Park-Kenwood with the rest of Chicago:

"... While the city increased [between 1948 and 1954] in total number of outlets for apparel, furniture, automobiles, buildings and drugs, Hyde Park-Kenwood declined. The number of liquor stores in the city tended to decrease, but those in the study area increased; and, while the city changed little in number of eating and drinking places, the study area increased."[2]

Feelings about the contribution of commercial arteries to the blight of the immediately adjacent residential housing were supported in a study of structural dilapidation conducted in connection with a community survey by the National Opinion Research Center in 1956. This NORC report allocated every structure in Hyde Park-Kenwood (excluding areas by then being cleared under the "Hyde Park A and B" plan, to be discussed shortly) to one of the following categories:[3]

"A" areas — where immediate and extensive renewal action seemed necessary from preliminary study and general observation.
"B" areas — where renewal action needed to be undertaken, but on a less extensive basis.
"C" areas — where a program of conservation needed to be inaugurated and maintained.

1 Peter H. Rossi and Robert A. Dentler, *The Politics of Urban Renewal*. Glencoe: The Free Press, 1961, p. 30.
2 Chicago Community Inventory, *Chicagoland's Retail Sales*. Chicago: University of Chicago, 1954. Cited in Rossi and Dentler, *Ibid.* p. 30.
3 National Opinion Research Center, *The Hyde Park-Kenwood Urban Renewal Survey*, Chicago: NORC Report No. 58, 1956.

As Figure 2.3 shows, the "A" areas demanding "immediate and extensive" clearance of incipient blight coincide closely with the commercial thoroughfares, especially when the zones already being cleared by the Hyde Park *A* and *B* projects are also considered. (See Figure 2.5).

Blight is clearly seen to be creeping inward from the skid rows, and in the case of "A-7" to be independently rooted in the only commercial strip penetrating the interior of the residential square mile. This latter phenomenon was specifically noted in the *Hyde Park Herald:*

". . . Hyde Park's newest embryonic slum centering on 53rd and Woodlawn is . . . starting around a commercial nucleus."[1]

Another trend associated with the deterioration of the residential periphery was a dramatic influx of Negroes. In 1950 the percentage of non-whites in Hyde Park-Kenwood was 6.1. By 1956, according to the NORC survey, this had leaped to

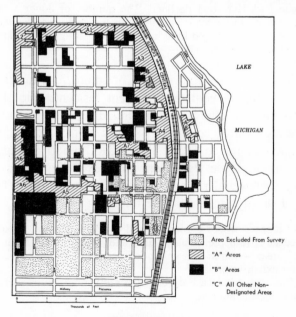

Figure 2.3
RENEWAL TREATMENT RECOMMENDED
BY 1956 N.O.R.C. SURVEY.

---

1 February 19, 1958, p. 22.

36.7. 19,989 whites had left the area and 23,162 non-whites came in during this period.[1]

The incoming Negro population concentrated in the north-western and western sections of the community adjacent to ghetto areas across Cottage Grove and 47th Street, as shown in Table 2.1, which should be related to Figure 2.4. This pre-

TABLE 2.1

NON-WHITE POPULATION BY SUBCOMMUNITIES AND TRACTS:
HYDE PARK-KENWOOD 1950, 1956 and 1960

Subcommunity	Tract	Percentage Nonwhite of Total Population		
		1950	1956	1960
University	617	16	61	67
Community	618	4	12	6
	619	3	1	4
	620	9	3	7
East Hyde Park	611	1	2	6
	612	2	6	4
	621	1	5	12
	622	1	7	—
Kenwood	596	20	94*	93
	597	3	70*	79
	598	5	46	61
	599	5	32	52
Village Core	608	31	95*	96
	609	3	73*	87
	610	2	13	58
	613	4	7	12
	614	4	31	43
	615	1	52	60
	616	6	83*	90

*Tracts showing highest influx

Source: Rossi and Dentler, *op. cit.* p. 27, as compiled from U.S. Census 1950 and 1960 and NORC *The Hyde Park-Kenwood Urban Renewal Study, op. cit.*

cipitous influx of non-whites signified to residents of Hyde Park-Kenwood a "loss in socio-economic distinctiveness"[2] and merging of the neighborhood with the squalid districts which lay beyond its commercial periphery.

One index of the level of anxiety concerning the various manifestations of neighborhood decline was the accelerated migration of residents to other parts of the city and to the sub-urbs. A study of migration in and out of the community be-

1 Rossi and Dentler, *op. cit.*, p. 26.
2 *Ibid.*, p. 26.

Figure 2.4
CENSUS TRACTS AND BLOCKS.

tween 1950 and 1956 undertaken by Rossi and Dentler revealed that:

> ". . . (M)igration concentrated on the apartment house areas in Ken-
> wood, the Village Core, and the border zones and made no appreciable
> inroads on East Hyde Park or the University Community."[1]

The loci of residential turnover were, in other words, the
zones which lay inside the "commercial rectangle."

The combination of factors leading to neighborhood deterioration—economic weakness, structural blight, crime, and
population turnover—were far more prevalent inside the commercial rectangle than elsewhere in Hyde Park. Because the
commercial fringe was in many minds identified as the cause
or source or at least the outward symbol of the community's
problems, its eradication was one of the major objectives of
urban renewal. Since 1955 virtually every structure fronting on
the four principal commercial streets within Hyde Park-Kenwood has been acquired and cleared. *Eighty per cent of the*

---

1 *Ibid.*, p. 33.

frontage formerly zoned for business and commercial uses has been re-zoned for noncommercial uses, primarily low and high rise housing, and institutions. However, three new shopping centers have also been constructed.

Undoubtedly, a significant decrease in the amount of commercial space in the community was justified by the vacancy and "secondary use" rates mentioned in the report of the Real Estate Research Corporation.[1] That study recommended an overall reduction by 20 per cent of available commercial floor area.[2]

Nevertheless, the clearance of the commercial rectangle and its appendages resulted in the displacement of 641 small businesses, of whom 207 went out of business when displaced, and of whom only 233 are still in business (83 in Hyde Park-Kenwood). One hundred ninety-four of the 641 were dislocated in the first wave of clearance, known as "Hyde Park A and B," which occurred between 1955 and 1958.[3] During this period no formal relocation guidance was available to displaced businesses; public attention was chiefly concerned with the plight of displaced families. Furthermore, before 1956, the concept of financial compensation for displaced business tenants, whose short-term leaseholds were valueless in the eyes of the law, had not yet been considered. The fact that both relocation guidance and reimbursement for certain expenses are now required by federal legislation testifies to the effect upon the public conscience of these small businessmen being turned out of their shops, in many cases, going out of business. (See later chapters for detailed discussion and analysis.)

However, such minimum standards of protection came too late and were essentially irrelevant to the plight of those displaced by Hyde Park *A* and *B,* although some assistance was afforded to businessmen dislocated by the subsequent Hyde

---

1 RERC, *op. cit.,* p. 20.
2 Specifically, their recommendations were as follows:

	Square Feet:
Current Estimated Ground Floor Area	1,471,145
Proposed Ground Floor Area	1,150,145
Retained	819,345
New	330,800

3 Jack Meltzer *et. al., Selected Aspects of Urban Renewal in Chicago; an Annotated Statistical Summary.* Chicago: Center for Urban Studies, The University of Chicago, 1965, p. 22.

Park-Kenwood urban renewal project. In both cases, though, *the primary need of those who were financially capable of staying in business was for commercial space in the community where they could relocate.* The efforts of certain displaced businessmen, together with community leaders, city and national officials, to put retail space back into the area is therefore the essence of the Hyde Park-Kenwood story of commercial renewal.

THE 55TH STREET–LAKE PARK SHOPPING CENTER

Hyde Park A and B: Total Clearance Projects

The earliest formal suggestion that the "string-like" shopping streets should be eliminated in favor of one or more shopping centers was included in an assessment of community resources and problems completed by the Hyde Park-Kenwood Community Conference in 1951.[1] This organization, formed in 1949, represented two thousand dues-paying members, plus several thousand additional families who were organized in "block groups" dedicated to neighborhood improvement.

The Conference's proposal relevant to commercial space was premised upon the parking and traffic difficulties and inconvenience of the existing streets. Its content was as follows:

"...Shopping facilities could be improved by the creation of a concentrated shopping center. Such a center, in a well-grouped layout, could offer goods and services not ordinarily found in local neighborhood areas. Thus time and effort for shopping would be minimized, and many shopping dollars would be kept in the area. This kind of project might be worked out as a cooperative venture by interested merchants, investors, and government agencies.

Still more time and energy might be saved by the provision of local neighborhood shopping centers, placed strategically throughout the community, each within short walking distance of family residences."[2]

However prophetic this analysis, the report as a whole, according to the Executive-Director of the Conference at the time, Mrs. Julia Abrahamson, "failed to produce the hoped-for result." In her book *A Neighborhood Renews Itself* she character-

1 Hyde Park-Kenwood Community Conference, *A Report to the Community.* Chicago: Mimeographed, 1951.
2 *Ibid.,* p. 22.

ized her organization as lacking the necessary influence to sponsor an actual planning effort:

"... (It was) felt, that the problems the community faced were primarily economic and political and that the money and power needed to solve them could never be attracted by the conference because business, real estate, and major institutional interests did not have confidence in its motives, goals, or leadership. They believed that a new organization could handle the power side while the conference worked at the grass roots."[1]

Alarm over a rising neighborhood crime wave in May 1952 brought about the creation of a new organization, the South East Chicago Commission (SECC). A major backer and participant in the Commission was the University of Chicago whose new chancellor, Lawrence A. Kimpton, had officially expressed the University's interest in reversing the deterioration of its environs. The University provided half the Commission's budget the first year, and thereafter ten thousand dollars annually, the remainder ($35,000) to be provided by contributions from the community it was to serve.

The Commission's original function, which continues today, was the suppression of crime and building code violations in its area of responsibility covering Oakland, Kenwood, Hyde Park, and Woodlawn. To this end, the full-time staff included a criminologist, Don Blackiston, and a Building and Fire Inspector. The Executive-Director of the Commission was and is attorney Julian H. Levi.

The role of the South East Chicago Commission as author of the plans for the redevelopment of Hyde Park-Kenwood commenced with the approval by the Marshall Field Foundation in March, 1954, of the University's application for a grant to establish a Planning Unit. The Foundation appropriated $100,-000 for this purpose, recognizing "that the university and the commission are committed to the development of a physically attractive, well-serviced, nondiscriminatory community where people with similar standards may live."[2] The Planning Unit was headed by Jack Meltzer, and performed the planning functions

1 Julia Abrahamson, *A Neighborhood Renews Itself.* New York: Harper Brothers, 1959, p. 190.
2 *Ibid.,* p. 194.

of the SECC on behalf of the University and the community.
The first planning efforts, "Hyde Park A and B," contemplated total clearance of two specially selected areas (Figure 2.5). The "total clearance" approach was dictated by the Illinois Blighted Areas Redevelopment Act of 1947, under which Hyde Park *A* and *B* were initially designed, although the Federal Housing Acts of 1949 and 1954 ultimately provided both the legal and financial base. The Illinois act provided for the acquisition (through settlement or condemnation proceedings), clearance, and resale to private redevelopers of "slum and blighted areas"[1] by a "Land Clearance Commission."[2]

The "A and B" plan was published June 30, 1954, three

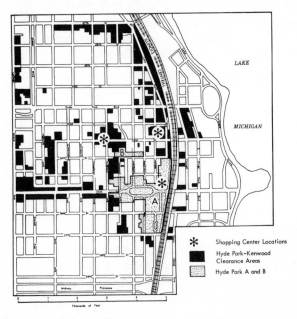

Figure 2.5
CLEARANCE AREAS AND LOCATIONS OF NEW RETAIL CENTERS.

---

1 "Slum and blighted area means any area of not less in the aggregate than two acres located within the territorial limits of a municipality where buildings and improvements, by reason of dilapidation, obsolescence, overcrowding, faculty arrangement or design, lack of ventilation, light and sanitary facilities, excessive land coverage, deleterious land use or layout or any combination of these factors are detrimental to the public safety, health, morals or welfare." Ill. Rev. Stat. Ch. 67 ½, § 65(j), (1947).

2 The method employed in the Hyde Park-Kenwood Urban Renewal Plan of 1958 was conservation and rehabilitation accompanied by spot clearance in an effort to preserve the entire community. This approach was sanctioned by the Urban Community Conservation Act of 1953 and will be discussed in the following section.

Plate 4
55TH STREET LOOKING WEST FROM ILLINOIS CENTRAL TRACKS
PRIOR TO CLEARANCE BY HYDE PARK *A* PROJECT.

Plate 5
55TH STREET IN MARCH, 1967.

months after the formation of the Planning Unit. It called for the clearance of approximately 47 acres contained in two irregularly shaped tracts. These sites comprised 6 per cent of the land area of Hyde Park-Kenwood but contained 40 per cent of the community's blighted buildings. Its boundaries, according to the SECC Report which promulgated the plan, were fixed according to two sources of information: a survey of housing and population conducted in the area by the Land Clearance Commission, and detailed structural inspection by the SECC building inspector and the architectural firm of Harry Weese.[1]

However selective the boundaries which cut through residential property, the *commercial* properties on both sides of 55th Street and Lake Park Avenue were squarely included in the area to be cleared (Figure 2.5). As mentioned earlier, 194 small businesses would eventually be displaced from the project area. Surprisingly, Hyde Park's 55th Street Business and Professional Men's Association quickly voted their overwhelming approval of the Plan.

Several factors were apparently responsible for this initially favorable response. First, many members of the Association were long-time residents of Hyde Park and were in sympathy with the goals of urban renewal. At a meeting of their Association in February, 1953, they had admitted to one another that their street was an irritation and an eyesore to the community.

In particular there was general approval of elimination of the 23 taverns which fell within the project boundaries, most of whose owners did not belong to the Association. Revocation of "late licenses" had long been sought by the Association.[2]

Furthermore, the project only included the eastern portion of 55th Street (extending five blocks on the south side and four blocks on the north). *Merchants outside the project limit did not apprehend that they might also be enveloped by later projects in succeeding years.* One such merchant told an interviewer recently that when he supported Hyde Park *A* and *B*, he "never realized that the whole street would go." His dry goods store was eventually cleared for a public park under what initially

---

1 South East Chicago Commission, *South East Chicago Renewal Project No. 1.* Chicago, 1954, p. 27.
2 "Late licenses" extend to 4 a.m. rather than 2 a.m.

was called "SECC Renewal Project No. 2," proposed later in the summer of 1954 and eventually incorporated into the Final Plan Hyde Park-Kenwood Urban Renewal Plan of 1958.

Not only were small businessmen unable to foresee the extent of the area which would be eventually cleared, but they were unaware of the lack of any compensation or aid for displacees. Most rented their premises on fairly short term leases which would be allowed to expire after the Land Clearance Commission acquired the building, precluding any claim for confiscation of the value of the leasehold. Further, no compensation was available before 1956 for moving expenses or loss of goodwill. (The latter is still not compensated).

In testimony to the House Select Committee on Small Business in 1956, a representative of the displacees characterized the dilemma resulting from this ignorance as follows:

". . . We gave our support in the belief that those merchants who were forced to relocate would be adequately compensated for moving and other related expenses. It never occurred to us that the Government could force a business tenant to move with no compensation whatever if he happened to be a tenant with only a short time left to run on his lease.

The owners of property are adequately protected under the law. Household tenants are paid moving expenses . . . But there is no protection for the business tenant with a short time left to run on his lease even if he has been in business in the community for 30 or more years. Even those businesses with some lease protection, and they are a rarity among small-businessmen, can recover nothing for moving expenses under the present law."[1]

Aside from public spiritedness and naivete concerning the hardship of being displaced, the primary reason for the initial receptivity of the 55th Street businessmen to the renewal of their street was the promise that a major shopping center would be an integral feature of the redevelopment plan. A survey by the *Hyde Park Herald* two weeks after release of the "A and B" proposal reported that businessmen were "confused and concerned by the plan" but that most "hoped and assumed" that they would be able to relocate into the new center.[2]

---

1 Testimony by Walker Sandbach, general manager of the Hyde Park Co-op Supermart, contained in Report of Select Committee on Small Business, House of Representatives, *Urban Renewal Projects and Slum Clearance.* Washington, D.C.: U.S. Government Printing Office, 1956, p. 8.
2 *Hyde Park Herald,* July 14, 1954, p. 1.

Such optimism stemmed perhaps from an early proposal for a shopping center drawn by architect Harry Weese for the Metropolitan Housing and Planning Council. That design "seemed to provide sufficient space for immediate and direct location of long-term resident businesses into a huge new shopping center."[1] Presented by the SECC to the 55th Street Association, that plan had "reportedly been favored strongly."[2]

The design incorporated in the "A and B" plan (again drawn by Weese) proposed a shopping center with 160,000 square feet of selling space with parking for 1000 cars. This center would be smaller than the earlier Weese proposal and represented a net reduction of commercial floor space in the 55th Street-Lake Park project area by 310,000 square feet or about 66 per cent.[3] Nevertheless, as grandly displayed in the *Hyde Park Herald,* this plan gave cause for optimism. Following exactly the recommendations of the Real Estate Research Corporation, the design included space for a small department store, two supermarkets, and a three block concourse containing many small shops.

The all-important question to the merchants of whether they would receive priority in getting into this new center was not explicitly confronted in the SECC proposal. However the following general statement seemed to infer that such a priority could be taken for granted:

". . . Two objectives need to be served by the relocation process: 1) a number of the commercial occupants need to be assisted during the period of transition *pending their relocation into the shopping center* and aid must be furnished the commercial tenants for whom the clearance will be a difficult change to which to adjust; and 2) convenience shopping must be continued during the transition period so that the surrounding residential area can continue to be served, uninterruptedly."[4] [*emphasis added*]

To achieve these two objectives the SECC plan contemplated undertaking clearance in four stages, approximately one year apart. The area scheduled for the shopping concourse, i.e., the north side of 55th Street, was designated as Stage One. Therefore the shopping center would in theory be ready by the time

1 Rossi and Dentler, *op. cit.,* p. 95.
2 *Ibid.*
3 SECC Report, *op. cit.,* p. 77.
4 SECC Report, *op. cit.,* p. 101.

the south side was cleared in Stages Three and Four. Again to quote the plan:

"... Since clearance of the south side of 55th Street would be left to the last stages, convenience shopping would be available during the periods of construction of the proposed center to the north. At no time would areas remain vacant for any period of time; and parking and open areas would be developed as the last item. In addition, there are at present a significant number of vacant stores on the south side and these will be available as interim locations for a number of stores required to relocate temporarily from the north side of 55th Street."[1]

In the light of these proposals the businessmen voted their approval of the plan.

However, Deputy Commissioner Phil Doyle of the Chicago Land Clearance Commission, meeting with the 55th Street Association two weeks after the plan was announced, firmly refuted the contention that the displaced merchants could receive any legal preference over outside concerns for places in the shopping center. Tenant selection, he stressed, would be entirely in the hands of the private redeveloper, who had not yet been chosen. He intimated however that it might be possible for the City to find a "friendly redeveloper" who would recognize a moral, if not a legal, priority in the displacees.[2]

Even were such the case, there would be no duplication of types: "The trend is to keep only one store of a type in a center and to maximize the efficiency and sales volume it enjoys."[3] His point was that many merchants were going to be left out, no matter how amicable the redeveloper. On the one hand, Doyle admitted the possibility that landowners in the project site, if financially eligible, might receive priority to act as redeveloper of their own land, thus anticipating in part the scheme used six years later by a group of merchants to develop Kimbark Plaza.

A new cause for concern among the merchants arose later in 1954 when the Redevelopment Plan of the Chicago Land Clearance Commission was prepared for submission to the City Council, the State Housing Board, and the federal Housing and Home Finance Agency (HHFA). The CLCC plan "closely followed" the boundaries and general land usage recommenda-

1 *Ibid.*
2 *Hyde Park Herald,* July 14, 1954, p. 1.
3 *Ibid.*

tions of the unofficial SECC "A and B" plan. However a change of the utmost importance to the businesses was a drastic alteration of the staging schedule. Whereas the SECC report had called for the clearance of the site for the new shopping center as Stage I, the CLCC scheme scheduled that area as Stage III. The entire south side of 55th Street within the project would be cleared in the first two stages in order to provide new housing at the earliest possible time.[1] This switch of precedence, from meeting the commercial need for space to suppling residential needs first, was explained by Commissioner Doyle as follows:

> ". . . Without closing our minds to the problems of the businessmen we believe it is the responsibility of a public agency to build housing before tearing it down wherever possible."[2]

This statement was in reply to a letter to the Land Clearance Commission from David Sutton, President of the 55th Street Businessmen's Association, asking reconsideration of the revised staging plan:

> ". . . May we point out that the merchant who rents his store has much more to lose than the property owner or the apartment dweller who has legal protection. A merchant who has spent years building up his business loses all if he is not permitted to return to the neighborhood.
> . . . We feel that many of the merchants now on 55th Street, Harper and Lake Park Avenue would prove to be excellent tenants for the shopping center and they should be given first consideration for stores in the new center.
> We consider it imperative that the shopping center be Stage No. 1 and that wherever possible existing business facilities be allowed to remain in operation until the new center is ready for occupancy."[3]

This letter was an exercise in futility. Doyle apparently had no faith in the staging concept, and besides, the Federal Government had two months earlier approved the Redevelopment Plan of the CLCC and had allocated a total of $6,548,547 as its two-thirds share in the cost of acquiring and clearing the land.[4]

---

1 Reprinted in *Hyde Park Herald,* November 3, 1954, p. 1.
2 Statement to *Hyde Park Herald* printed in issue of April 20, 1955, p. 9.
3 Letter to CLCC from 55th Street Businessmen's Association. Reprinted in *Hyde Park Herald,* April 13, 1955, p. 10.
4 The federal share of local urban renewal projects is normally *two-thirds* of the "net project cost," as determined by statutory formula, unless the LPA contracts to absorb all administrative expenses, in which case the federal share is three-quarters. Housing Act of 1949, §103(a)(2), 63 Stat. 416, as amended, 42 U.S.C.A. §1453(a)(2) (Supp. 1965).

The Land Clearance Commission had thereupon begun the process of acquiring the property involved, through negotiation or condemnation. Demolition would begin with a ceremonial house-smashing to be observed by the Board of Directors of the SECC on May 10, 1955.

Ironically, all these arguments as to the order of staging proved moot; *it turned out to be impossible to acquire the 167 separate parcels of real estate in accordance with any pre-determined schedule.* In its year-end report for 1955 the SECC summarized the progress of the Land Clearance Commission as follows:

> ". . . By year's end, 5 properties had been demolished, 37 properties had been acquired, options had been taken for acquisition on 41 properties, and condemnation proceedings were pending on 57 parcels . . .[1]

At the end of *1956,* the SECC reported:

> ". . . By year's end, 147 parcels had been acquired by the Land Clearance Commission. Of the 20 parcels remaining to be acquired, 10 are covered by agreements on price and executed options. Condemnation judgments have been entered on 2, leaving only 8 properties where condemnation proceedings were to be completed or where price negotiations were still under way."[2]

Pursuant to the irregular progress of acquisition, demolition proceeded spasmodically for three years, reaching substantial completion in March, 1958. Construction of the Hyde Park Shopping Center did not begin until later that year. The 194 businesses of the project area were therefore displaced one by one, over a three-year period without any clear predictability about when the notice to vacate would come and, unlike displaced families, without the provision of alternative quarters. Julia Abrahamson has fittingly characterized the small merchant as the "chief victim in Hyde Park's redevelopment program."[3]

Legislative Relief for Displaced Merchants

The first effort to alert public attention to the problems threatening the businesses was a series of articles in the *Hyde Park*

---

1 South East Chicago Commission, *Annual Newsletter,* December, 1955.
2 South East Chicago Commission, *Annual Newsletter,* December, 1956.
3 Abrahamson, *op. cit.,* p. 232.

Herald during the summer of 1955 entitled "Businessmen and Bulldozers." While thoroughly endorsing the "A and B" plan, the *Hyde Park Herald* portrayed the merchant as "the left-out fellow of urban renewal."[1] In considering the plights of individual businesses in separate articles, the series illuminated the unequal impact of displacement upon businesses of diverse character such as a restaurant, an automobile dealer, a book store, and a beauty parlor.

An immediate result of the publicity thus accorded to the commercial situation in the project area was the mounting of a public effort to procure financial aid for the merchants as they became displaced. The Land Clearance Commission, regardless of the personal sympathy of its officials, "had neither the money nor the legal power to aid the merchants,"[2] although within its capacity could have been more favorable consideration of the staging idea. Since the Illinois State Legislature would not meet until 1957, a campaign was undertaken in the Fall of 1955 to obtain the passage of necessary legislation at the federal level.

Strategy for such an effort was the subject of a meeting held September 21 at the South Side Swedish Club, arranged by Julian H. Levi, and attended by Commissioners Bach and Doyle of the Land Clearance Commission, Alderman Despres, Congressman O'Hara, State Senator Korshak, and members of the 55th Street Association's "Committee. on Redevelopment." Senator Paul Douglas telegraphed from Washington: "As you know, Hyde Park is dearer to me than any other place under the sun and I want to do everything I can to help."[3]

The political process started with the introduction of a resolution by Hyde Park's Alderman Despres requesting the City Council to authorize a study of the 55th Street situation by its Committee on Housing and Planning. The object of the study would be to prepare "a full presentation" of the problem for the attention of the Sub-committee on Housing of the House Committee on Banking and Currency which had scheduled hearings in Chicago for late November.[4]

---

1 *Hyde Park Herald,* April 15, 1955, p. 1, *et. seq.*
2 *Hyde Park Herald,* November 9, 1955, p. 1.
3 *Hyde Park Herald,* September 21, 1955, p. 3.
4 *Hyde Park Herald,* October 12, 1955, p. 1.

Accordingly, the city committee held a hearing on November 9 where the questions of financial payments and the need for priority of selection for the eventual shopping center were aired. In particular, Julian Levi of the SECC attacked the extent to which federal restrictions and controls served to "hamstring" the Land Clearance Commission in its efforts to choose a redeveloper with whom the displaced merchants might negotiate. Additionally, he blasted Government's role in overseeing all phases of renewal plans saying that this greatly slowed up and complicated the program.[1]

Two weeks later, on November 21, the Congressional Subcommittee on Housing convened in Chicago. Among its members was Hyde Park's Congressman Barratt O'Hara. Presentation of the 55th Street situation was made by Alderman Despres:

> "...There is one pressing problem...which is incidental to the whole problem, but vital to the people it affects. It is the problem of giving justice to the small displaced and dispossessed business tenant who receives no compensation for condemnation of the real estate, and who finds himself suddenly faced with removal, although were it not for the urban renewal project he would continue his business indefinitely . . . Condemnation and land acquisition require months and perhaps years. As some buildings are torn down, the neighborhood becomes a less satisfactory source of business and the tenant's income declines.
>
> The tenant has no assurance that he will be admitted to the business center. He has heavy moving expenses which no one will reimburse him for. He has equipment and merchandise which are valuable to a going business and have a fair cash market use value that is far higher than the knockdown price he will get if he has to sell. If he finds a new location, he must pay dearly for any credit used to buy equipment and stock, and he can get only short-term credit which puts him, if he can get it at all, at the mercy of high-interest finance houses. Upon moving to another location, the tenant may lose incalculable goodwill."[2]

Despres' testimony was supported by a legal opinion from the Chicago Corporation Counsel and a survey of 41 businessmen affected by the project. The opinion said in essence that

---

1 Testimony reprinted in *Hyde Park Herald* November 9, 1955.
2 Subcommittee on Housing, Committee on Banking and Currency, House of Representatives, *Hearings, Chicago*, November 21-23, 1955. Washington, D.C.: U.S. Government Printing Office, 1955, p. 213.

"under present Federal and State law, there is no relief whatsoever for the displaced and dispossessed small-business tenant with a short term lease."[1] The survey reported the terms of leases, the length of time in the neighborhood, the value of fixtures and equipment and the personal comments of each merchant.

In February, 1956, Representative O'Hara and Senator Douglas (a resident of Hyde Park) introduced parallel bills in their Houses calling for the reimbursement of displaced businesses of moving expenses up to $2000 and for three per cent 20-year loans to be made available to displacees under the "disaster" powers of the Small Business Administration. On May 3, 1956, a hearing was held in Washington on the O'Hara bill by a subcommittee of the Select Committee on Small Business of the House of Representatives. Testimony on behalf of Hyde Park was offered by Commissioner Bach, Alderman Despres, Julian Levi, Bruce Sagan, publisher of the *Hyde Park Herald,* and Walker Sandbach, general manager of the Hyde Park Co-operative Supermarket.

The Housing Act of 1956, signed into law on August 7, 1956, authorized the payment of "reasonable and necessary" moving expenses up to $2000 (but with the "disaster" loan provision deleted.)[2] Thus, the situation in Hyde Park, as publicized by its leaders (alongside, it must be noted, parallel experiences in Connecticut, New York and Pennsylvania), directly inspired the creation of a new instrument in the nation's urban renewal program. Legislation in subsequent years sponsored by O'Hara and Douglas gradually increased the "moving expenses" ceiling to its present level of $25,000. The Small Business Loan concept was revived and passed into law in 1961. And in 1964 a special displacement payment of $1500 (raised to $2500 in 1965) was authorized for independent businesses having an annual net taxable income between $1500 and $10,000. This sequence of enactments is reviewed in detail in Part II of this study.

---

1 *Ibid,* p. 215.
2 Altogether, this law and its successors eventually authorized reimbursement on 123 claims from Hyde Park "A" merchants amounting to $225,000. (*Hyde Park Herald,* November 13, 1957, p. 1.)

Survival of the Fittest

Meanwhile in 1956, as the political process labored to produce "justice" for displaced merchants, the conditions described by the testimony in the various hearings were in fact taking place. The plight of the *A* and *B* displacees was ultimately to significantly change urban renewal law and concepts of "just compensation," but for the businessmen concerned the plight was serious indeed. No commercial relocation representative existed in the city administration at the time; relocation efforts of the Land Clearance Commission were entirely concerned with families. With reference to that situation an official of the Chicago Department of Urban Renewal recently told an interviewer:

> ". . . Presumably because of the lack of attention and the authoritative manner of CLCC there was very little trouble getting commercial tenants to vacate within a very short time. Of course, there were a great many more failures as a result. Once his establishment was earmarked for an urban renewal project, the marginal businessman resigned himself to failure, knowing that he could not possibly afford to move, and simply vacated with little more ado."[1]

And according to the findings of Rossi and Dentler:

> ". . . Demoralization among the merchants — chiefly a conviction that businessmen had been "sold a bill of goods," or among others, "that we had no voice" — deepened into bitterness."[2]

The economically viable businessmen fended for themselves in various ways between 1956 and 1958. A few, such as Havill's TV Ltd. or Watson Jewelers, were able to find space in the few "safe" commercial structures scheduled to be left standing. Others such as David Sutton's moving company (Peterson Movers) eventually left the community permanently. But many emulated the Hyde Park Coop Supermarket by moving to temporary quarters, when necessary, in order to await construction of the new shopping center. *A recurring theme in the commercial story of the "A and B" project was the necessity of making two moves if a merchant wished to stay in business in Hyde Park.*

---

1 Interview with Fred Levandoske conducted by Staff of Center for Urban Studies, Summer, 1965.
2 Rossi and Dentler, *op. cit.*, p. 94.

A matter of vital concern to those who hoped to get into the shopping center was the selection of a private redeveloper. According to Rossi and Dentler:

". . . It became increasingly evident during 1956 that critical decisions bearing on the fate of local businessmen and precisely how the "A and B" sites should be redeveloped rested with neither the Land Clearance Commission nor with the South East Chicago Commission, but with the private redevelopers bidding for the job. Moreover, their bids had to be considered principally in terms of costs, quality of plans, and ability to carry out plans, rather than in terms of "friendliness."[1]

In November, 1955 Julian Levi had criticized the delay in choosing a redeveloper:

". . . One of the major problems before the merchants resulted from their not knowing who the redeveloper would be. If they had this information they could negotiate with him and perhaps receive some shopping center preference by themselves."[2]

Furthermore, until a redeveloper was selected, the completion date for the center could not be estimated, thus placing a great risk upon those businesses, such as the Hyde Park Coop, who moved into temporary quarters in other buildings scheduled for demolition upon the assumption that they would get into the center.

Finally, the very size and character of the shopping center would be speculative until a redeveloper's plan was accepted. Bidders would not be bound to follow the exact specifications of the previously adopted Land Clearance Commission plan (based on the SECC proposal). Rather, the design of the successful bidder would become "Revision No.1" to the CLCC plan, and would itself be submitted in ordinance form to the City Council, and thereafter to the State Housing Board and the HHFA for approval. No aspect of the center therefore was certain in 1956 except that there would be one: bids would be prescribed only to that extent.

On July 24, 1956, seventeen months after federal approval of the project, the Land Clearance Commission formally invited bids to be submitted on "A and B" prior to September 24. Bids

---

1 Rossi and Dentler, op. cit., p. 94.
2 Testimony to Committee on Planning and Housing, Chicago City Council, November 9, 1955.

were submitted by Harry Applegate and Co., Harry Trevalyan and Herbert S. Greenwald, all of Chicago, and from Lambert and Co. and Webb and Knapp of New York. The designs were examined by a panel of architects designated by the City, under the direction of Louis Wetmore. Despite their controversial high rise block of apartments located in 55th Street and dubbed "Monoxide Island" by rival Greenwald, the Webb and Knapp plan became the apparent favorite by the end of the year.

Enter the Developer: Webb and Knapp

From the merchants' viewpoint, the latest version of the ever-shrinking shopping center, now scheduled to be 60,000 square feet, was unacceptable. David Sutton, president of the newly formed Hyde Park Business and Professional Men's Association, wrote an angry letter to Mayor Daley excoriating the handling of commercial displacement by the Land Clearance Commission, and deploring the repeated reduction of the shopping center. He intimated that the businessmen were "willing to arrange funds to buy the entire 160,000 square feet contemplated in the original SECC and CLCC designs. "[Even] 103,000 square feet might be ample, but 60,000 was definitely too small."[1]

The sole member of the Association to vote against the statement was Walker Sandbach, general manager of the Hyde Park Coop. A week later, Sandbach joined Bruce Sagan and Alderman Despres in praising the work of Commissioners Bach and Doyle. He pointed out that both men "warned from the start that legal protections for businessmen were non-existent and both have done all possible to help."[2]

Sandbach's siding with the "opposition" on this issue did not necessarily indicate alienation from the Association which he had represented in Washington a few months earlier. However he sincerely felt that some of the merchants were shrinking from investing in their own survival and were attempting to shift the blame to the CLCC. Furthermore, cooperation with the officials of CLCC was vital to the survival of the Co-op.

---

1 Letter reprinted in *Hyde Park Herald*, December 19, 1956, p. 14.
2 *Hyde Park Herald*, December 26, 1956, p. 1.

On January 23, 1957 the Land Clearance Commission submitted "Revision No. 1" (Webb and Knapp's plan) to the City Council. The Council's Committee on Planning and Housing reported favorably on the revision on February 13, and the change was approved by the City Council itself on April 3. Pursuant to state and federal approval Webb and Knapp was officially selected as redeveloper. However sale of the land to Webb and Knapp was not consummated until February 5, 1958 after the various prerequisite resolutions had passed through the long succession of steps required by the governments involved.

Being assured of their eventual selection, however, Webb and Knapp opened a project office in Chicago on May 1, 1957. They initiated their own market studies to determine the actual commercial floor space to be incorporated into the final "working plans."[1]

Webb and Knapp's public statements on tenancy of the center were equivocal. In January, with their plan under consideration by the City Council, a Webb and Knapp spokesman stated that the center would be a "neighborhood operation" and was "not to be utilized by chains."[2] The stated intention of Webb and Knapp in January was "to recruit local establishments." Moreover, other community facilities (a restaurant, a theater and a university inn) were at that time scheduled to be built across 55th Street.

The hospitable tone of these public statements was qualified in June by Webb and Knapp's president, William Zeckendorf, speaking to the annual meeting of the South East Chicago Commission. He promised priority of selection to local merchants "if they can meet the financial requirements" but there would be no rent reductions below the level prevailing in other centers.[3]

In actuality, prospective tenants from among the displaced businesses were given cause for discouragement during the summer of 1957. The Continental Gourmet, an extremely popular restaurant which had been displaced a year before, was informed by Webb and Knapp that negotiation of leases would have to

---

1 *Hyde Park Herald,* June 19, 1957, p. 1.
2 *Hyde Park Herald,* Jan. 9, 1957, p. 1.
3 *Hyde Park Herald,* June 19, 1957, p. 1.

COMMERCIAL RENEWAL IN HYDE PARK-KENWOOD   41

await the execution of a contract between Webb and Knapp and the CLCC, as well as the preparation of a "Master Plan".[1] Despite the endorsement of the CLCC itself, as well as the South East Chicago Commission, the Continental Gourmet was sufficiently discouraged by this implication of yet more delays to relocate in a different part of Chicago.

Role of the Hyde Park Co-op

The primary tenancy question was the selection of a supermarket. Both the SECC and the CLCC expected that the Hyde Park Co-op would be the logical candidate. However it became apparent that regardless of the hospitable tone of Webb and Knapp statements towards local businesses, Zeckendorf assumed all along that he would be able to select an outside chain store to fill the supermarket spot, because of the difficulty of financing independents and the time required to put deals together. Indeed, his financing plans were dependent upon procuring an "AAA" chain to bolster his credit-worthiness; no shopping center had previously been built without an "AAA" tenant, and the high costs of land in urban renewal projects, plus time delays in working with the local public agency, raise costs substantially. Zeckendorf's mis-estimation of the importance of the Co-op to the community produced a year-long series of negotiations which further delayed the beginning of construction.

Although the Co-op did not belong to a chain, it nevertheless represented a force to be reckoned with. Its gross sales in 1956 amounted to nearly two million dollars; its 2200 stockholders included many persons of influence both in Chicago and nationally.

Manager Sandbach had anticipated a struggle when he moved the Co-op in 1954 from its old grocery store on 57th street to premises on Harper Avenue, two and a half times as large.[2] On the Opening Day in this new location, "Hyde Park A and B" was published, scheduling the Harper Avenue structure for demolition. Sandbach had been forewarned by Julian Levi, but considered that the bargaining advantage to be gained by demonstrating the growth potential of the Co-op offset the risk of

1 *Hyde Park Herald,* August 28, 1957, p. 1.
2 Interview with Mr. Walker Sandbach, September, 1966.

being forced to make another temporary move.[1] Additionally, Sandbach had tacit assurance from the CLCC that the Harper Avenue store would stand until the Center was ready. The promise was kept; that building was one of the last four out of 194 to be demolished.

The Co-op's prime competitors for space in the center were the A & P, National, and Hi-Lo chains, each of whom was eventually to lose a store on 55th Street. The Co-op's eligibility in preference to the chains was endorsed by the SECC, CLCC, the *Hyde Park Herald,* and the Hyde Park-Kenwood Community Conference. However after several months of negotiating, Webb and Knapp still thought the Co-op was too small.

The impasse was finally resolved by the Co-op's offer to obtain financing from its own sources to construct the part of the center which the supermarket would occupy. A promise of $580,000 was obtained from the Nationwide Insurance Company, which specialized in financing cooperatives, in exchange for a mortgage on the Co-op.

Furthermore, Sandbach agreed that the Co-op would meet Webb and Knapp's asking rent of $75,000 minimum on its first $5 million of business. This seemed an exorbitant figure for the Co-op's 1957 level of business which fell between $2 and $3 million. The additional rental term of 1.5 per cent of all business above $5 million, according to Sandbach, "proved to be extremely economical when the Co-op's business eventually did exceed that level in 1964."[2]

Webb and Knapp finally submitted to political pressure and the Co-op's own determination by entering into a 20 year lease with the Co-op in July, 1958. In addition to the aforementioned terms, the agreement included a very favorable rate of 8c per square foot for use of the proposed 600 car parking lot, and a provision which precludes either party from establishing a supermarket within a two mile radius.[3]

---

1 *Ibid.*
2 *Ibid.* However, a 1.5 per cent lease for a supermarket is high in the food industry, regardless of sales, according to industry representatives and location research analysts.
3 The latter provision was the basis of a lawsuit during 1967 in which the Co-op successfully prevented Webb and Knapp's successor, Arthur Rubloff and Co. from leasing an adjoining site, C-10, to the National Tea Co. for erection of a rival supermarket. At this writing, National has dropped its plans and the site has been offered to a building firm for construction of a high rise apartment building.

Physically the new Co-op was to be the largest supermarket in Chicago at the time of its opening. Its 46,000 square feet included a selling area of 22,000 square feet and space for a Credit Union and meeting hall in the basement, together with a coffee bar in the center of the store. Designed by Harry Weese, the building proved to be significantly modern rather than the "warehouse style" typical of shopping center supermarkets. Construction began in August, 1958 and the Co-op opened amidst piles of rubble, dust and construction materials, on October 13, 1959.

Other Tenants

Once the supermarket issue had been settled, Webb and Knapp in 1958 finally invited applications for the remainder of the center. This proved to be quite a different story: discouraged perhaps by the difficulty experienced by the Co-op and by the deserted aspect of the rest of the shopping center site for over a year (demolition had been largely completed in March, 1958) and by the changing tone of Webb and Knapp's statements, the local aspirants for admission to the center had lost interest. According to Walker Sandbach, "there was a general belief in 1959 that the neighborhood was going down." Furthermore, discussion of an additional center elsewhere in Hyde Park had become serious in 1959, and was attracting the interest of the more viable displacees.

Therefore Webb and Knapp's informal overtures to local businessmen such as hardware retailer "Ted" Anderson were simply ignored. Since tenants had to be procured before financing could be obtained, Webb and Knapp began to sign up chain stores. On April 29, 1959, announcement was made that tenants would include Woolworth's, Walgreen's, Rothschild's (clothing), Fannie Mae Candies, Neumode stockings, Wimpy's "and other chains." In a complete reversal of the initial concept, no small local merchants were expected to enter at all.[1]

On the same day announcement was made of a construction loan of $1.8 million to Webb and Knapp by Chicago City Bank

---

1 *Hyde Park Herald*, May 7, 1958, p. 1.

and Trust Company. This loan supplemented funds already committed to construction of the shopping center from Nationwide Insurance Company ($580,000) and Bankers Life and Casualty ($1.2 million).[1]

In May the Book Nook, Flair Cleaners, Lake Park Currency Exchange, and the Marco Polo Travel Agency were announced.[2] Of these the Book Nook was owned by a local merchant doing business at 1453 East 53rd Street, but who was not displaced by urban renewal. In early July a displaced optometrist, Dr. Aaron Zimbler, was added to the list.[3]

Inquiry into the efforts to fill the center by Webb and Knapp and its leasing agent Arthur Rubloff and Company indicates that difficulty was encountered at every turn. The Real Estate Research Corporation study had reported the 55th Street-Lake Park Avenue location to be ideal for a medium sized clothing and department store. Several major stores, including Rothschild's mentioned above, were approached with those findings in hand. All eventually lost interest. The clothing store space was finally divided between a women's apparel shop, Albert's, and a men's store, Cohn and Stern. The former was a new business; the latter was one of the four displaced businesses that ultimately became the tenants of the center. (The others: the Co-op, Lowe's Records, and Dr. Zimbler). Like the Co-op, Cohn and Stern had made two moves within five years, having weathered the 55th Street demolition by moving to temporary quarters on 53rd Street.

A restaurant was planned for the center, although this was not finally decided until the community facilities planned for the other side of 55th Street were eliminated from the plan in favor of townhouses. The Continental Gourmet had long since moved away (to 525 W. Arlington Street), and no other candidate could be found. Finally, the space reserved for a restaurant was divided between Wimpy's Hamburgers and the Marco Polo Travel Agency.

Some difficulty was even experienced in signing up Wal-

1 *Hyde Park Herald*, May 1, 1958, p. 1.
2 *Hyde Park Herald*, May 15, 1958, p. 1.
3 *Hyde Park Herald*, July 4, 1958, p. 1.

green's and Woolworth's, despite the fact that both chains lost stores on 55th Street. Walgreen's was particularly reluctant to reestablish on 55th Street due to neighborhood opposition to its liquor department. However the store now profitably operates the only liquor outlet in the center.

Several spaces in the center were leased for uses not usually found in a shopping center, namely doctors' offices, a new Hyde Park Savings and Loan Association, and a brokerage office.[1] The RERC study of 1954 had explicitly advised against such low volume tenants:

> ". . . There are a number of types of facilities which it is important to have convenient to the Shopping Center, but it is equally important that they not be inside or adjacent to the Center. This is true, for example, of a medical center, doctors, dentists, and similar facilities. This is not a use compatible with a high volume retail area. Parking at medical facilities is of long duration and . . . only a small fraction of shoppers couple visits to the doctor . . . with a shopping trip."[2]

The presence of such non-retail enterprises in the center serves as further evidence that commercial prospects for the center had become limited when leases were being written in the maximum period of neighborhood uncertainty in 1959. For example, the Hyde Park Savings and Loan Association was not chartered until May 24, 1961. Before that time its office space had stood vacant for a year.

The New Hyde Park Shopping Center Today

In contrast, the New Hyde Park Shopping Center today is filled and evidently prosperous. Its concourse and mall are thronged by residents of the adjacent new living units as well as by shoppers from other parts of Hyde Park and the City. Its straggling parking lot is often filled. (Parenthetically, the Co-op claimed in a 1967 lawsuit against Arthur Rubloff and Company involving development of a rival supermarket that the latter has actually provided only 446 parking spaces, whereas the lease calls for 718.)

---

1 Replaced in 1964 by "The Shoe Corral."
2 RERC findings reprinted in SECC Report, *op. cit.* p. 75. This recommendation was made because Webb and Knapp had already leased several spaces to non-retail uses, because they could not get their asking rents from either chain or local independent retailers, although non-retailers were willing to pay the rent demanded.

Plate 6
CORNER OF 55TH STREET AND LAKE PARK AVENUE IN SEPTEM-
BER, 1967. *Photo provided by Department of Urban Renewal, City of Chicago.*

Plate 7
INSIDE NEW HYDE PARK SHOPPING CENTER, 1963. *Photo provided
by Office of Public Relations, The University of Chicago.*

Manifestly, the prime generator of this prosperity is the Hyde Park Co-op, whose twelve check-out counters are frequently crowded. The Co-op as an institution serves to assimilate the Center to the community.

Yet the role of the Center in providing quarters to businesses displaced by "Hyde Park A and B" was obviously slight. Of 194 businesses displaced, four independents and two chains ended up in the center. Excluding the Co-op and the optometrist, only two of the independents could be considered "typical" small business displacees. Neither of the latter, Cohn and Stern and Lowe's Record Store, were signed up until after the main effort to obtain tenants in 1959 had failed to fill the center.

Of course, many of the 194 displacees managed to relocate individually: One hundred and twenty-three survived temporarily, although only one-quarter (31) remained in business until 1967 (See Chapter 3). Certain of these, such as an automobile dealership, were unsuited to the shopping center by definition, and thus were not affected by the delay in its construction. Others who might have been tenants, such as the Continental Gourmet, preferred reestablishment in other parts of Chicago to an indefinite period of waiting for the center. In such cases, the merchant gave up his local goodwill and the community lost the merchant.

The history of the New Hyde Park Shopping Center therefore is a study in disappointed expectations for displacees, despite the financial success of the center and the growth of the Hyde Park Co-op. Hopes raised by the early "large center" proposals turned to hostility as political, legal, and financial contingencies eroded the space to be devoted to a shopping center. Much of the difficulty, such as the failure of staging of clearance, was due to the unprecedented scale and character of the project and the priority assigned to residential as opposed to commercial objectives: "Hyde Park A and B" was in every sense a pioneer project. However, the peremptory methods used by the Land Clearance Commission to dislodge businesses and the fact that Webb and Knapp, in 1957, courted local merchants verbally while ignoring them in fact during the prolonged periods of planning and negotiation, were largely responsible for substantial disaffection of local merchants with urban renewal. (See Chapter 4).

Out of the disillusionment thus engendered, however, there arose among the more solvent merchants in the late fifties a desire to find a more effective solution to the problem of surviving in business in Hyde Park. Out of this desire emerged a novel center, Kimbark Plaza—an experiment which itself is proving to be of importance and significance to commercial renewal planning elsewhere.

KIMBARK PLAZA

The Hyde Park-Kenwood Urban Renewal Plan

In 1956, while the highly selective *A* and *B* projects were being executed by the Land Clearance Commission, the planners turned to the remainder of Hyde Park-Kenwood. On January 12, the University entered into a contract with the Community Conservation Board of the City of Chicago (CCB) under which Jack Meltzer and the University's Planning Unit would prepare a preliminary plan and, subject to federal approval, a final Hyde Park-Kenwood Urban Renewal Plan.

The area of concern for this plan was bounded by Cottage Grove Avenue, 47th Street, Jackson Park, and the Midway, excluding the University campus and the "A and B" project zones (Figure 2.5). This area comprised 855 acres and contained 3100 structures housing 65,000 people. It was officially designated as a "Conservation Area" pursuant to the Urban Community Conservation Act of 1953[1] by the CCB after public hearings were held in April and May, 1956.

As its designation connotes, the objective of this plan, in contrast to *A* and *B*, was the "conservation" of the existing community. Clearance would be applied only selectively in furtherance of this objective.

Nevertheless, the Preliminary Plan delivered to CCB on July 5, 1956 by the South East Chicago Commission called for thorough clearance along Cottage Grove, 47th Street, and the relocation of Lake Park Avenue against the Illinois Central

---

1 Ill. Rev. Stat. Ch. 67½, §§91.8-91.16 (1953).

right-of-way. When added to the clearance already underway in Hyde Park *A* and the acquisition by the University of the south side of 55th Street between University and Cottage Grove Avenues under the terms of its Southwest Hyde Park project, the clearance anticipated by this latest plan would entirely eliminate the old "commercial rectangle."

To quote the language of the Plan:

> ". . . The proposed street program results in the removal of the existing retail establishments, principally along 47th, Cottage Grove, 55th and Lake Park. While special problems will thus be created with respect to some long time retail occupants, these streets are currently characterized by a substantial number of store vacancies, and by a large number of substandard structures housing these retail establishments."[1]

The actual number of vacancies in Hyde Park-Kenwood, according to the 1956 RERC study relied upon by the SECC, was 112.[2] As of 1964, execution of the Final Urban Renewal Plan accounted for the recorded displacement of 447 businesses in addition to the 194 already displaced by Hyde Park *A* and *B*.[3]

No promise was made in the Preliminary Plan that this legion of commercial displacees could be accommodated in any shopping center. However the intention was made explicit that independent businesses would be encouraged:

> ". . . The objective of attracting the independent merchant will depend in major part on the ability to develop a disposition package which is within the financial capacity of the independent merchant. This is consequently the critical question to be determined from final planning studies."[4]

Provision in the Preliminary Plan for restoration of a limited amount of commercial space to the community was prompted not merely by a desire to help displaced businesses but also in order to avoid depriving 65,000 people of their neighborhood walk-in shops. Consequently the Plan designated ten scattered sites to be sold for future commercial redevelopment.[5] The

---

1 University of Chicago Planning Unit, *Preliminary Project Report.* Chicago: Mimeographed, 1956, p. 88.
2 RERC Report, *op. cit.*, p. 12.
3 Meltzer, *op. cit.*, p. 22.
4 Planning Unit, *op. cit.*, p. 88.
5 According to Rossi and Dentler, *op. cit.*, p. 213: "Without doubt, the addition of scattered commercial facilities represents an instance of a successful citizen influence upon the planner."

locations of these sites were governed by the recommendations of the Real Estate Research Corporation. (See Figure 2.6.)

When added to the 55th-Lake Park Center and the limited strips of businesses remaining on 51st, 53rd, and 57th Streets, these facilities were deemed sufficient to satisfy the community's need for convenience shopping:

"... These small centers would include the necessary minimum convenience and personal service establishments, e.g. drugs, groceries, filling station, barber and beauty, shoe repair, and the like."[1]

Essential to the fulfillment of this design was the acknowledged power of the acquiring authority (in this case the Community Conservation Board) to restrict disposition of each site to the kind of redeveloper which it deemed desirable for the particular location.

The Preliminary Plan was transmitted to the Housing and Home Finance Agency by the CCB on August 31, 1956, and

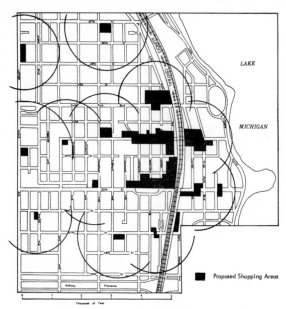

Figure 2.6
SHOPPING AREAS PROPOSED FOR HYDE PARK
BY REAL ESTATE RESEARCH CORPORATION.

1 Planning Unit, *op. cit.*, p. 88.

approved by HHFA on December 20 with instructions to proceed with completion of a Final Plan. $25,835,000 was set aside as the federal share of the cost of the project. The next step was an appraisal of all property scheduled to be acquired, cleared, and re-sold under the plan. The valuation report prepared by the firm of Jack Witkowsky included recommendations of changes in the uses proposed for various tracts. Several small commercial sites were deemed to be more usable (i.e. salable) for other purposes such as institutional use or low-rise housing. Altogether Witkowsky's recommendations amounted to a net reduction by 23 per cent of the amount of land area scheduled in the Preliminary Plan for commercial re-use.[1] In accordance with his recommendations both commercial sites on Cottage Grove Avenue and a single one on 47th Street, together with a sliver at 53rd and Lake Park, were changed in the Final Plan to noncommercial uses.

Significantly however, at the suggestion of Witkowsky and SECC, one low-rise and one parking site on 53rd Street were redesignated for commercial use. Together with an 82,000 square foot tract (C7) already designated at 53rd and Woodlawn, this change created a three acre commercial package in the very heart of the community. Severed only by Kimbark Avenue and a single structure exempt from acquisition, this site provided an excellent location and adequate space for a new center in the Final Plan that was passed into law by the City Council on November 7, 1958 (Figure 2.7).

Formation of the Redevelopment Corporation

Not only was the site at Woodlawn and 53rd ideally located for a shopping center but the ordinance contained a novel proposal as to its disposition, inserted at the suggestion of SECC:

"... It is recommended that C-6 and C-7 be made available to local merchants affected by proposed clearance activities in the Hyde Park-Kenwood area."[2]

---

1 Jack Witkowsky, *Report of Valuation of Various Properties in Hyde Park-Kenwood*, Nov. 1, 1957, p. 35.
2 *Proposed Ordinance to Approve Hyde Park-Kenwood Urban Renewal Plan* . . . etc. (Passed November 7, 1958), Chicago: 1958, p. 8.

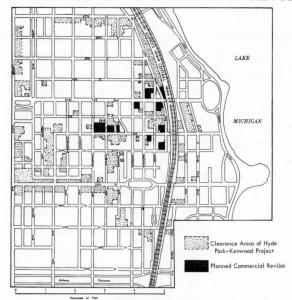

Figure 2.7
1958 PLAN FOR COMMERCIAL RE-USE IN THE
HYDE PARK-KENWOOD RENEWAL AREA.
(Subsequently modified, see Fig. 7.1)

According to Jerray A. Elsinger, the Commercial Relocation
Officer of the Chicago Department of Urban Renewal:

"...This marked the beginning of a new era in the city in commercial relocation for businesses affected by urban renewal. Prior to that
time, the only assistance rendered to commercial establishments had
been in the filing of their commercial relocation claims."[1]

The source of the proposal and subsequent recommendation
clearly was public demand. The only opposition came from
chain stores, who complained that the proposal unduly favored
small merchants, and from professional developers, who argued
that they should be permitted to do the construction, for occupancy by displacees. The local demand prevailed. In April 1958,
at the high point of bitterness toward Webb and Knapp and the
55th-Lake Park Center, the Hyde Park Business and Professional Men's Association held a meeting at which legal priorities
for displaced businesses were discussed. Senator Douglas, Representative O'Hara, and Julian Levi all spoke in favor of such

---

[1] Jerray A. Elsinger, "Chicago Small Business Relocation," *The Journal of Housing,*
Vol. 8 (October, 1966), p. 448.

a principle. Levi on behalf of the SECC suggested that the final plan might provide for redevelopment of the Kimbark site by local displaced merchants.

On May 21, Douglas and O'Hara introduced bills in the Congress to establish a policy of giving priority to local merchants in new commercial structures. These bills did not mature but the principle was recognized "de facto" in the provision suggested by Levi which was incorporated in the plan.

Everett Ramsey, owner of the Hyde Park News Service, who was familiar with legal techniques, took leadership in implementing the recommendation of the city. He could not move his business out of Hyde Park because his franchises for the distribution of newspapers were limited to that neighborhood.[1] Furthermore, Ramsey's interest in rebuilding on his own in Hyde Park was forestalled by the fact that no single lots were being sold for redevelopment.[2] The Land Clearance Commission, which owned all the cleared land from the "A and B" projects, preferred to sell the entire package to one redeveloper, Webb and Knapp.

Therefore Ramsey, in collaboration with attorney Sidney Salins, developed the notion of forming a group of like-minded displacees to incorporate and bid collectively on one of the larger sites to become available under the Hyde Park-Kenwood Urban Renewal Plan. The site of greatest potential was, of course, the Woodlawn-53rd Street, although there was some talk of a smaller commercial tract at Woodlawn and 55th, should the campus tavern ("Jimmy's") ever be dislodged.

Ramsey looked to the HPBPA, of which he was a member, to find the sort of men he needed. Interested merchants were invited to stay after the regular Association meetings to hear Ramsey's ideas. He paid for dinners to promote further discussion and participation by the businessmen. Gradually a "club" of about fifteen emerged as the principle enthusiasts.

Ramsey sought particular criteria in prospective members. An obvious requirement was intention to stay in Hyde Park; he

---

[1] This problem also affected automobile dealers and other enfranchised businesses displaced by urban renewal.
[2] Interview with Mr. Everett Ramsey, summer, 1965.

requested "letters of intent" to this effect from each candidate. Secondly he needed younger men who would be able to undertake twenty-year mortgages. Thirdly, he sought complete diversity amongst the goods and services to be offered and amongst the members of the group in order to forestall criticism and receive "special consideration" by the City.

Most importantly, since the members individually and collectively would have to attract heavy financing, he needed men of known solvency and sound business reputation.[1] One member recently interviewed said that the group finally formed comprised "the most solvent merchants on 55th Street."[2]

Dues at first were $10 per month to cover incidental expenses. The group raised this amount to $25 and then to $50 prior to incorporation to pay for legal costs. The club incorporated on March 23, 1960, as the "53rd Street-Woodlawn-Kimbark Shopping Center Inc."

Some turnover in membership was experienced both before and after incorporation as individual businesses found independent solutions to their relocation problem. Connor's Hardware, originally at 1306 E. 55th Street, withdrew from the group to relocate further down 53rd Street. His place was taken by A. T. ("Ted") Anderson. Another business that lost interest in Kimbark Plaza was Watson Jewelery, located for 40 years at 55th and Woodlawn. Watson "could not afford to wait for the Plaza" and found permanent quarters in the Chevrolet garage building across 55th Street from Webb and Knapp's shopping center. (Neither Connor nor Watson are still in business.)

Two businesses that withdrew from the Kimbark group after incorporation were Havill TV and Radio Ltd. and Duncan's Stationary. Both of these enterprises relocated permanently in older buildings on 53rd Street. Another prospective member, the Woodlawn Currency Exchange, failed to be granted a license to continue in the area.

The merchants who finally carried the project through to realization and the locations from which they were displaced

1 *Ibid.*
2 Interview with Mr. A. T. Anderson conducted by the writer, August, 1966.

(with interim locations if more than one more was involved) were the following:

Everett Ramsey, "H. P. News Service," 1210 E. 55th Street
(interim: 1159 E. 55th Street)
Gus and "Stevie" Breslauer, "Breslauer's" Department Store,
1312-1314 E. 55th Street
A. T. "Ted" Anderson, "Anderson's Hardware," 1455 E. 55th Street
(interim: 1215 E. 55th Street)
Gabe Stern, "Gabe's Men's Clothing," 1334 E. 55th Street
Nick DeBello, "Nicky's Pizza," 1235 E. 55th Street
Mitzie Horky, "Mitzie's Florist," 1301 E. 55th Street
(interim: 1340 E. 55th Street)
Julius and Louis Gerstein, "Mr. G's Certified Food Mart," 1226 E.
53rd Street (interim: opened store in Prairie Shores Shopping Center—the Kimbark supermart became a second store)
Harold Jacobson, "Kimbark Liquors," 1220 E. 53rd Street
H. and M. Weinstein, "Par Rexall," 5500 Kimbark Avenue
L. and M. Steiner, "Public Cleaners" (chain, no former address)
Floyd Cohen, "Kimbark Plaza Launderette and Cleaners" (chain, no former address)
W. C. Siegrist, Jr, "American Radio and T.V. Lab.," 6321 S. University Avenue
Dr. J. E. Jones, moved from elsewhere in the City
Dr. K. Rosenbaum, 1132 E. 55th (interim: 1207 E. 55th Street)
Dr. Sydney Bild, 1229 E. 55th Street

It will be noticed that four of the foregoing businesses were forced to make interim moves before finally settling in Kimbark Plaza. Anderson's first relocation to 1215 E. 55th Street (beyond the reach of Hyde Park "A" but still within the clearance zone of the later Hyde Park-Kenwood Renewal Plan) was accomplished on November 7, 1957 by a parade of 60 Hyde Parkers who transported their merchandise in shopping carts, amid considerable fanfare. This was the first business displaced in Hyde Park.

Mr. G's and Kimbark Liquors were both displaced in 1961 from the very site to be occupied by Kimbark Plaza. The Gersteins took refuge in a new store in the Prairie Shores Shopping Center; the Kimbark Liquor proprietors took other jobs for 2½ years until the Kimbark center was ready.

Ramsey's "club" also included lawyer Sidney Salins and architect Donald Olivieri who offered their services at no fee until the project became a reality.

The actual organization of the corporation is described in an article by Jerray Elsinger of the Department of Urban Renewal as follows:

"...The Hyde Park merchants decided to create an organization owned, paid for, maintained, and managed as cooperatively as was possible under the framework of a corporation organized under the Illinois business corporation act...Only displaced merchants were allowed to subsribe for shares of stock. Approximately 15 people signed a pre-organization subscription agreement.

In order to determine the number of shares that each shareholder was to be ultimately issued, it was agreed that the group had to first determine the percentage of the shopping plaza structure to be occupied by each shareholder. Once this was determined, th corporation could calculate for each participant the percentage of land it could use, its share of stock ownership of the corporation, the strength of its voice in the corporation management, its rent and share of the mortgage. Thus the businessman who wanted elaborate construction on his space would have to pay more on a square foot basis than the one who wanted simple construction. Excess cost per square foot was treated as tenant's expense."[1]

Additionally the Corporation's by-laws established a "Merchants Association" in which each tenant, regardless of size, exercises one vote. This Association is responsible for the actual "housekeeping" decisions and day-to-day management of the Center. 53rd Street merchants outside the Center, who do not belong to the Corporation, may be accepted into the Association, as in the case of the nearby Mobil Station which shares in snow removal contracts.

Acquisition of the Site

Although the Ramsey group received assistance from the Department of Urban Renewal, particularly through attorney Jerray Elsinger, who at that time was working with the group, the land owned and cleared by the City could not simply be donated to the Corporation. Open bidding was required by law, although some modification was authorized in this case to offset the Kimbark group's limited bargaining position.

Therefore the first task of the Kimbark Corporation was to secure financing both to acquire the land and, if successful, for

---

1 Elsinger, *op. cit.*, p. 448.

construction of the center. As in the case of the Webb and Knapp center, no major chain was represented among the Kimbark members; indeed each was an independent merchant (except for Public Cleaners and the launderette). However, after some negotiation, the Connecticut General Life Insurance Company was persuaded to back the group by virtue of the latter's assurance of full occupancy and the good business record of its members. Accordingly, a loan for $500,000 was extended in exchange for a mortgage on the center. This amount was subsequently raised to $600,000 to cover increased costs. With financing thus assured, the Kimbark merchants were in a position to bid on the 53rd Street site.

Since several other organizations and supermarket chains were desirous of acquiring the same site, the success of the Kimbark Plan required a modification of the normal standard of "highest bid." Accordingly officials of the Department of Urban Renewal and Hyde Park citizens urged Mayor Daley to introduce in the City Council a resolution stating that the 53rd-Woodlawn site might be sold to a less-than highest-bid if that bidder offered more benefit to the local community in terms of providing space to displaced businesses.[1] Accordingly on October 18, 1961, the Mayor introduced an ordinance specifying the following criteria for selection of a redeveloper for the site:[2]

1) Accommodation of the greatest possible number of local merchants compatible with economic use of space.
2) Balanced distribution of merchants and services to provide a desirable diversification.
3) Provision for ownership of shops rather than leasing arrangements.
4) Sound architectural and landscape, planning in accord with plan objectives.
5) Financial ability of the developer to carry out the terms of the agreement.
6) The price offered in relation to land values.

These requirements meant that the site affected could be

1 The Land Clearance Commission and the Community Conservation Board were merged in January, 1961 to produce the Department of Urban Renewal of the City of Chicago.
2 *Hyde Park Herald,* Oct. 20, 1961, p. 1.

redeveloped only on behalf of merchants displaced by the Hyde Park urban renewal plan.

The measure was passed by the City Council on November 1, 1961. The Department of Urban Renewal invited bids on February 7, 1962 for the three parcels, C-6, C-7 and (separated by a single structure) C-5.

Five bids were submitted on various combinations of these parcels.[1] Ramsey's group offered $2.02/square foot for the contiguous lots C-6 and C-7, comprising about 100,000 square feet. The American Oil Company offered $4.27/sq. ft. for C-6 alone. Other bids by Urban Renewal Associates and local newspaper publisher, Bruce Sagan, on both parcels were less than Ramsey's. The intention of the latter bidders was to organize a local development corporation composed of local merchants. A fifth bid by Jewel Tea of $2.05/sq. ft. on C-7 was the highest offer on that parcel.

The bid by the Kimbark group was accepted. Theirs was not the highest among the bids applicable to C-6 and C-7: *the novel principle of "community benefit" governed the selection.*

Construction of the Center

The Kimbark merchants could not afford to waste time. Sites C-6 and C-7 were conveyed to them on October 30, 1962. Ground was broken November 28; the Center opened for business less than a year later on October 15, 1963. This rapid schedule was made possible by completing both architectural and financial planning prior to the submission of their bid on the land.

In addition to the Connecticut General loan undertaken collectively, each merchant had to arrange "front money" for the outfitting of his own premises. Most obtained private bank loans. Ted Anderson, whose hardware store was to be a "simple box with shelves," managed on his own resources.

Two businesses, "Mr. G's" and Breslauer's, successfully applied for major loans under the displacement loan program, created by the Small Business Act of 1961. These two loans for

---

1 Except for C-5 which is now owned by the Mobil Oil Co. which prevailed in subsequent bidding on that site alone.

approximately $50,000 each were among the first to be granted to non-agricultural applicants.[1] Additionally, "Mr. G's" received a "regular" long term SBA loan for approximately $150,000. Two architectural plans were drawn up by Donald Olivieri, one allowing Kimbark Avenue to pass through the Center, the other to be used if the City closed Kimbark. After construction had commenced, closure of the street was enacted by the City Council and Olivieri's second plan was implemented taking advantage of the "bonus" of 8,000 square feet thereby created.

Altogether the Plaza consists of two structures, containing a total of 44,000 square feet of commercial space, which form an "L" around a 167 car parking lot. The actual cost of construction and paving has been estimated at $1.5 million in addition to the site acquisition cost of $204,564.

Kimbark Plaza Today

Kimbark Plaza is eminently prosperous today; as a neighborhood convenience center it flourishes despite the presence of the New Hyde Park Shopping Center and the Co-op about six blocks away.[2] In a recent survey, *every respondent in Kimbark Plaza indicated satisfaction with the improvement of his business over his former location.*

Certain problems common to new shopping centers in renewal areas deserve mention, however. The parking lot at Kimbark Plaza, while adequate perhaps for actual shoppers, is vulnerable to use by neighborhood residents for temporary or even permanent parking. As a private lot, the city police are not empowered to ticket automobile violations occuring therein, unless "abandoned for seven days or creating a hazard." Furthermore a traffic hazard has been created where the parking lot empties onto 53rd Street. So far, no light or stop sign has been installed at that point.

Another problem is the use of the Center as a gathering point for motorized youths at night, many of whom are attracted by

---

1 Mr. Breslauer is an elderly businessman (about 68 when the 20-year SBA displacement loan was received).
2 However, over 70 per cent of the customers at Kimbark Plaza are Negro, whereas the proportion is much less in Hyde Park Shopping Center, reflecting the northwestern concentration of Negro residences within Hyde Park-Kenwood.

Plate 8
KIMBARK PLAZA ON OPENING DAY. *Photo provided by Department of Urban Renewal, City of Chicago.*

the pizza restaurant which remains open until 2 A.M. Apparently vandalism has become more of a problem to a business located in such a center than to the same business located inconspicuously on a traditional commercial street.

Notwithstanding such problems, the Kimbark idea has succeeded and is serving as a model for other centers for displaced businesses in Chicago.[1]

HARPER COURT

The Kimbark Plaza concept provided only a partial solution to the problem of keeping local businesses in business locally after displacement by urban renewal. Such a cooperative venture clearly can only be undertaken by enterprises capable of raising capital. Survival is not likely to be a problem for such businesses; their main concern is how to stay in the same community.

---

1 The concept is being utilized in three other centers today, notably Jeffro Plaza, at 26th and State, and Lincoln Park.

Plate 9
BRESLAUER'S ON 55TH STREET BEFORE BUILDING WAS DEMOL-
ISHED. *Photo provided by HUD.*

Plate 10
BRESLAUER'S IN NEW QUARTERS IN KIMBARK PLAZA. *Photo provided by HUD.*

Displaced Artists and Craftsmen

In the case of the marginal, low-volume merchant, survival itself becomes paramount and the cooperative type of center is out of the question; even the Small Business Administration requires proof of ability to repay its loans. The Small Business Displacement Payment of $1500 (raised to $2500 in 1965) has provided modest capital to very small businesses displaced since January 27, 1964, over and above compensation for actual moving expenses. But the sheer unavailability of cheap space in a community undergoing renewal may force the craftsman or family business to move elsewhere or to liquidate.

Before urban renewal Hyde Park was unusually abundant in tiny specialty enterprises offering "old fashioned" services and products. A famous enclave of such shops and studios was known as the "Art Colony," housed in decaying buildings left over from the Columbian Exposition of 1893. Apocryphal former tenants of the Art Colony included Carl Sandburg, Ben Hecht, and James Farrell.[1] Located near the Museum of Science and Industry, the "Colony" enjoyed constant circulation of visitors and very low rents.

Announcement of the impending demolition of the Art Colony for urban renewal purposes in 1962 dramatized to the community that its specialty shops would not survive unassisted. The neighborhood weekly publicized the dilemma in an article entitled "Will Hyde Park lose its Artisans?"[2] Sympathy for the craftsmen themselves and concern about losing the convenience and prestige afforded by the shops promoted community interest in establishing a low rent center especially designed for craftsmen.

A proposal for such a center had been made in 1955, in connection with "Hyde Park A and B", by Harvey S. Perloff, at that time Professor of City Planning at The University of Chicago:

". . . The Arts and Building Center, as its name suggests, would bring together in one place activities and services related to the fine and applied arts and to the improvement and furnishing of homes. The

---

1 Muriel Beadle, *The Hyde Park-Kenwood Urban Renewal Years.* Chicago: 1965, p. 2.
2 *Hyde Park Herald,* April 4, 1962, p. 1.

Plate 11
THE "ART COLONY" ON 57TH STREET

center would provide two types of units: stores and shops for the "building" phase fronting on the main street, and studios of varying sizes for the various "arts" activities, without street frontage. The former would highlight and ease the task of home improvement — a critical aspect of a "renewal" program; the latter would bring to the fore the cultural attractions of the community.[1]

The actual proposal which led to Harper Court was made by the Hyde Park-Kenwood Community Conference in May, 1962. This proposal was based upon a survey of artisans and craftsmen in the area who faced displacement. The committee which conducted the survey found that rents paid by craftsmen averaged $1.50-$1.66/square foot, and recommended that a new center should strive to offer similarly low rates.

Later in 1962, a committee of twenty prominent residents was formed to galvanize community interest. The members included experts in the pertinent fields of law, real estate, and business, who agreed to furnish their talents at no cost. Heading the committee were Mrs. George Beadle, wife of the President

---

1 Harvey S. Perloff, *UUrban Renewal in a Chicago Neighborhood,* Chicago: Hyde Park Herald, Inc., 1955, p. 23.

of the University of Chicago, and Bruce Sagan, publisher of the *Hyde Park Herald.* Architect John Black, also a resident of Hyde Park, was commissioned to design the Center. The plans which he completed in cooperation with Ezra Gordon and John Vandermeulen were revealed in March, 1963.[1]

Actual development of Harper Court was based upon use of three novel devices. The first of these translated community enthusiasm into activity through the incorporation of the Harper Court Foundation under the "Not for Profit" Corporation Law of Illinois, and the sale of low-yield debentures to community residents. The Foundation's board of directors consisted entirely of residents, headed by Mrs. Beadle.

In a fund drive held in the Fall of 1963, the Foundation raised $120,000 in six weeks through the sale of 6 per cent, 25-year bonds to 430 residents. The University of Chicago pledged to buy a maximum of $35,000 towards the $120,000 goal. Sales to private residents exceeded expectations, resulting in the actual purchase of $27,000 worth by the University.

The yield of these debentures, according to Bruce Sagan, was deliberately set below market rates to minimize the annual rate of return to investors, thereby permitting lower rents to be charged to tenants.[2] Additionally, the bonds were subordinated to any other debts incurred by the Foundation. In this way *community enthusiasm was converted into a subsidy.*

With the $120,000 equity secured, the Foundation formally applied to the Small Business Administration in Washington, D. C. for a loan under Section 502 of the Small Business Development Act of 1958. This was the second device. Section 502 authorizes SBA to make loans to "state or local development corporations" to be used "to assist an identifiable small business concern and for a sound business purpose as approved by the Administration."[3] According to Sagan, the Foundation's application was unprecedented in two respects: 1) a not-for-profit corporation had never before applied for recognition as a "development corporation;" and 2) Section 502 had been designed

---

1 *Hyde Park Herald,* March 13, 1963, p. 1.
2 Testimony of Bruce Sagan on June 11, 1965 before the Subcommittee on Housing, Committee on Banking and Currency, House of Representatives.
3 72 Stat. 511, 15 U.S.C. 690 (1958).

to support minor industry and had not before been employed to help artisans.[1]

Notwithstanding these novelties, SBA agreed to furnish a loan covering 80 per cent of the cost of Harper Court, about $480,000, at 5 per cent, payable over 25 years. The Hyde Park Bank and Trust Co. provided 10 per cent of the loan in participation with SBA. Sagan testified that the best rates available in the commercial market for this kind of project would have been 15 years at 6 per cent which would have required the Foundation to charge 22 per cent higher rentals to its tenants.[2]

In addition to low-yield debentures and favorable terms on the SBA loan, a third device was employed to enable Harper Court to rent space at low rates. A rental formula was established whereby approximately one-third of the total floor space would be rented to two restaurants at higher than average rates, since their profits also would presumably be higher than average, because many restaurants had vanished from the area during urban renewal. The remaining two-thirds of the floor space would be divided into about two dozen small shops and rented at various rates below market average, according to what a business had been paying before, or what his profits were expected to be.

Selection of Tenants

The selection of tenants for Harper Court was performed by a special committee while financing was being raised. The purpose of the center was widely publicized and the selection committee both invited applications and actively sought out small enterprises throughout Chicago. They interviewed and received applications from "literally hundreds" of candidates, from which twenty-nine were finally chosen.[3] The Foundation had adopted, in 1964, a policy statement to guide it in choosing tenants, excerpts of which follow:

". . . In the event that a choice must be made between two equally qualified prospective tenants, the priorities implicit in the following order of listing shall tend to obtain . . .:

---

1 Sagan testimony, *op. cit.*, p. 116.
2 *Ibid.*
3 Telephone interview with Mr. Bruce Sagan, August, 1966.

1. Creative and instructional enterprises, especially in the arts. (Painters, ceramicists, weavers, musicians, dancers, photographers of recognized artistic stature; and those offering individual or group instruction in these and similar arts.)
2. Purveyors of esthetic or intellectual materials. (Book stores, art galleries, dealers in music; suppliers of materials for thoughtful and creative hobbies; and enterprises "servicing" the above, such as picture framers or musical instrument repairers.)
3. Quality craftsmen and artisans. (Cabinet makers, lamp-makers, landscapers, confectioners, tailors.)
4. Retailers in unusual and superior commodities. (Importers, outlets for regional crafts, specialty food shops or restaurants where food is regarded as a creative product for the discriminating consumer.)
. . . . When renting space to generally conventional enterprises at the higher rentals which help to provide sufficient income to support the project as a whole, the enterprise must be compatible with the cultural and intellectual component of community life for which Harper Court seeks to provide; it must demonstrably add to the scope and convenience of the goods and services offered by Harper Court as a whole; and it must offer goods and/or services which, by virtue of their special character or level of quality, are not — nor are likely to be—available elsewhere in the immediate neighborhood."[1]

Besides the policy statement, the committee followed two sources of authority in making its selection. One was the results of a questionnaire, completed by the Hyde Park public, which revealed 26 types of shops which the community wanted or needed. Of these, the committee was able to satisfy 19 choices[2] (See Table 2.2).

TABLE 2.2
HARPER COURT TENANTS

Name of shop and owner	Former Address, if any
Acasa (Books, stationery, and gifts) Miss Clarinda Buck (deceased)	1322 E. 55th Street
American Designers Galleries (now discontinued) Ray Williams	
Andrews and Lee Gallery (paintings and antiques) Partnership dissolved shortly after opening. Now bankrupt, space to be used by Book Center.	
Animal Clinic (veterinarian) Adam C. Kostecki (professional veterinarian)	
Art Directions (Art supply and picture framing) William Erick Erickson	
Book Center (new books) Mr. Jack Mosoff	

1 *Hyde Park Herald,* Oct. 9, 1963, p. 9.
2 Memorandum of the Harper Court Foundation, mimeographed, 1965.

TABLE 2.2 (continued)

Name of shop and owner	Former Address, if any
Borkeramik (handmade pottery) Albert J. Borch	
The Cage (Pet supplies) (now discontinued) Theodore James Drake	1352 E. 53rd St. (not displaced)
Chances R (pub-type restaurant) Other premises at: 1533 N. Wells Avenue	
Clothes Closet (new fashions) Miss Marta Devins	
Contemporary Prints and Drawings (now discontinued) Mrs. Helen Schlien	
Cooley's Candles (commercial and hand-dipped candles) Mr. George Cooley, Department of Development and Planning	
Court House (Gourmet Restaurant) Mr. Hans Morsbach also owns Medici Coffeehouse 1450 E. 57th Street	
Eclectic (Objets d' art from demolished houses) Now dissolved	
Fabyar (Fabric and Yarn) Mrs. Katherine Colman and four partners	
Fensin Lamps Ray Fensin	
Fret Shop (Stringed instruments) Peter Leibundgath	1551 E. 57th St. (Art Colony) 1547 E. 53rd St.
Fine Arts Faculty Gallery (closed subsequently) Cooperative—36 partners	
Harper Gallery Mr. Jan Messinger Mr. and Mrs. Charles F. Custer	53rd St. & Lake Park (not displaced)
Maison Henri (now closed) Mr. and Mrs. Henri Neurath	
One of a Kind (antiques) never opened space to be used by Art Directions	
Plants Alive Nathan Morris, Department of Urban Renewal	
Rosemary Mitchell Interiors Miss Rosemary Mitchell	
Ruyell Ho (portrait photography) Ruyell Ho (now out of business)	
Totville (children's clothing and related items) Mrs. Jean K. Lutz (now discontinued) also owns store at 1643 E. 87th St.	
Sticks and Stones (primitive art and crafts) Alphonso M. Westbrook	
Van Tellingen's (used books) Rudolph A. Van Tellingen	1555 E. 57th St. (Art Colony) 1544 E. 53rd St.
Wall and Window (wallpaper and drapery) Mr. Bert N. Cohn	

The other source of guidance was the Small Business Administration. Approval by SBA of the proposed tenants of Harper
Court was required for two reasons. First the over-all $480,000
loan from SBA would actually comprise 29 separate loans made
to the Foundation *on behalf of* each of the 29 individual businesses. The unacceptability of any of the tenants to SBA would
deny the Foundation a corresponding fraction of the $480,000
upon which it was planning. Furthermore, many of the tenants
would need individual loans from SBA, independent of the
Foundation, in order to finance the costs of opening in the center.[1] Therefore, each candidate was examined to determine
whether he or she could overcome the SBA requirement that a
loan cannot be made "if it will subsidize inferior management."[2]

In practice, the tenant selection committee consulted SBA in
doubtful cases. Reciprocally, an SBA official admitted that the
Administration was able to relax its standards in certain instances
due to the economic advantage of collecting many specialty
shops in one center. In other words, certain marginal concerns
were approved in the context of Harper Court which would not
have passed SBA standards if applying individually.[3]

Acquisition of the Site

The acquisition of a site for Harper Court, as in the case of
Kimbark Plaza, required suport and assistance from the city
urban renewal authorities. Part of the land on which it was eventually built had been acquired and cleared by the City for a fire
station and police station. These facilities were subsequently
located elsewhere, leaving a site (I-8) vacant which extended
from Harper to Lake Park Avenue along 52nd St.

In order to create a "clustered" pattern, the Foundation
wanted only the western half of this site which fronted on Harper,
directly opposite another "institutional" site which it intended
to acquire. Additionally it wanted an adjacent parcel on Harper,
then owned by the Chicago Parking Lot Authority and not available for sale.

---

1 Sagan interview.
2 13 C.F.R. §108.502 (1) (1958).
3 Interview with officials of Small Business Administration, August, 1966.

Accordingly a three-way swap was engineered by the Department of Urban Renewal involving another site in the same block, which was zoned for eventual use by a gas station. The latter parcel was transferred by DUR to the Parking Lot Authority in return for the latter's parking lot on Harper. The unwanted eastern half of I-8 was re-zoned by DUR for a gas station. The western half of I-8 was combined with the adjacent former parking lot and site I-10 across Harper Avenue to form a "package," custom-made for Harper Court.

The bid documentation for this land was even more restricted than in the case of Kimbark Plaza. The City Council authorized sale of the land to a bidder which proposed to build a "not for profit" center for artisans.[1] Harper Court Foundation, as the sole bidder, acquired the land for $135,672.

After this amount was used for acquisition of the site, the remainder of the Foundation's assets of $600,000, comprising the proceeds of the bond issue and of the SBA loan, was spent for construction of three two-story buildings, containing a total of 36,000 square feet of commercial space. The architect, John Black, characterized them as "modernized versions of the converted brownstone."[2] They surround a small brick pedestrian mall created by the closing of Harper Avenue for half a block. A fourth building of similar design was completed in August, 1967 for use by the Hyde Park Cooperative Society as a furniture store.

The time schedule of the development of Harper Court, once the idea had taken, was rapid. The sale of bonds by 124 volunteers was completed by May 7, 1964. Approval by the City Council of the site disposition in accordance with the above described arrangements was obtained on June 1, 1964. The land was conveyed to the Foundation in November, 1964 and construction began with a ceremonial "bricklaying" (inside Bruce Sagan's Harper Theater!) on December 1.

Opening and Subsequent Events

Official completion of the center was marked by a gala eve-

1 Sagan testimony, *op. cit.*, p. 117.
2 Testimony of Mrs. George Beadle, before Subcommittee on Housing, *op. cit.*, p. 111.

ning on July 29, 1965, complete with balloons, fireworks, and music by the Fifth Army Band. Unfortunately, no businesses, displaced or otherwise, had yet opened their doors for business. The first two tenants to open (on August 21) were Sticks and Stones, a primitive art shop, and the Andrews and Lee Gallery, Ltd.[1]

The remaining 26 tenants opened between September, 1965 and April, 1966, except for one called "One of a Kind" which never opened.

An early disappointment among the tenants was "The Eclectic" which specialized in bric-a-brac from homes in the community which were being demolished by urban renewal. Its proprietor received considerable advance publicity from "dashing around in a hearse to collect objets d'art." Eclectic lasted only a few months and its space is still vacant.

As mentioned, the tenant selection committee was able to produce 19 of the 26 types of businesses requested in the neigh-

Plate 12

HARPER COURT. *Photo provided by Department of Urban Renewal, City of Chicago.*

---

[1] Operation of this gallery was severely limited by the departure of partner Lee and the enterprise went bankrupt within a year.

Plate 13
INSIDE HARPER COURT. *Photo provided by Department of Urban Renewal, City of Chicago.*

borhood questionnaire. However, despite the effort to rush the project to completion, it was found impossible to implement the center's original purpose—to rescue Hyde Park's artisans and small shopkeepers displaced by urban renewal. Among the 29 businesses chosen for Harper Court, only three fitted that description. Two of them, the Fret Shop (stringed instruments) and a used book store, had been displaced when the Art Colony was cleared in 1963. Both had weathered the intervening 2½ years in temporary quarters provided by the Department of Urban Renewal in buildings scheduled for demolition. DUR attempted to evict Rudolph A. Van Tellingen, the book dealer, shortly before Harper Court was completed. In the related court proceedings, Van Tellingen was granted extra time by the judge, enabling him to stay until his new store was ready.

The third displacee to reach Harper Court was the Acasa Book and Gift Shop, owned by Miss Clarinda Buck. Miss Buck's former premises on 55th were preserved after its neighbors were demolished, by virtue of a local office of DUR on the second

Plate 14
THE LAST STORES ARE DEMOLISHED ON 55TH STREET. Acasa
moved directly from this building into the new Harper Court.

floor. Acasa was able to move directly from its old location to
Harper Court and received both moving expenses and the $2500
payment authorized for small businesses displaced after August
10, 1965. *This was the only "model" example of relocation of a
small, marginal concern in the entire Hyde Park-Kenwood renewal story.* Fittingly, the shop was a tradition in the neighborhood, precisely the sort of enterprise which Harper Court was
designed to rescue. However, the store's future is presently uncertain due to the death of Miss Buck, only a year after her move
to Harper Court.

It is too early to assess the over-all success of Harper Court.
Its prosperity differs from one business to another, and certain
problems such as business inexperience may be alleviated with
time. The Small Business Administration has attempted to hold
seminars in business practices for the benefit of the amateurs
among the tenants.

As of March, 1968, many changes in Harper Court's composition have occurred, consisting mainly of expansions of existing businesses into space vacated by the least successful of the

original entrants, and a trend away from art and towards women's apparel and gifts. Cooley's Candle Shop moved into the larger space vacated by the departure of the Faculty Fine Arts Gallery and expanded its merchandise to include general Scandinavian wares. Cooley's former space was taken over by Sticks and Stones which also enlarged its gift inventory. Another former art gallery, that of Andrews and Lee, was replaced by an expansion of the Book Center. Contemporary Prints and Drawings also succumbed and its space is now occupied by a leather crafts business, which was displaced by clearance for a new high school project on Hyde Park Boulevard. The bakery, "Maison Henri," closed and its space is now occupied by a boutique. "Art Directions" also expanded into a vacant space intended for "One of a Kind." During March, Totville, The Cage and American Designers also departed, the first two due to repeated floodings of their basement space because of poor storm drains, and Totville to consolidate with another store. Wall and Window has expanded into American Designers' space.

Thus the original 29 store spaces of the center are now reduced to 21 through expansions, and the principle of substantial diversity amongst the businesses has been somewhat eroded under the test of market conditions. However, the evident prosperity of certain businesses, regardless of the original merchandising criteria is consistent with Harper Court's other goal of being able to "carry" certain less profitable but worthy craftsmen.

Difficulties with the initial managing agent, Draper and Kramer,[1] have been reduced by replacing them with a partnership of two local residents, wives of Chicago real estate experts, who are trying to procure new, efficient, tenants to fill the new vacancies. Nevertheless, continuing difficulties remain obvious. Parking is virtually non-existent except in the adjacent city lot. The latter, however, is often filled by non-customers and its charge, though nominal, discourages motorized passers-by. As for pedestrians, Harper Court is not very centrally located. In

---

1 Several tenants had gone on a rent strike, charging that Draper and Kramer had failed to provide any services during their management term. General dissatisfaction with the assistance and concern of the company led quickly to their replacement.

winter, few local residents stroll in this direction. Furthermore, persons approaching from 53rd Street must pass the shops of 53rd Street, many of which now anticipate what Harper Court has to offer. In fact, 53rd Street, now the primary shopping thoroughfare in Hyde Park, offers stiff competition to several Harper Court shops.

Another kind of effect is noticeable at the Harper Avenue approach to Harper Court. A "31-flavor" ice cream parlor has ousted a local "figure," Benny the Tailor (who now has a shop in the Hyde Park YMCA). A pub-type bar with a late liquor license is installed across the street. Together with Bruce Sagan's Harper Theater, the street has assumed an atmosphere which the

Plate 15

NEW DEVELOPMENT ON 51ST STREET. *Photo provided by Department of Urban Renewal, City of Chicago.*

Chicago Daily News (Nov. 14, 1965) characterized as the "Old Town of the South"—a product of the stimulus of Harper Court.

Aside from the three main shopping centers, the only other nucleus of new commercial space is the "Village Center" located at Lake Park Avenue and Hyde Park Boulevard. The development currently consists of a new A & P Supermarket with a sixty car parking lot. An adjacent three story structure, formerly housing a bowling alley, is undergoing modernization to serve as a professional offices center with space for a restaurant on the ground floor. The plans for the remaining land assigned to the Village Center are presently in flux.

Plate 16
OPPOSITE THE VILLAGE CENTER, CLARK AND CLARK, ONE OF HYDE PARK'S FIRST DISPLACEES, IS DISPLACED AGAIN AND THE STORE DEMOLISHED FOR A NEW HIGH SCHOOL (April 1, 1968).

CHAPTER THREE

Mortality Experience of The Hyde Park-Kenwood Displacees

Hyde Park *A* and *B* and Hyde Park-Kenwood Urban Renewal Program displaced six hundred and forty-one businesses from land to be cleared. Thirty-one per cent of these (207) went out of business when they were dislocated, consistent with the national average. An additional thirty per cent (201) reestablished themselves for only a brief time after relocation, but ceased operations before the end of 1966. Of the 233 still in business, 83 are still operating in Hyde Park (23 of them in one or another of the three new shopping centers—slightly more than one-third of the 61 businesses in these centers), 86 relocated to adjacent communities, 55 moved elsewhere in the Chicago metropolitan area, and 9 migrated outside the area. Table 3.1 provides details by project. Figure 3.1 shows the complex reshuffling that took place within Hyde Park-Kenwood, and Figure 3.2 the relocation patterns of displacees moving elsewhere within Chicago.

These are the kinds of figures seized upon by the opponents of urban renewal as evidence of a profound and deleterious impact of renewal activity upon small business. They indicate, it is said, the high social costs that stem from the physical means of renewal planning. The presumption is that liquidation rates of thirty per cent or more are excessively high.

A quotation from the Hearings before Subcommittee No. 5 of the Select Committee on Small Business of the House of Representatives, conducted in Chicago on June 11-12, 1965, will illustrate. Mrs. Florence Scala, an opponent of urban renewal, is speaking:

"...The small business in our urban community is truly in real trouble. Indeed, the whole urban community is in trouble because of the effects of government clearance but particularly because of urban renewal clearance ... We have allowed the urban renewal law to be

TABLE 3.1

DISPOSITION OF DISPLACEES

Project	Total Workload	Liquidated	Relocated	Liquidation after Relocation[a]
Hyde Park A	190 (100%)	51 (26.8%)	31 (16.3%)	108 (56.8%)
Hyde Park B	4 (100%)			4 (100%)
Hyde Park-Kenwood	447 (100%)	156 (34.9%)	202 (45.1%)	89 (19.9%)
TOTALS	641 (100%)	207 (32.3%)	233 (36.3%)	201 (31.4%)

[a]Differences in rates reflect in part differences in the period of time elapsed since Hyde Park A and the Hyde Park-Kenwood project.

used in such a way that it literally destroy thousands of small businesses yearly . . ."[1]

The crux of the matter is whether the liquidation rate among small business displacees is "excessive." Although there is considerable variability from one renewal project to another, the modal percentage liquidating upon displacement in the United States as a whole exceeds twenty-five and the mean is close to thirty-three (refer back to Chapter 1). Losses are highest among food-related retail units, the smallest stores, stores whose owners entered business from the lowest socio-economic levels, and

---

1 Parenthetically, Mrs. Scala also took the opportunity to attack this study: ". . . I include a footnote . . . (concerning) . . . the Hyde Park clearance program to emphasize the sham that this program has become. I am quoting from the "Urban Renewal Review," published by the Department of Urban Renewal, volume 4, No. 2, April-May 1965, city of Chicago:
"The city council has approved an ordinance authorizing the department to file an application for a demonstration grant from the Federal Housing and Home Finance Agency. The funds would be used to study small business relocation experiences in the city with special emphasis on the Hyde Park-Kenwood project. The gathering and analysis of the data would be done under contract with the Center for Urban Studies of the University of Chicago."
"The interesting thing about this is that the Center for Urban Studies is headed by a former city employee, the city planner who designed the Hyde Park urban renewal plan which cleared out 600 small businesses . . ." The U.S. Congress, Subcommittee No. 5 of the Select Committee on Small Business, *Hearing, Small Business Problems in Urban Areas*, 89th Congress, 1st Session, pp. 169-172 (hereafter cited as *Hearings, Chicago*). The latter reference is to Jack Meltzer, Director of the Center for Urban Studies. Such an attack, levied before this study was even started, made us constantly aware of the need for objectivity and accuracy. Indeed, the very inference that because federal research funds supported the study, the investigators would produce a "whitewash," made us both meticulous in the scientific style of our inquiry and assertive of the freedom of our investigations and conclusions, however unpalatable they were likely to be to either the friends or foes of public policy. Our conclusions are our own, and for them we accept complete responsibility. If they are inadequate, it is because our science is weak, and not because of any overt or implicit censorship. We take it as a mark of courage on the part of the public agency that they were willing to support research on these terms, to provide an objective body of evidence about the effects of displacement by urban renewal on the small businessman.

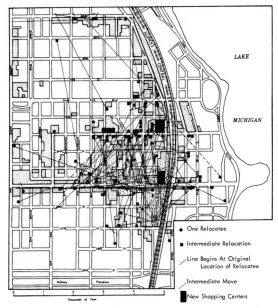

Figure 3.1
RELOCATION OF DISPLACEES
WITHIN HYDE PARK-KENWOOD.

stores whose owners are closest to retirement.[1] Yet these are the
kinds of business declining most rapidly in the country at large.[2]
Does the high liquidation rate simply reflect national small business trends, perhaps with some hastening of the inevitable for
a few, or is it greater among businesses dislocated by urban renewal than might reasonably have been expected if renewal had
not taken place? Only in the latter case can any assertion of
excessive liquidation rates be supported.

If there were some standard against which the mortality rates
of displacees had been compared, the assertions of the earlier
"impact" literature and those who attack renewal activity might
be valid. But heretofore such data have not been available, and
small business is undergoing great changes because of increasing
scale of retailing, increasing consumer mobility, and rising real
incomes, all of which are contributing to the competitive success
of large or more specialized retailing units and business centers,

---

1 Basil G. Zimmer, *Rebuilding Cities.* Chicago: Quadrangle Books, 1964. Eric W.
Meyer, *The Effect of Business Displacement Due to Urban Renewal.* New York:
Pratt Institute, 1967.
2 Brian J. L. Berry, *Commercial Structure . . . , op. cit.*

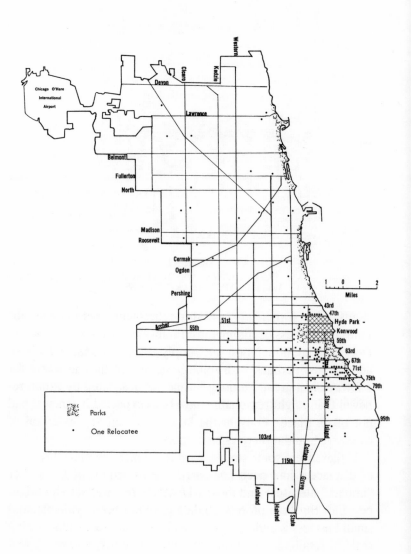

Figure 3.2
RELOCATION OF DISPLACEES
OUTSIDE HYDE PARK-KENWOOD.

and the gradual elimination of those that are smaller and less viable.

Clearly, analysis is required. Thirty-one per cent of the Hyde Park-Kenwood displacees liquidated, while at the same time some dramatic new experiments in commercial renewal were being undertaken. Was the liquidation rate excessive? This question can only be answered analytically and comparatively.

SMALL BUSINESS TRENDS

The analytic problem that is raised is a complex one, for a variety of studies have documented the fact that several secular trends are now leading to the decline of small business in the central city quite independently of urban renewal, and regardless of the social characteristics of the neighborhood involved.[1] Figures 3.3 and 3.4 show, for example, the changes in retail businesses in the Chicago metropolitan area in the periods 1948-1958 and 1958-1963. There is retail growth in suburbia, but elsewhere the number of retail units is declining rapidly. Figures 3.5 and 3.6 relate the changes to the broad ecological zones of the metropolis.

This being so, the question then becomes whether the liquidations would have taken place in any case—in short, whether the liquidation rates among displacees are excessive when compared with what might be expected from the ongoing processes of retail change thought to be operating.[2]

Retail Change in Chicago

In a separate study,[3] the senior author of this book clarified these processes of retail change in Chicago. This previous study showed that only 50 years ago the Central Business District

---

1 Edward D. Hollander and others, *The Future of Small Business*. New York: Frederic A. Praeger, Publishers, 1967.

2 The critics then reply that business in slum areas is *different*, oriented to ethnic or racial communities that are cleared by urban renewal, so that such a comparison "may be unrelated to the issue here. Slum businesses and other small business are quite different in their ability to survive. Small businesses of the white middle class areas lose out because larger units are more attractive, offer more choice, etc. Such things do not operate among slum dwellers." (Basil G. Zimmer, in writing to the authors, 1967). The evidence we present later is a convincing rejoinder to such a critique.

3 Brian J. L. Berry, *Commercial Structure . . .*, *op. cit.* This section summarizes the findings of the earlier study, completed as a resource paper for Chicago's Community Renewal Program.

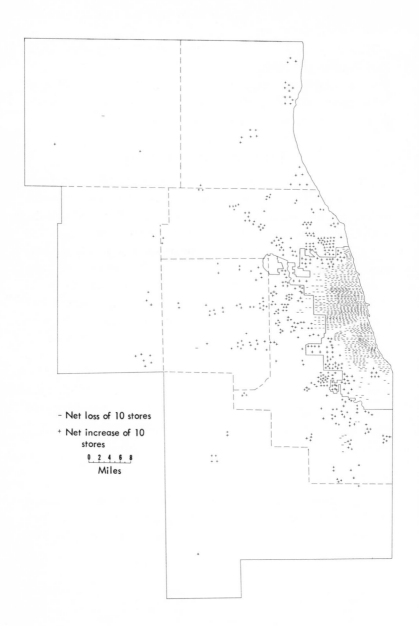

Figure 3.3
NET CHANGES IN RETAIL BUSINESS IN
METROPOLITAN CHICAGO, 1948-1958.

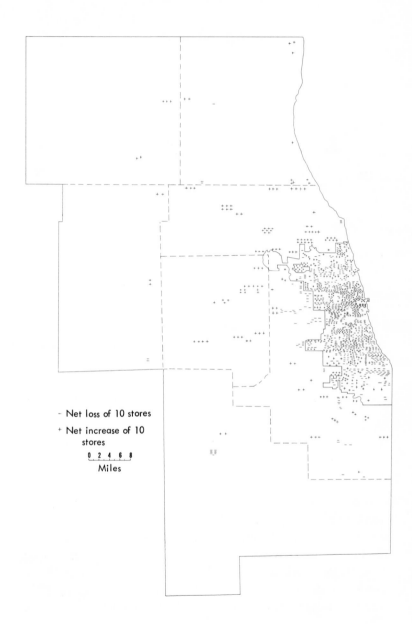

- Net loss of 10 stores
+ Net increase of 10 stores

0 2 4 6 8
Miles

Figure 3.4
NET CHANGES IN RETAIL BUSINESS, 1958-1963.

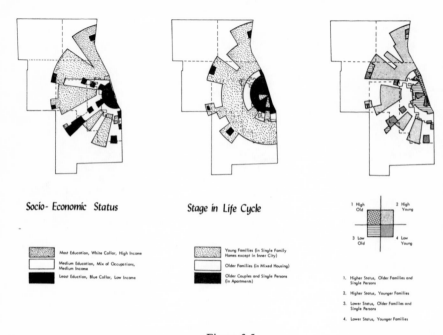

Figure 3.5
SOCIAL AREAS OF METROPOLITAN CHICAGO, 1960.

provided almost all the goods and services demanded by the residents of Chicago, despite earlier beginnings of neighborhood business street developments. Following 1910 a complex array of outlying business centers and commercial ribbons developed to serve the residents of the city, evolving so that by 1958 the Census of Business reported that in that year all but 14.6 per cent of Chicago's retail transactions were completed outside the CBD.

Two periods in the development of the City of Chicago's outlying commercial structure can be distinguished. The first

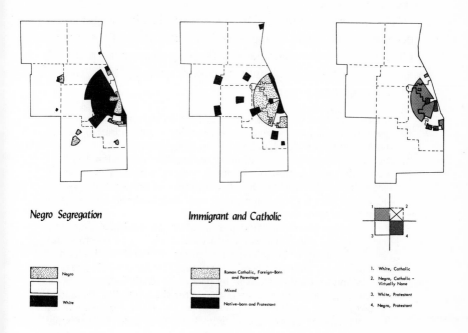

Negro Segregation

Immigrant and Catholic

Negro

White

Roman Catholic, Foreign-Born and Parentage

Mixed

Native-born and Protestant

1. White, Catholic
2. Negro, Catholic – Virtually None
3. White, Protestant
4. Negro, Protestant

Figure 3.6
PRINCIPAL ETHNIC PATTERNS
IN METROPOLITAN CHICAGO, 1960.

spans the quarter century of continued explosive growth of the city following 1910, and ends in the depression years and wartime. During this period the essential features of retailing to be seen today in most parts of the city developed. Commercial land uses extended along more than 500 miles of ribbons occupying most of the section line and half section streets. At fairly regular intervals (the principal street intersections) some 70 outlying business centers developed in the familiar hierarchy of neighborhood, community, and regional centers. Whereas service and convenience uses predominated in the ribbons, the centers emphasized provision of shopping goods for different segments of the urban market.

This pattern remains today, but is experiencing severe stress because of the many changes in American life and the city of Chicago that have characterized the second postwar phase of growth and decline of the outlying commercial structure. Among these changes have been:

1) *Suburbanization.* Consumers with medium to high purchasing power favor residences and convenience shopping in the suburbs, leaving the lower income communities in the older central city.

2) *Increasing mobility.* A continuing automobile revolution has promoted the new pattern of shopping centers, which in turn favors larger businesses with high credit ratings. In the central city the old corner store, strip commercial and neighborhood convenience shopping patterns remain.

3) *Rising real incomes.* As Americans have become wealthier, they have demanded the superior quality and greater variety of commodities found only in larger stores and/or more specialized shops, both types of which favor shopping center locations. The automobile provides the customer with the means to by-pass older smaller stores in favor of newer larger business centers that offer the centrality demanded by large retail outlets, and appropriate locations for retailers of specialty and/or luxury goods, who have little potential for scale economies. Accompanying the income shift is also a rising demand for personal services.

4) *Changing technology of retailing.* Increasing costs of labor relative to those of land and capital have hastened the rate at which businessmen have taken to larger scale, more automated forms of retailing. In addition, larger-scale high-volume establishments can operate on slimmer margins, offering lower prices to cost-conscious consumers. This has meant powerful, often fatal, competition for the smaller retailer, and the success of the larger stores in the new planned shopping centers and of the discount houses. Larger stores, in turn, have easier access to credit and financing than their smaller competitors.

5) *Social change in the central city.* The classical picture of the social geography of an American city is one in which the less wealthy live around the center, the middle-income groups at the periphery, and the highest income groups in sectors extending outwards from the city core to the edge of the metropolis. Central areas provided homes for new immigrants who, as they prospered, moved outwards to wealthier neighborhoods. As the city grew, lower income neighborhoods extended outward from the city center encroaching upon older parts of the higher income zones. Urban ecologists have described these processes using such concepts as "succession" and the

"filtering down" of housing. Negroes, in particular, living in congested, segregated slums, were only able to extend their residential area by gradual extension at the periphery, a process which accelerated with increasing migration of Negroes to Chicago from the South during the 1950s. The results are clear. In 1940, out of a city population of 3.4 million, 300,000 were Negro and 3.1 million were white. In 1950 the city's population reached 3.6 million, still with a 3.1 million whites, and with 500,000 Negroes. In 1960 the white population had fallen to 2.7 million and the Negro population was over 800,000. Today, the number of Negro residents of Chicago approaches 1 million. What does this mean for retailing? Very simply loss of markets, for Negro family income averages approximately two-thirds that of the white population of Chicago, Negro families are larger, and the incidence of unemployment (including a growing pool of technologically-unemployed unskilled southern immigrants and of young high school dropouts) among Negroes is greater. Growth of the Negro population has meant declining retail markets throughout the city.

The story of the transition from middle- to low-income status (and coincidentally in the contemporary city, from white to black) is an interesting one, because it holds the key to understanding the development and persistence of commercial blight in the city's communities. In fact, there is not one equilibrium pattern for retailing in the city of Chicago, but two—one in the middle and higher income periphery, and one in the central lower income zones. In the outer and higher income zone the hierarchy of business centers has four levels (neighborhood, community, smaller shoppers goods, and regional) but in the central lower income zone it only has two (neighborhood and smaller shoppers) because of the smaller demands for specialized commodities at the lower income levels.

Population turnover such as we have described involves the replacement of the higher income equilibrium by the lower, with effects expressed in the centers which previously served the higher income residents. The transition actually takes place in several stages:

1) *The anticipation of neighborhood transition.* During the phase two important things happen. First, the normal replacement of businesses which fail, or close because the owners retire or die, ceases. Vacancy rates begin to rise. Second, a "maintenance gap" appears. Property owners cease normal repairs, or reduce maintenance expenditures, because of growing uncertainty about prospective revenues. There

are thus the beginnings of dilapidation, especially among the vacant shops, and a generally rundown appearance prevails.

2) *During the period of population turnover.* In this phase demands drop precipitously, particularly for the more specialized, higher quality kinds of goods. The more flexible stores change their price lines, but the smaller more specialized shops do not have such flexibility, and go out of business. Vacancies in centers rise, reaching between one-third and one-half the stores in the worst cases.

3) *The stabilization phase.* The neighborhood then settles down into its lower income character. There has been a maintenance gap there, too, and now, with lower incomes, it is difficult to restore previously sound building conditions. Thus, the areas surrounding business centers are at best "seedy" and more usually continue to deteriorate. Rents in the business centers drop, and the more viable establishments from the ribbons move in and fill up the vacant space. Vacancies mount in the ribbons, settling down at around 20 per cent of all establishments, and usually concentrated in the most dilapidated buildings, which through lack of use deteriorate even more. Lower income zones are thus criss-crossed with ribbons of unwanted, blighted commercial property.

Graphic testimony to these changes is provided in Table 3.2, showing how, under the simultaneous impact of each of these forces, the retail complement of city business declined between 1948 and 1963.

TABLE 3.2

CHANGE IN NUMBERS OF BUSINESSES, 1948-1963

	United States		City of Chicago	
	Retail	Selected Services	Retail	Selected Services
1948	1,668,479	559,559	43,540	20,485
1954	1,721,650	785,589	32,222	20,952
1958	1,788,325	975,195	35,910	22,146
1963	1,707,931	1,061,673	29,775	21,597

Since urban renewal usually enters the scene in this atmosphere of accumulating commercial blight, the relevant question about liquidations among displacees seems to be whether they are simply a reflection of the larger trends in the retail industry, brought to a head in a limited period of time by dislocation, or whether they include viable businesses that have been forced to liquidate and that might have survived if alternative public policies had been in effect.

A WORKING MODEL OF CHANGE

Clearly, small business is consumer-oriented, and extremely sensitive in a very short period of time to changes in market conditions. A substantial amount of painstaking statistical analysis in the earlier study[1] came to the following conclusions about the precise impact of each source of change in Chicago:

1) If nothing else changed except the level of technology and consumer mobility, the annual drop in retail establishments due to scale changes would be 5.87 per cent.

2) Real income increases of 3.2 per cent per annum offset this decline in numbers by 2.7 per cent per annum (a 1-per cent shift in real income means a shift in retail establishments of 0.86 per cent).

3) Social turnover in a city neighborhood, by which a middle-income group is replaced by a low-income group reduces demands to the extent that numbers of retail establishments will decline at the rate of 2.2 per cent per annum during the decade of change.

4) A 1.0 per cent change in the population of a community will generate a change of 0.98 per cent in the number of retail establishments.

If these figures are drawn together they mean that stable higher income communities in the city are experiencing 2.0 per cent annual rates of decline of retail establishments, stable low income neighborhoods have declines of 4.0 per cent per annum, and areas in transition from middle to low income have rates of decline exceeding 5.0 per cent per annum.

Because some of these declines in establishments are accompanied by scale increases, rates by which demands for retail floor area are declining are not quite as bad—zero net change in the stable higher income zones, 2 per cent decline in stable low income neighborhoods, and a 3-per cent decline in areas of transition. The only areas of retail growth are outside the city limits, in expanding suburbia, where the population is increasing in new residential subdivisions.

A Basic Equation

The basic equation produced in the earlier study, drawing together the statistical findings to describe these retail changes is

$$C_E = -7.71 + 0.9778\,C_P + 0.8638\,C_I \ (R^2 = 0.95)$$

where C_E is the average annual rate of change in retail establish-

---

[1] Berry, *op. cit.*

ments, and C_P and C_I are the respective rates of change for population and median incomes.

This equation, computed for the period 1950-1960, is uncorrected for price shifts, but if they are taken into account, so that the median income term is replaced by real incomes, the intercept (assuming constant inflationary pressures for all population groups in the city) becomes -5.87.

Since we will make some use of this equation in the analysis that follows, it is worthwhile to review some of the econometric problems that such use presents. We assume that the constant term includes net loss from secular forces, assumed in turn to exert a uniform pressure on all areas of the city, in contrast to the considerable variability of population and income shifts from place to place. Any error in these assumptions will therefore seriously alter the conclusions.

Use of the constant term in this way leads, in effect, to the argument that one or more variables have been omitted from the equation and are subsumed in the intercept. Now if the remaining variables are positively correlated with the missing variable, the intercept will be biased downward, meaning that

1) Estimates of the coefficients of C_P and C_I will be too high if the secular trends are positively correlated with C_P and C_I, and conversely.
2) The estimate of the constant term is biased downward if the secular trends are positively correlated with C_P and C_I.[1]

However, the correlation of the secular trends with population changes in neighborhoods is close to zero (some neighborhoods are growing and some declining, irrespective of income and mobility shifts), and the correlation with C_I is negative (income shifts generate more stores, technological changes less). Therefore, the equation actually provides a *conservative* base for estimating what might have happened to the Hyde Park businessman in the absence of intervention by urban renewal.

COMPARATIVE CASE STUDIES

The retail change equation captures the effects of the forces affecting the retail structure of communities in Chicago. To

---

1 I am indebted to George S. Tolley and John H. Makin for making me spell out these implications carefully.

determine exactly what might have happened to business in Hyde Park-Kenwood if urban renewal had not taken place, estimates of the likely values assumed by the determining forces must be added. This we achieve by analyzing a variety of materials relating to small business mortality in Hyde Park-Kenwood and in three neighboring Chicago communities during the period 1953-1967. Each case exemplifies a different socio-economic condition or condition of socio-economic change, and taken together, they enable us to draw comparative conclusions about the liquidation of Hyde Park businesses, and thus to assess whether the reported rates are indeed excessive. In brief, the required standard is provided, by comparing what happened to business with what would have been likely to happen if urban renewal had not taken place in Hyde Park.

The four communities are South Shore, Oakland-North Kenwood, Woodlawn, and Hyde Park-Kenwood. See Figure 3.7 and Table 3.3. Until the years following 1960 South Shore was a relatively stable middle-income white community of more than 70,000 population and 30,000 housing units, although since

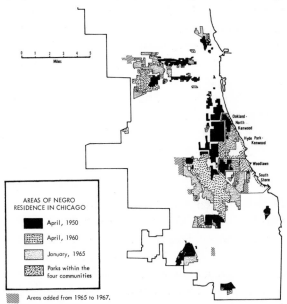

Figure 3.7
AREAS OF NEGRO RESIDENCE IN CHICAGO THROUGH 1967.

TABLE 3.3

**POPULATION AND INCOME CHANGES IN FOUR
SELECTED CHICAGO COMMUNITIES**

Community	Population			Median Family Income[a]		
	1950	1960	% Change	1950	1960	% Change
Hyde Park	55,206	45,577	—17.45	4,754	6,772	+42.44
S. Kenwood	16,300	19,100	+17.17	4,500	5,900	+31.11
N. Kenwood	19,100	22,300	+16.75	3,500	4,400	+25.11
Oakland	24,464	24,378	— 0.37	2,683	3,412	+27.17
Woodlawn	80,699	81,279	+ 0.71	3,473	4,769	+38.12
South Shore	79,336	73,086	— 7.88	5,298	7,888	+48.88

[a]Change not adjusted for shifts in the price level.

1960 it has experienced a substantial influx of nonwhite population. Oakland-North Kenwood had a population of 42,000 in 1960, having undergone a transition from white to low income Negro in the period 1940-1950 in all except its southern fringe. In 1950 the population was 80 per cent black, and by 1960 the percentage exceeded 95 as the "turnover process" was completed. Woodlawn had 30,000 housing units in 1960, and a population of 81,000. In 1950, 38 per cent of its population was Negro (concentrated west of Cottage Grove Avenue), but by 1960 this had increased to 90 per cent. The 1950-1960 period was thus for Woodlawn one of "engulfment" by the ghetto, and replacement of Loop commuters, elderly white apartment dwellers, and University of Chicago faculty and students, by a low income nonwhite group.

Hyde Park had a population of 50,000 in 1940. This increased to 55,000 in 1950, when the nonwhite population was only 3 per cent. In the years following 1950, population continued to increase, and the nonwhite percentage reached 37 in 1956. Because of renewal clearance, however, the population was cut back to 45,000 in 1960, although the nonwhite proportion remained approximately the same. Additionally, South Kenwood (south of 47th Street) had a population of 22,000 in 1960, of which the largest proportion was nonwhite. This, together with Hyde Park, comprises the renewal area under study. Before 1950 Hyde Park had been a middle-income white community. Renewal activity was initiated because the community began to deteriorate severely in the early part of the 1950-1960 decade, when one-third of its population changed to nonwhite.

The comparative cases thus provide a spectrum of the stable middle-income white community Hyde Park had been (South Shore), the low-income Negro community it was in process of becoming before renewal entered the scene (Oakland), and what the transitional period from middle to low-income and from white to Negro would have been like if permitted to run its course completely (Woodlawn, 1950-1960). Small business mortality experiences can be arrayed against this income, race and stability spectrum, and the Hyde Park displacement process compared with the array. The questions to be answered are, in this context, whether urban renewal led to liquidation rates that were any different from what might be expected, given the position of Hyde Park within the socio-economic spectrum of Chicago communities, and/or what Hyde Park might have become if renewal had not taken place.

THE DATA

The data we were able to assemble on business in the four communities related to the passage of some 15,000 businesses through the 8,600 stores and offices located in the communities in the 13-year period 1953-1966. Only a little over 5 per cent of these businesses remained in the same store or office for the whole period, less than 27 per cent of the 15,000 remained in operation in the same community, while another 13 per cent relocated to some other community in the city by 1965. Tables 3.4-3.7 show that of all businesses that had operated in the four areas at some time in the period, sixty per cent had liquidated by 1965. In Oakland the figure was 65 per cent, in Woodlawn 63 per cent, in Hyde Park 60 per cent, and in South Shore 50 per cent. *A very high proportion of all businesses went out of business after operating for less than two years: in Hyde Park 31 per cent, Oakland 36 per cent, Woodlawn 38 per cent, and South Shore 28 per cent.*

Such information is not readily available in conventional catalogs or published sources. It has to be acquired through pains-

TABLE 3.4

HYDE PARK: GROSS BUSINESS EXPERIENCE 1953-1965

LENGTH OF STAY IN STORE BUILDING OR OFFICE	BUSINESSES OPERATING IN 1965				BUSINESSES OUT OF OPERATION BY 1965						TOTAL	
	IN THIS STORE		RELOCATED ELSEWHERE		SMALL BUSINESS LIQUIDATED IN 1954-1965		CHAIN STORE CLOSED IN 1954-1965		NOT KNOWN			
	No.	Pct.	No.	Pct.	No.	Pct.	No.	Pct.	No.	Pct.	No.	Pct.
1 Year	90	2.67	152	4.51	656	19.48	16	.48	33	.98	947	28.13
2 Years	57	1.69	99	2.94	328	9.74	11	.33	14	.42	509	15.12
3 Years	44	1.31	105	3.12	247	7.34	15	.45	11	.33	422	12.53
4 Years	44	1.31	81	2.41	186	5.52	11	.33	12	.36	334	9.92
5 Years	54	1.60	68	2.02	126	3.74	8	.24	7	.21	263	7.81
6 Years	35	1.04	30	.89	64	1.9	5	.15	12	.36	146	4.34
7 Years	32	.95	37	1.10	55	1.63	2	.06	4	.12	130	3.86
8 Years	28	.83	42	1.25	54	1.60	4	.12	3	.09	131	3.89
9 Years	22	.65	19	.56	52	1.54	6	.18	3	.09	102	3.03
10 Years	25	.74	13	.39	42	1.25	1	.03	1	.03	82	2.44
11 Years	35	1.04	14	.42	17	.5	2	.06	4	.12	72	2.14
12 Years	33	.98	8	.24	11	.33	2	.06	0		54	1.6
13 or more years	168	4.99							1	.03	169	5.02
TOTAL	667	19.81	668	19.84	1838	54.59	83	2.47	105	3.12	3361	
	Total Now Operating in Community		Total Still Operating Elsewhere After Period in Area		Total Small Businesses That Liquidated 1954-1965		Total Chain Outlets Closed 1954-65				Total Number of Separate Businesses in Community 1953-1965	

TABLE 3.5

OAKLAND: GROSS BUSINESS EXPERIENCE 1953-1965

LENGTH OF STAY IN STORE BUILDING OR OFFICE	BUSINESSES OPERATING IN 1965				BUSINESSES OUT OF OPERATION BY 1965						TOTAL	
	IN THIS STORE		RELOCATED ELSEWHERE		SMALL BUSINESS LIQUIDATED IN 1954-1965		CHAIN STORE CLOSED IN 1954-1965		NOT KNOWN			
	No.	Pct.	No.	Pct.	No.	Pct.	No.	Pct.	No.	Pct.	No.	Pct.
1 Year	35	2.05	78	4.57	360	21.1	18	1.05	21	1.23	512	30.
2 Years	31	1.82	43	2.52	212	12.42	9	.53	12	.7	307	17.99
3 Years	29	1.7	32	1.88	118	6.91	7	.41	5	.29	191	11.19
4 Years	23	1.35	24	1.41	64	3.75	3	.18	9	.53	123	7.21
5 Years	20	1.17	13	.76	65	3.81	0		7	.41	105	6.15
6 Years	20	1.17	12	.7	53	3.11	1	.06	6	.35	92	5.39
7 Years	28	1.64	18	1.05	35	2.05	2	.12	5	.29	88	5.16
8 Years	11	.64	9	.53	28	1.64	4	.23	6	.35	58	3.4
9 Years	6	.35	6	.35	18	1.05	0		2	.12	32	1.88
10 Years	15	.88	14	.82	16	.94	1	.06			46	2.7
11 Years	39	2.29	2	.12	10	.59	1	.06			52	3.05
12 Years	13	.76	1	.06	3	.18	1	.06			18	1.05
13 or more years	81	4.75									81	4.75
TOTAL	351	20.57	252	14.77	982	57.55	47	2.75	73	4.28	1705	
	Total Now Operating in Community		Total Still Operating Elsewhere After Period in Area		Total Small Businesses That Liquidated 1954-1965		Total Chain Outlets Closed 1954-65				Total Number of Separate Businesses in Community 1953-1965	

TABLE 3.6

WOODLAWN: GROSS BUSINESS EXPERIENCE 1953-1965

LENGTH OF STAY IN STORE BUILDING OR OFFICE	BUSINESSES OPERATING IN 1965				BUSINESSES OUT OF OPERATION BY 1965							TOTAL	
	IN THIS STORE		RELOCATED ELSEWHERE		SMALL BUSINESS LIQUIDATED IN 1954-1965		CHAIN STORE CLOSED IN 1954-1965		NOT KNOWN			TOTAL	
	No.	Pct.	No.	Pct.	No.	Pct.	No.	Pct.	No.	Pct.		No.	Pct.
1 Year	175	3.61	171	3.52	1232	25.38	7	.14	25	.52		1610	33.17
2 Years	99	2.04	103	2.12	545	11.23	6	.12	12	.25		765	15.76
3 Years	95	1.96	68	1.4	368	7.58	3	.06	8	.16		542	11.17
4 Years	88	1.81	53	1.09	244	5.03	3	.06	11	.23		399	8.22
5 Years	83	1.71	34	.7	170	3.5	4	.08	6	.12		297	6.12
6 Years	75	1.55	34	.7	115	2.4	4	.08	4	.08		232	4.78
7 Years	58	1.19	31	.64	99	2.04	4	.08	4	.08		196	4.04
8 Years	48	.99	23	.47	65	1.34	3	.06	2	.04		141	2.9
9 Years	57	1.17	13	.27	54	1.11	3	.06	1	.02		128	2.64
10 Years	39	.8	12	.25	40	.82			1	.02		92	1.9
11 Years	87	1.79	4	.08	19	.39						110	2.27
12 Years	63	1.3	2	.04	14	.29			1	.02		80	1.65
13 or more years	257	5.29										257	5.29
TOTAL	1224	25.21	548	11.29	2965	61.08	37	.76	75	1.55		4849	
	Total Now Operating in Community		Total Still Operating Elsewhere After Period in Area		Total Small Businesses That Liquidated 1954-1965		Total Chain Outlets Closed 1954-65					Total Number of Separate Businesses in Community 1953-1965	

TABLE 3.7   **SOUTH SHORE: GROSS BUSINESS EXPERIENCE 1953-1965**

| LENGTH OF STAY IN STORE BUILDING OF OFFICE | BUSINESSES OPERATING IN 1965 | | | | BUSINESSES OUT OF OPERATION BY 1965 | | | | | | TOTAL | |
| | IN THIS STORE | | RELOCATED ELSEWHERE | | SMALL BUSINESS LIQUIDATED IN 1954-1965 | | CHAIN STORE CLOSED IN 1954-1965 | | NOT KNOWN | | | |
	No.	Pct.	No.	Pct.	No.	Pct.	No.	Pct.	No.	Pct.	No.	Pct.
1 Year	218	4.14	228	4.33	898	17.06	26	.49	30	.57	1400	26.6
2 Years	167	3.17	187	3.55	459	8.72	18	.34	30	.57	861	16.36
3 Years	134	2.55	126	2.39	281	5.34	14	.27	11	.21	566	10.75
4 Years	103	1.96	96	1.82	186	3.53	16	.3	5	.1	406	7.71
5 Years	103	1.96	88	1.67	163	3.1	11	.21	4	.08	369	7.01
6 Years	74	1.41	68	1.29	117	2.22	5	.1	4	.08	268	5.09
7 Years	75	1.43	48	.91	77	1.46	6	.11	4	.08	210	3.99
8 Years	66	1.25	44	.84	58	1.1	5	.1	4	.08	177	3.36
9 Years	71	1.35	35	.67	70	1.33	12	.23	5	.1	193	3.67
10 Years	82	1.56	34	.65	46	.87	6	.11	1	.02	169	3.21
11 Years	96	1.82	22	.42	24	.46	4	.08			146	2.77
12 Years	45	.86	12	.23	24	.46	1	.02			82	1.56
13 or more years	396	7.52									396	7.52
TOTAL	1630	30.97	988	18.77	2403	45.66	124	2.36	98	1.86	5243	
	Total Now Operating in Community		Total Still Operating Elsewhere After Period in Area		Total Small Businesses That Liquidated 1954-1965		Total Chain Outlets Closed 1954-65				Total Number of Separate Businesses in Community 1953-1965	

taking business-by-business, store-by-store, year-by-year use of street and other directories,[1] and careful cross-tabulation and checking. Thus, the data themselves should be of some general interest, regardless of the light they cast on renewal impact upon small business.

BUSINESS HISTORIES: AGGREGATE CHANGE

Tables 3.8-3.11 introduce the business histories of the four study areas, showing how the stock of stores and offices changed from year to year. Figures 3.8-3.11 depict the trends graphically. In all four communities the number of operating businesses declined rapidly, as one would expect from the combined impact of secular trends operating and the population and income changes that took place. Compared with the end of 1953, at the beginning of 1966 there were 56.8 per cent less businesses in Hyde Park-Kenwood, 55.6 per cent less in Oakland, 28.8 per cent less in Woodlawn and 16.2 per cent less in South Shore. Moreover, whereas the comparative cases show smooth declines, Hyde Park's business history is "bumpy," with the "dips" coinciding with the two periods of renewal clearance. In the three comparative cases, declines in operating businesses were accompanied by increases in the amounts of vacant commercial space. In Hyde Park, however, LPA demolitions succeeded by 1966 in eliminating all except some fifteen vacant stores.

Expected Histories

These actual trends can be compared with changes in the business composition of the areas expected on the basis of secular trends, population redistribution, and the changing socio-economic character of the communities. The 1950-1960 differences in population and income are recorded in Table 3.3. Tables 3.12 and 3.13 show the results of inserting these changes into the equation describing retail change in Chicago, and Figures 3.8-3.11 contain the expected trends (extrapolated

---

1 The basic source of data was the street address telephone directories prepared each year by the Donnelley Corporation. 1953 was an enforced starting date, because all directories for earlier years had been destroyed. Nevertheless, the processing of the 1953-1966 materials took three full man-years of work!

TABLE 3.8

NATURE OF BUSINESS TURNOVER: HYDE PARK-KENWOOD

At the end of the year:	There were:			Of the operating businesses:		Of the vacant stores:	
	Total businesses operating	Vacant stores	There all the year	Replaced an existing store	Occupied a vacancy[a]	In a new building	Vacated during year
1954-1955	1490	692	1110	104	276	..	181
1955-1956	1494	761	1279	103	112	..	198
1956-1957	1260	a	1052	94	114	..	239
1957-1958	1117	a	988	66	63	..	192
1958-1959	1099	a	949	62	88	..	115
1959-1960	1051	a	927	41	74	9	130
1960-1961	912	a	791	52	61	8	202
1961-1962	788	a	696	45	66	1	156
1962-1963	708	a	637	32	38	1	126
1963-1964	674	a	590	21	53	10	82
1964-1965	644	87	570	35	37	2	68
1965-1966		17			70	25	

aPrecise numbers unclear because of LPA activity

TABLE 3.9

NATURE OF BUSINESS TURNOVER: OAKLAND-NORTH KENWOOD

At the end of the year:	There were:		Of the operating businesses:			Of the vacant stores:	
	Total businesses operating	Vacant stores	There all the year	Replaced an existing store	Occupied a vacancy		Vacated during year
1954-1955	767	397	466	64	237	294	103
1955-1956	741	420	626	47	68	315	105
1956-1957	671	496	575	39	57	379	117
1957-1958	617	551	532	33	52	447	104
1958-1959	577	590	490	37	50	495	95
1959-1960	548	610	457	36	55	525	85
1960-1961	501	656	428	28	45	559	97
1961-1962	448	705	397	21	30	625	80
1962-1963	384	766	338	19	27	665	101
1963-1964	383	779	329	16	38	733	46
1964-1965	348	789	312	13	23	765	33

TABLE 3.10

NATURE OF BUSINESS TURNOVER: WOODLAWN

At the end of the year:	There were:		Of the operating businesses:		Of the vacant stores:	
	Total businesses operating	Vacant stores	There all the year	Replaced an existing store	Occupied a vacancy	Vacated during year
1954-1955	1757	952	1235	135	387	760	192
1955-1956	1654	1048	1351	126	177	822	226
1956-1957	1592	1082	1314	135	143	888	194
1957-1958	1530	1137	1290	123	117	950	187
1958-1959	1501	1173	1244	123	134	1022	151
1959-1960	1456	1205	1204	107	145	1022	183
1960-1961	1399	1257	1176	106	117	1086	171
1961-1962	1360	1297	1120	117	123	1133	164
1962-1963	1308	1329	1134	61	113	1191	138
1963-1964	1248	1365	1079	62	107	1233	132
1964-1965	1271	1340	1092	69	110	1212	128

TABLE 3.11

NATURE OF BUSINESS TURNOVER: SOUTH SHORE

At the end of the year:	There were:		Of the operating businesses:			Of the vacant stores:	
	Total businesses operating	Vacant[a] stores	There all the year	Replaced an existing store	Occupied a vacancy		Vacated during year
1954-1955	1831	1507	1350	134	347	1161	157
1955-1956	1811	1694	1496	113	202	1104	198
1956-1957	1764	1718	1507	106	151	1149	211
1957-1958	1752	1655	1476	107	169	1165	179
1958-1959	1773	1686	1490	117	166	1172	196
1959-1960	1722	1644	1456	93	173	1188	188
1960-1961	1737	1615	1433	127	177	1194	182
1961-1962	1669	1614	1395	118	156	1210	219
1962-1963	1635	1576	1380	92	163	1276	196
1963-1964	1588	1542	1340	99	149	1316	202
1964-1965	1530	1507	1302	82	146	1375	205

aIncludes stores, offices, and homes and apartments that moved in and out of business use.

TABLE 3.12

ESTIMATING EQUATIONS: GROSS BUSINESS CHANGE

All rates in average annual percentages. The basic equation used is C_E $= -7.71 + 0.9778\ C_P + 0.8638\ C_Y$, where C_E, C_P and C_Y are the changes, respectively, in establishments, population, and income.

Hyde Park

$$C_E = -7.71 + 0.9778\ (-1.745) + 0.8638\ (4.244)$$
$$= -5.75\%$$

Aggregate decline of 45.0% in 11 years.

Oakland

$$C_E = -7.71 + 0.9778\ (-0.037) + 0.8638\ (2.717)$$
$$= -5.40\%$$

Aggregate decline of 42.5% in 11 years.

Woodlawn

$$C_E = -7.71 + 0.9778\ (+0.071) + 0.8638\ (3.812)$$
$$= -4.348\%$$

Aggregate decline of 36.7% in 11 years.

South Shore

$$C_E = -7.71 + 0.9778\ (+0.0788) + 0.8638\ (4.888)$$
$$= -3.411\%$$

Aggregate decline of 29.3% in 11 years.

after 1960). The observed trends in business in the communities parallel expectations based upon the ecological changes.

Through 1960, transitional Woodlawn's actual experience is very close to the expected, but thereafter flattens off as the community stabilizes. On the other hand, stable South Shore changed substantially less than expected in the years before 1960, but in the transitional years after 1961 expectations based upon the later base are identical to actual. Hyde Park shows rates of decline of operating businesses far greater than might have been expected if the community had changed smoothly between 1950 and 1960, with, in particular, precipitous drops away from the expected coinciding with the two periods of

TABLE 3.13

EXPECTED CHANGES IN NUMBERS OF BUSINESSES OPERATING IN THE FOUR COMMUNITIES

	Hyde Park-Kenwood	Woodlawn	Oakland	South Shore	South Shore 1961 Base
1954-1955	1490	1757	767	1831	
1955-1956	1404	1681	726	1769	
1956-1957	1323	1608	687	1709	
1957-1958	1247	1538	650	1651	
1958-1959	1175	1471	615	1595	
1959-1960	1107	1407	582	1541	
1960-1961	1043	1346	551	1488	1737
1961-1962	983	1287	521	1437	1678
1962-1963	926	1231	493	1388	1620
1963-1964	873	1177	466	1341	1565
1964-1965	823	1126	441	1295	1515

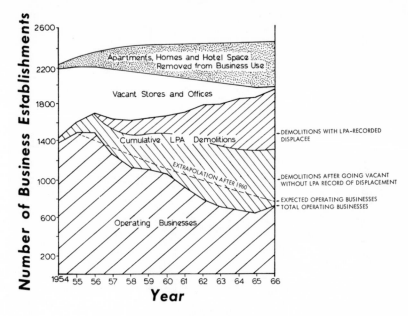

Figure 3.8
HYDE PARK-KENWOOD BUSINESS HISTORY.

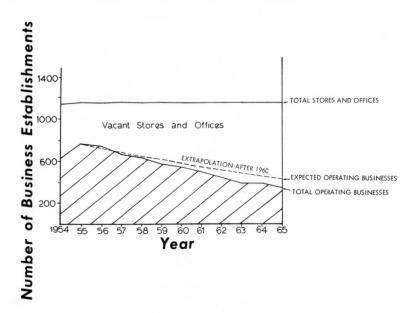

Figure 3.9
OAKLAND BUSINESS HISTORY.

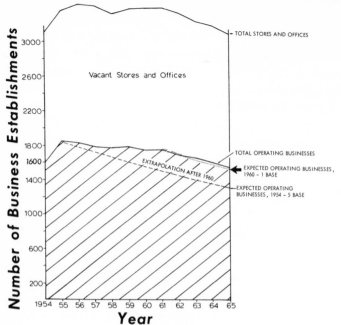

Figure 3.10
SOUTH SHORE BUSINESS HISTORY.

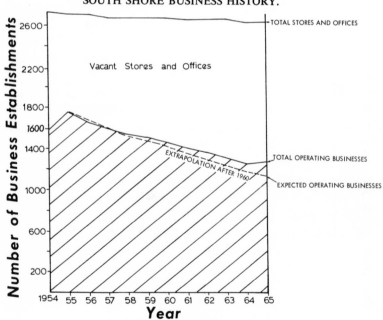

Figure 3.11
WOODLAWN BUSINESS HISTORY.

clearance. However, by 1960 new construction had restored the number of operating businesses very close to the number the equation indicates to be needed to serve the renewal-created market. But these rates of change for Hyde Park were calculated using population and income data already affected by the urban renewal projects. If Hyde Park had remained a stable middle-income community like South Shore, the rate of decline would have been substantially less, and even if it had "turned over" to low-income status like Woodlawn it would still have more businesses than it does today.

Thus we can conclude that Hyde Park's retail businesses declined in numbers far more rapidly than in neighboring stable communities, or even in communities experiencing transition from middle to low-income (56.8 per cent compared with 20 or 30 per cent). On the other hand, the decline was compatible with the changes in population and income produced by urban renewal in the residential community, and continuing secular trends. Further, recent filling of vacancies as residential areas have been rebuilt, together with the opening of Harper Court in the 1966-1968 period, have actually reduced the 56.8 per cent figure which held at the beginning of 1966 to 51 per cent today, while, of course, continuing secular trends have raised the expected rates of decline close to this figure. If urban renewal had the effect of raising liquidation rates, then, the principal source of the change lay in population and income shifts introduced in the market, rather than in displacement of businesses *per se,* for today the supply of businesses in Hyde Park-Kenwood is entirely consistent with the population levels and income characteristics created by the program of residential renewal.

Urban renewal had two effects additional to alterations in markets, however, and it is in these contexts that the issue of the liquidation rate is most frequently raised. It displaced businesses, many of which liquidated. It also cleared many store and office buildings, removing the opportunity for new businesses to move in. The business histories provide the additional opportunity of determining whether the rapid decline of business in Hyde Park caused by renewal-engendered market changes was due to an excessive liquidation rate among displacees, or a reduction in business opportunities for new entrants because commercial land was cleared.

ENTRY, EXIT AND LIQUIDATION RATES

From the business histories one can compute aggregate annual entry, exit and liquidation rates for businesses in the four communities. An *entry* occurs when a business occupies a store or office, whether it is a "birth" or has relocated from elsewhere in the city or other commercial space within the community. An *exit* occurs when a business leaves a particular store or office, either to relocate or to liquidate. The *entry rate* is the proportion of the stores in an area that had new occupants in a given year. The *exit rate* is the proportion of businesses leaving stores or offices in an area in any year. This exit rate exceeds the *liquidation rate,* the proportion leaving and going out of business, by the amount of relocations (analogously, the true *birth rate* is less than the entry rate by the amount of relocating entrants). The sum of the entry and exit rates can be called the *turnover rate*.[1]

Tables 3.14-3.17 record the relevant entry and exit data for the four communities, and Table 3.18 translates these into rates. Figures 3.12-3.15 graph the changes in rates over the years. The rates confirm the very high mobility and mortality characteristics of small business, regardless of public intervention.

In Figure 3.12 Hyde Park's post-1956 entry rate is seen to be somewhat more variable from year to year and also lower than those of the comparative cases. This is consistent with the argument that the most pervasive long-term supply-side effect of urban renewal on business in a community is the control of new entrants, because low-rent space conducive to speculative or marginal business ventures is eliminated. Initially, Woodlawn's entry rate was the greatest, followed by South Shore and Oakland. However, in the period after 1960, when Woodlawn stabilized as a low-income Negro community and South Shore started its transition process, South Shore's rate has exceeded

---

1 The data include all businesses in each area (i.e. they are not biased by omitting very long-lived businesses which neither opened nor closed from the calculations).

TABLE 3.14

ENTRY AND EXIT DATA: HYDE PARK-KENWOOD

During the year:	There were:		The departing businesses:		In property subsequently demolished there were:				Cumulative store removals
	New entrants	Departing businesses	Liquidated	Relocated	LPA-recorded displacees In Year	Cumulative	Other departures, store going vacant In Year	Cumulative	
1953-1954	288	241	185	56	2	2	48	48	50
1954-1955	380	263	192	71	3	5	56	104	109
1955-1956	215	294	217	77	15	20	77	181	201
1956-1957	208	328	241	87	105	125	83	264	389
1957-1958	129	258	195	63	37	162	61	325	487
1958-1959	150	171	122	49	3	165	52	377	542
1959-1960	124	166	127	39	14	179	46	423	602
1960-1961	121	249	177	72	74	253	106	529	782
1961-1962	112	212	130	82	128	381	69	598	979
1962-1963	71	153	103	50	57	438	47	645	1083
1963-1964	84	117	73	44	74	512	27	672	1184
1964-1965	74	100	60	40	9	521	19	691	1212
1965-1966	70+ Harper Ct.								

TABLE 3.15
ENTRY AND EXIT DATA: OAKLAND-NORTH KENWOOD

During the year:	There were:		The departing businesses:	
	New entrants	Departing Businesses	Liquidated	Relocated
1953-1954	170	144	117	27
1954-1955	311	164	137	27
1955-1956	115	153	128	25
1956-1957	96	152	120	32
1957-1958	85	133	110	23
1958-1959	87	132	96	36
1959-1960	91	122	100	22
1960-1961	73	122	89	33
1961-1962	51	97	70	27
1962-1963	46	117	84	33
1963-1964	54	59	48	11
1964-1965	36	54	40	14

TABLE 3.16

ENTRY AND EXIT DATA: WOODLAWN

During the year:	There were:		The departing businesses:	
	New entrants	Departing Businesses	Liquidated	Relocated
1953-1954	339	331	279	52
1954-1955	522	345	294	51
1955-1956	303	357	303	54
1956-1957	278	344	293	51
1957-1958	240	332	292	40
1958-1959	257	274	224	50
1959-1960	252	303	247	56
1960-1961	223	287	231	56
1961-1962	240	282	230	52
1962-1963	177	220	173	47
1963-1964	169	195	148	47
1964-1965	179	202	156	46

TABLE 3.17

ENTRY AND EXIT DATA: SOUTH SHORE

During the year:	There were:		The departing businesses:	
	New entrants	Departing Businesses	Liquidated	Relocated
1953-1954	355	331	266	65
1954-1955	481	277	198	79
1955-1956	315	302	226	76
1956-1957	257	308	223	85
1957-1958	276	290	197	93
1958-1959	283	299	206	93
1959-1960	266	304	217	87
1960-1961	304	303	202	101
1961-1962	274	337	244	93
1962-1963	255	316	209	107
1963-1964	248	324	205	119
1964-1965	228	298	186	112

TABLE 3.18

ANNUAL ENTRY, EXIT AND LIQUIDATION RATES

Year	Hyde Park			Woodlawn			South Shore			Oakland		
	Entry	Exit	Liquid.	Entry	Exit	Liquid.	Entry	Exit	Liquid.	Entry	Exit	Liquid.
1953-1954	.209	.175	.134	.214	.209	.176	.218	.203	.163	.277	.234	.191
1954-1955	.255	.176	.128	.297	.196	.167	.263	.151	.108	.405	.214	.179
1955-1956	.144	.190	.145	.183	.215	.183	.174	.167	.124	.155	.206	.173
1956-1957	.165	.260	.191	.175	.216	.184	.145	.174	.126	.143	.226	.179
1957-1958	.115	.230	.174	.157	.216	.190	.157	.165	.112	.138	.216	.178
1958-1959	.136	.155	.111	.171	.183	.149	.159	.168	.116	.151	.228	.166
1959-1960	.118	.158	.121	.173	.208	.169	.154	.176	.126	.166	.222	.182
1960-1961	.132	.273	.194	.159	.205	.165	.175	.175	.116	.146	.243	.177
1961-1962	.142	.269	.167	.176	.207	.169	.164	.202	.146	.114	.216	.156
1962-1963	.100	.216	.145	.135	.168	.132	.156	.193	.128	.121	.304	.218
1963-1964	.124	.173	.108	.135	.156	.118	.156	.204	.129	.141	.154	.125
1964-1965	.114	.155	.093	.141	.158	.123	.149	.195	.122	.103	.155	.115

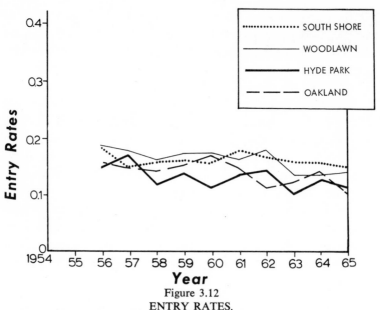

Figure 3.12
ENTRY RATES.
Proportion of businesses in each year who are new entrants. See Table 3.18.

that of Woodlawn, and Oakland's rate became less than that of Hyde Park.[1]

The exit rates shown in Figure 3.13 are quite different, being highest in Oakland until 1960, followed by Woodlawn, Hyde Park and South Shore, in approximate income and racial array. However, Hyde Park shows great "bursts" of exits corresponding to the two periods of clearance activity, Hyde Park "A and B" and the later Hyde Park-Kenwood project, with much lower compensatory rates following each burst. If a running average is taken, the smoothed curve lies between Woodlawn and Oakland on the one hand and South Shore on the other, at least until 1960. In aggregate terms, then, Hyde Park's liquidation rates were quite consistent with its social and economic character, and the most that can be said is that urban renewal hastened liquidations for some by a year or two. The years following 1960 confirm the impression.

1 On the transition process in South Shore, see Harvey Molotch, *Community Organization to Control Racial Change: A Transition Area Competes for Whites*. Ph.D. dissertation, University of Chicago, 1967.

First, the Oakland rate increases in 1962-1964 as a result of
renewal activity in its northern sections, and then drops to the
level of Woodlawn and Hyde Park, repeating the latter's experience with a compensatory lag. Then, the South Shore rate rises
rapidly with the onset of racial transition in that community.

Total turnover rates are shown in Figure 3.14. They reveal
that turnover variability from year to year is largely a function
of the exit characteristics. Further, the liquidation rates shown
in Figure 3.15 mirror overall exit rates. They are highest in the
transitional middle-to-low income communities and in the stabilizing low-income Negro areas. The lowest rates are in the
stable middle-income areas. *In spite of renewal, Hyde Park's
liquidation rate only equals that of the transitional and low-income areas at the height of displacement activity, and there are
compensatory succeeding drops in the liquidation rate to levels
lower than that of the stable middle-income community.*

LIFE SPANS OF BUSINESSES

Given such great mobility and turnover, what is the expected

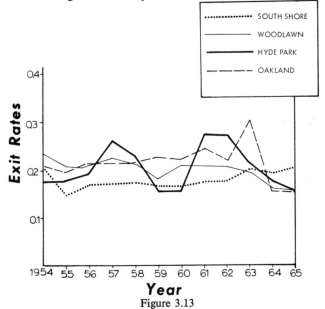

Figure 3.13
EXIT RATES.
Proportion of businesses exiting in the year. See Table 3.18.

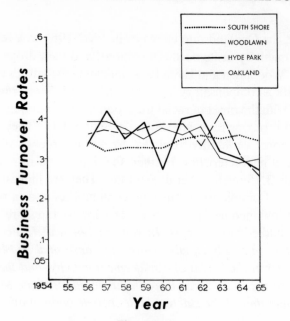

Figure 3.14
BUSINESS TURNOVER RATES.
Sum of the annual entry and exit rates. See Table 3.18.

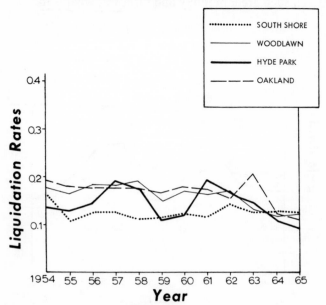

Figure 3.15
LIQUIDATION RATES.
Proportion of businesses liquidating each year. See Table 3.18.

life-span of a retail store or an office? Obviously, this depends
upon many variables, but given any store selected at random, it
should be possible to attach probabilities to longevity, and to
determine whether urban renewal has different effects on different kinds of business.

Relevant data are presented in Tables 3.4-3.7, which record
the number of years of operation of all businesses which opened
and/or closed in the four communities in the 1953-1967 period,
or which stayed in operation for the whole time.[1] Note the dis-
tinctions made between longevity of businesses still in operation
in the communities, those still operating after relocation elsewhere, and those liquidating. Note also, in the Hyde Park case,
that there were 3361 businesses which operated in the community in the period, of which 1838 liquidated and 668 relocated elsewhere. Of these, 641 were displacees, of whom 408
have now liquidated. Only 83 of the 667 businesses operating
in the community today are displacees. Table 3.19 provides a
convenient comparative summary. Displacement and control
of new entrants by removal of store space has meant that Hyde
Park-Kenwood, approximately the same size as South Shore,
has only thirty-seven per cent as many businesses (Tables 3.8
and 3.11).

TABLE 3.19

SUMMARY CHARACTERISTICS OF
BUSINESSES IN HYDE PARK-KENWOOD

	Displacees	Other Businesses, Not Displaced	TOTAL
Businesses operating in 1966:			
In Hyde Park	83	584	667
Elsewhere in city	141	527	668
Other	9		
No longer in business:			
Small business	408	1513	1838
Chain store closed			83
Unknown	—	—	10
TOTAL	641	2729	3361

---

1 Similar tables were prepared for each of 39 types of business—principal results are
shown in the accompanying illustrations.

Reference to Table 3.8 and Figure 3.16 will show how the probabilities of longevity in a given store *(turnover probabilities)* and of period in operation *(liquidation probabilities)* can be derived. Twenty-eight per cent of the businesses in Hyde Park stayed in a given store one year or less; nineteen per cent liquidated after a year or less in operation. Thus, seventy-two per cent of the businesses stayed in a given store at least a year, and eighty-one per cent remained in operation for at least that period of time. Similar figures can be derived for at least two years, three years, . . . etc.

If the results are plotted in a graph with proportion of businesses on the ordinate and length of stay on the abscissa, and the points linked, curves such as are depicted in Figure 3.16 result. The curves look like radio-active "decay" curves and can be analyzed like them. One can read off, for example, the number of years that have to elapse before half the businesses can be expected to move (the lower "turnover" curves in the graph) or, alternatively, liquidate (the upper curves — higher and not

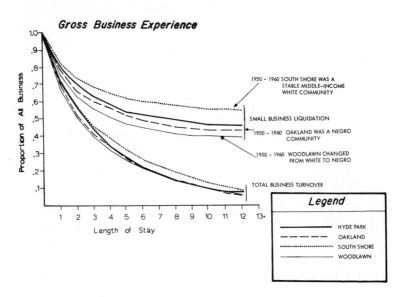

Figure 3.16
TURNOVER AND LIQUIDATION EXPECTATIONS:
LONGEVITY CURVES FOR ALL BUSINESSES IN
FOUR CHICAGO COMMUNITIES.

as steep because the liquidation rate is less than the turnover rate). This figure is called the "half-life." Alternatively, for a business selected at random, one can develop probabilities for relocation or liquidation.

A set of half-lives is presented in Table 3.20 for each type of business in each community. The community in which the half-life is least is indicated in each case. Thus, half the eating places in Woodlawn either relocate or liquidate each year — half of the entrants liquidate in less than two years.

Businesses with the shortest life-spans in Oakland have been: miscellaneous food stores, apparel stores, barbers, laundries, real estate offices, insurance offices, miscellaneous retailing, miscellaneous personal services, auto repair and miscellaneous services. In Woodlawn the most rapid rates of liquidation have been for: groceries, drugstores, eating places, furniture stores, beauty shops, dentists, financial establishments, entertainment facilities, auto dealers, business services, printing shops, utility offices, transport garages, construction contractors, and "other types." Amongst the four communities Hyde Park experienced the highest rates of liquidation among the following business types: drinking places, general merchandise stores, physicians, other professional services, auto accessory stores, radio-television repair and other repair services, building materials and hardware stores, veterinaries, educational establishments, wholesalers, manufacturers, and hotels and boarding houses. There were no instances in which the liquidation rate was highest in South Shore.

These findings are consistent with the observation that retail uses are extremely sensitive to changes in purchasing power incident upon racial change. Such was the case in Woodlawn and in Oakland.[1] *The activities with the shortest life-spans in Hyde Park, on the other hand, are exactly those which the renewal projects sought to eliminate in a clearance program directed at perceived sources of blight. These included taverns (which ex-*

---

1 Further, they are confirmed by other studies of negro business. Robert B. McKersie, *The Negro and Economic Activity*, University of Chicago, 1968. Real Estate Research Corporation, *Retail Location Analysis Manual: Small Business in Low Income Areas.* Chicago: Small Business Opportunities Commission, 1967. Walter J. Raine, *Los Angeles Riot Study. The Ghetto Merchant Survey.* Institute of Government and Public Affairs, University of California, Los Angeles, 1967.

TABLE 3.20
EXPECTED HALF LIVES OF BUSINESSES, BY TYPE

HALF LIVES IN YEARS

Type of Business	IN A GIVEN STORE BUILDING				UNTIL BUSINESS LIQUIDATED			
	Woodlawn	Oakland	Hyde Park	South Shore	Woodlawn	Oakland	Hyde Park	South Shore
ALL BUSINESS	2.1	2.2	2.6	2.6	4.2	5.7	7.5	>12
Groceries	3.2	3.4	3.2	2.5	4.5	6.5	6.7	8.0
Other food	2.3	1.7	3.6	4.2	3.3	2.6	7.7	8.1
Drugs	6.3	7.5	7.4	7.5	>12	>12	>12	>12
Eating places	0.9	1.0	1.4	1.2	1.9	2.0	3.9	3.7
Drinking places	0.9	1.2	2.7	2.3	5.2	3.3	3.2	3.8
General merchandise	2.6	3.5	3.5	1.8	>12	10.0	9.0	>12
Apparel, etc.	2.5	2.5	3.1	3.6	5.6	3.3	4.8	>12
Furniture, etc.	1.0	2.5	0.9	1.1	2.6	3.1	6.6	>12
Beauty	2.5	1.9	2.7	3.9	5.7	6.5	>12	>12
Barber	2.1	2.6	3.0	3.0	7.4	6.2	>12	>12
Laundry, dry cleaning	2.9	2.4	3.7	3.1	7.0	5.6	9.6	>12
Physicians	2.5	1.5	2.3	4.1	>12	>12	>12	>12
Dentists	2.8	4.0	3.2	5.5	>12	>12	>12	>12
Real estate	2.5	2.3	3.5	3.6	>12	>12	>12	>12
Insurance	2.1	1.0	2.4	2.1	>12	1.0	>12	>12
Other retail	2.5	3.0	3.0	3.6	5.0	4.8	9.0	>12
Other personal services	2.3	2.7	2.9	3.1	4.6	4.5	9.3	>12
Other professional services	3.0	2.0	2.2	4.0	>12	>12	>12	>12
Other finance	3.4	1.8	4.2	2.5	>12	>12	>12	>12
Entertainment, etc.	1.8	4.3	1.8	2.9	2.8	4.5	6.0	>12

TABLE 3.20 (cont.)

EXPECTED HALF LIVES OF BUSINESSES, BY TYPE

Type of Business	IN A GIVEN STORE BUILDING				UNTIL BUSINESS LIQUIDATED			
	Woodlawn	Oakland	Hyde Park	South Shore	Woodlawn	Oakland	Hyde Park	South Shore
Motor vehicles	1.3	6.5	3.2	2.0	1.8	>12	3.5	2.0
Auto accessories	11.0	1.7	2.0	2.0	>12	>12	2.0	>12
Auto repair	1.6	1.4	2.2	1.8	3.9	1.7	2.9	7.0
Radio–TV repair	2.1	1.7	1.4	2.1	9.3	>12	2.7	6.2
Business services	1.6	0.9	2.5	2.9	10.2	>12	>12	>12
Other repair services	2.5	2.0	2.3	2.0	7.0	>12	4.0	5.5
Printing, etc.	1.2	3.0	1.6	3.6	1.8	>12	>12	>12
Building materials, hardware	3.6	5.5	4.4	4.4	11.8	5.5	8.3	>12
Veterinary	3.0	..	1.5	3.4	9.0	>12	1.5	>12
Utilities	2.0	2.5	..	..	3.0	..	..	10.0
Transport	0.9	0.8	1.2	1.8	4.5	>12	12.0	..
Education services	1.6	3.7	3.3	1.9	>12	9.5	8.8	>12
Contract constructs	2.0	1.3	1.6	2.4	>12	>12	>12	>12
Miscellaneous services	1.8	1.8	1.9	2.6	12.0	6.0	>12	>12
Wholesalers	1.9	2.5	1.8	2.2	6.6	>12	3.2	>12
Manufacturing	2.3	2.0	1.9	1.9	4.0	4.7	3.9	>12
Mining offices	..	9.0	..	4.7	..	..	..	>12
Residential uses (hotels, etc.)	4.5	3.2	5.5	>12	8.0	10.0	7.2	>12
Business NEC	1.1	2.3	1.9	1.6	1.3	4.5	2.9	1.9

perienced an additional licensing problem) and "ribbon businesses," including most automobile dealers (where there were franchise problems), as well as wholesalers and manufacturers. All of these business type find their most economical location in the stores and offices available at the lowest rents — generally in the oldest and most deteriorated structures.

These half-life differences extend to the whole longevity and liquidation curves. Thus, Figure 3.16 shows Woodlawn consistently to have the higher turnover and liquidation probabilities (the curves provide empirical estimates of the probability that a business will stay in a given store for a specified period or more), followed by Oakland, Hyde Park and South Shore. The progression is of some interest, for it attaches the briefest lifespan to businesses located in the community undergoing racial transition, followed by the stabilizing Negro community of Oakland, then by Hyde Park, and finally by what had been the stable middle-income white community of South Shore, with the greatest longevity. Even if displacement did cause two "bulges" of liquidation in Hyde Park (Figure 3.13), liquidation rates still, at their most extreme, barely equalled those consistently characteristic of the low-income Negro communities. Thus, under conditions of urban renewal, small business mortality experience was *less* in the community as a whole than it might reasonably have been expected to become. The exceptions to this statement are those particular kinds of business in the ribbons that the renewal project sought to eliminate. In no case, on the other hand, were Hyde Park's liquidation rates less than in stable South Shore.

Figure 3.17 shows those individual kinds of business following the overall pattern of Figure 3.16. Figure 3.18, on the other hand, indicates that longevity was least in Hyde Park for taverns, auto repair and accessory stores, residential hotels, dealers in building materials and in general merchandise, a variety of service occupations — veterinary, business, miscellaneous repair — for wholesalers and manufacturers, and for doctors and dentists. Most of those are businesses requiring the low rent space that was eliminated when the "commercial rectangle" was cleared. The doctors and dentists were among the first to leave

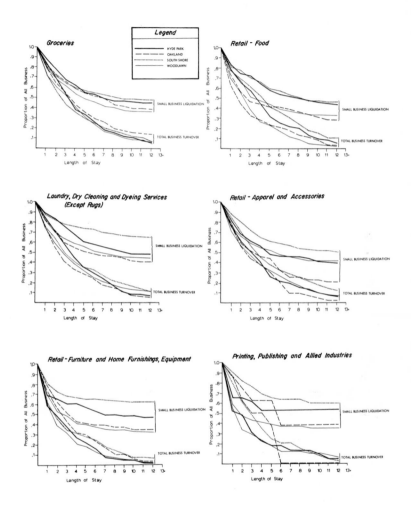

Figure 3.17
TURNOVER AND LIQUIDATION PROBABILITIES
FOR TYPES OF BUSINESS IN WHICH LONGEVITY
FALLS AS COMMUNITY INCOME DROPS.

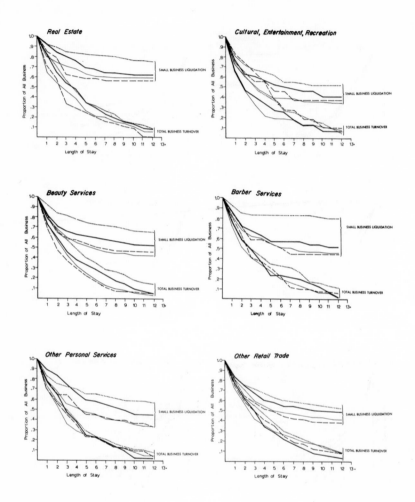

Figure 3.17
(CONTINUED)

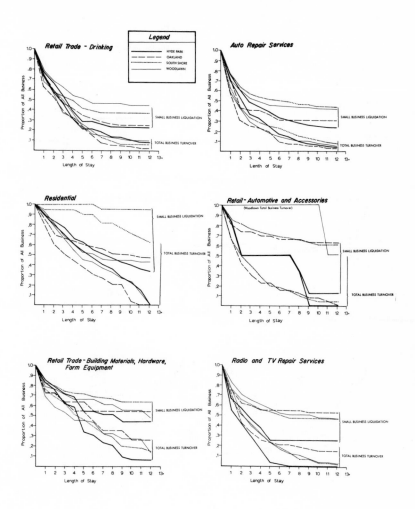

Figure 3.18
TURNOVER AND LIQUIDATION PROBABILITIES
FOR TYPES OF BUSINESS SHOWING GREATEST RATES
IN HYDE PARK.

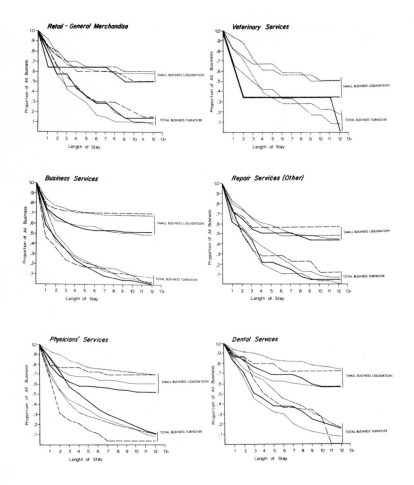

Figure 3.18
(CONTINUED)

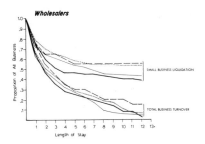

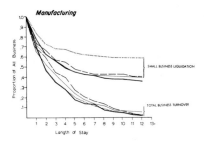

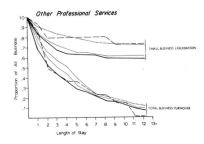

Figure 3.18
(CONTINUED)

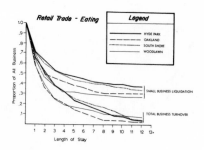

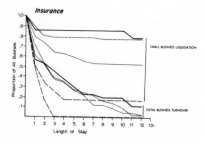

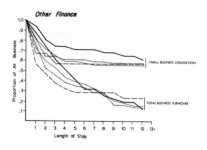

Figure 3.19
TURNOVER AND LIQUIDATION PROBABILITIES
FOR TYPES OF BUSINESS SHOWING GREATEST STABILITY
IN HYDE PARK.

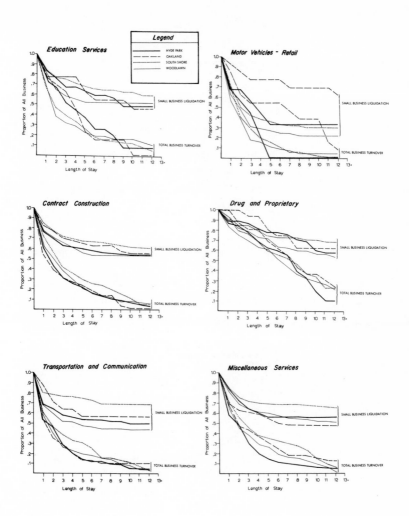

Figure 3.20
TURNOVER AND LIQUIDATION PROBABILITIES:
MISCELLANEOUS OTHERS.

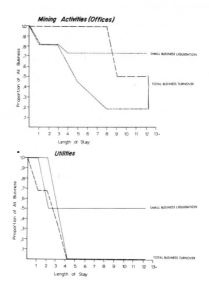

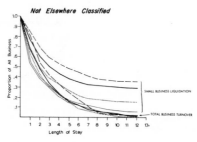

Figure 3.20
(CONTINUED)

the community in the early years when the prospect of racial transition loomed large. Taverns lost their licenses.

WAS THE LIQUIDATION RATE IN HYDE PARK-KENWOOD EXCESSIVE?

Was the thirty-one per cent liquidation rate among Hyde Park-Kenwood displacees excessive? No absolute or unequivocal answer can be provided. Certainly, *retail business declined more rapidly in Hyde Park-Kenwood in the period 1953-1967 than one might have expected if the community had retained a stable middle-income character,* or even if it had undergone complete racial transition to low-income status.

On the other hand, by 1967 it was clear that *the aggregate amount of change was exactly consistent with the nature of the market that had been created by urban renewal.* The principal reason for the change in market conditions was the alteration in residential patterns — of population densities and income levels —accomplished by the renewal project.

The reduction in business in the community was accomplished in two ways:

(a) Substantial tracts of commercial land were cleared. The long-term effect of clearance was to reduce the rate of entry of new business into the community to levels substantially lower than those of surrounding communities.

(b) Merchants were displaced by clearance. In all, there were 641 displacees, 207 of whom immediately liquidated. The liquidation rate shows peaks associated with the principal periods of clearance, but low compensatory rates between, and the moving average is perfectly consistent with the socio-economic status created for the community by the renewal program. Hyde Park-Kenwood businesses had lower liquidation rates and longer life-spans than businesses located in nearby transitional or low-income communities (where continued high entry rates had a compensatory effect and resulted in lower overall rates of decline than in Hyde Park), but greater than those in the stable middle-income areas. At worst, then, displacement in the aggregate hastened the inevitable for a few by a year or two.

Within the aggregate, *there were important differences between types of business* (Chapter 4 discusses differences between businesses and businessmen within types). In particular, *life spans were much shorter in Hyde Park-Kenwood than elsewhere for those kinds of business occupying commercial properties perceived as blighted* or blighting by the drafters of the community's renewal plans. These include taverns, residential hotels, automobile-related business, and "ribbon" concerns such as service, repair, and household supply establishments of most kinds, wholesalers and manufacturers. The greater liquidation rates for these types are clearly related to the goals that were set for Hyde Park-Kenwood's urban renewal program, and are among the sources of discontent of displacees with urban renewal.

CHAPTER FOUR

The Businessmen and The Public Agency

AGGREGATE RESULTS VS. INDIVIDUAL DIFFERENCES

The common presumption that urban renewal resulted in undue mortalities among small businessmen is thus invalid in the aggregate. If urban renewal had not taken place, changes in the social and economic characteristics of the area's residents would have resulted in substantially shorter life spans for community businesses. To be sure, the rates in Hyde Park-Kenwood rose to the level of transitional communities during the main periods of displacement as the life-span of some displacees was shortened, and the rate of entry of new businesses would have been greater without the massive clearance of commercial land. But the compensatory rates that followed clearance indicate the displacement period involved a relatively brief compression of trends. Only for those types whose removal was required by the broader community and residential goals of the renewal plan were mortality rates higher than elsewhere.

In the long-run, the most profound problem for small businesses in Hyde Park and similar renewal areas — although not, parenthetically for chain stores — does not involve the liquidation of existing enterprises but the drastic reduction in the entry rate of *new* business by removal of low-rent property. Such property while it is generally felt to lead to many deleterious community impacts also provides opportunities for new businesses to find their feet and for innovators to get a start. One might ask what opportunities a renewed area provides for small "indigenous business" for example if location opportunities in new commercial property produced by redevelopment of clearance areas are only provided for:

(a) chains and other triple-A stores in conventionally-financed and developed centers such as the New Hyde Park Shopping Center;
(b) the most viable and solvent of displacees cooperating in joint redevelopment ventures such as Kimbark Plaza;
(c) the exotic and the "contributors to culture," in community-subsidized undertakings like Harper Court.

All this is small consolation for the displacees, however. Could any of the displacees who liquidated have been saved by alternative public policies? Were there businessmen who were outside the renewal project clearance area (and therefore not displaced) who were either adversely or positively affected by the renewal program? What did relocation do for the displacees who did not liquidate? What were the subsequent fortunes of the merchants who went out of business? Did renewal result in differential and uncompensated losses?

Such issues as these raise a whole series of additional questions that must be answered in the context of *individual differences* among businessmen, their businesses, and their particular relationships to the renewal program and the Public Agency. Focus must therefore be switched from the aggregate community level to that of the individual businesses. Among the individual variations of concern are type, size, whether or not they were displaced and if they were, when, or if they were not, for what period they operated in the community, from what location relative to the renewal projects, and whether or not they are a "new entrant." Fortunes before, during and after the renewal projects need to be assessed, taking into account the varying backgrounds and capabilities of the businessmen themselves, and, if they were displaced, their differing experiences with the public agency, and the perceptions and opinions they are left with.

The inquiry is important, because small businesses do not exist in a vacuum. Urban renewal transforms the community to which the enterprise had adjusted. If too many of the relationships to community are destroyed, special help and compensation may be required if the owner wishes to stay in business. What can be learned from the merchants themselves and from the Local Public Agency about alternative policies and programs, their limitations and prospects?

THE SMALL BUSINESSMEN

In the twelve months of June 1966 — June 1967 an attempt was made to interview owners or operators of a sample of the 3361 businesses which moved through the declining stock of stores and offices in Hyde Park-Kenwood in the period 1953-1966 (recall that there were 1490 businesses operating in 1954, but barely 700 in 1966). The questionnaire appears in an appendix, along with a review of problems encountered in conducting the interviews and the categories of information finally coded and keypunched for purposes of analysis and comparison. Sampling rates are outlined in Table 4.1.

The observations were weighted heavily in favor of displacees, and the sampling rates were also affected by the short life-span and ephemeral character of many of the businesses — fully 45% of the concerns no longer in business operated for less than two years, and most have now vanished without trace.

All the displacees still in business were contacted by the interviewers, together with half the displacees no longer in business. Of the latter, half had refused to be interviewed on first contact, and many of the remainder refused to respond when the interviewers arrived for an appointment. A variety of reasons were given: "Too busy." "Urban renewal has not affected us." "Damned spying and prying by the University of Chicago." Difficulties were encountered because three other individuals or research groups were trying to interview the same businessmen at the same time. One day, for example, our interviewer arrived at a business in Harper Court at the appointed time, and found there at the same time, or just departed, one student from Roosevelt University who was doing a master's thesis on the role of the Hyde Park-Kenwood Community Conference in commercial renewal, one University of Michigan planning student working on his thesis on Harper Court, and a Small Business Administration staff member visiting for regular surveillance of a business with an SBA loan. Not surprisingly, we never did complete an interview there! Similar circumstances also resulted in refusals, and we cannot be sure that the responses we did receive were unaffected by them.

Despite all attempts to persuade businessmen otherwise, many

TABLE 4.1

SAMPLING RATES

Displacees	Total Businesses	Interviewed	Some data from LPA files	RATE	No information Available	RATE SOUGHT
In Hyde Park in 1966	83	68	15 (15)[b]	100%	—	100%
Operating Elsewhere in 1966	150	57	93 (93)[b]	100%	—	100%
Liquidated	408	14	180[a](178)[b]	47.5%	214	50%
Other Hyde Park Businesses						
In Hyde Park in 1966	584	99	—(47)[b]	16.1%	485	25%
Operating Elsewhere in 1966	527	10	—(16)[b]	1.9%	517	5%
Liquidated	1612	12	—(40)[b]	0.6%	1612	2.5%
TOTALS	3361	248	288 (389)		2828	

N = 536

[a]Includes 9 deaths, 2 cases of sickness, 8 retirements. Twenty-five had relocated before liquidating, 15 outside Hyde Park and 10 inside.

[b]Refused to permit detailed interview.

of the refusals stemmed from fear that the interview would be a precursor to further renewal, from unspecified but very evident anger at the University of Chicago's role in the earlier renewal program, or from disaffection with renewal in general. Feelings ran highest among businesses denied relocation opportunities in Hyde Park by clearance of the community's business ribbons. It is difficult to convey the intensity of feelings or the pungency of some of the refusals without tempting the pen of the censor.

Characteristics of Survivors and Liquidatees

Most of the businesses in Hyde Park-Kenwood were owned and run by individuals who worked long hours, had little help and no additional form of income. Those who owned grocery stores, taverns or eating places as likely as not had little reserve capital, and, with the scarcity of alternative relocation sites in Hyde Park or the loss of their business license, went out of business once their property was acquired. Those who were in the general merchandise, furniture, real estate or hardware lines were more likely to relocate along with repair and supply shops who were forced to relocate out of Hyde Park. Those who remained in Hyde Park were usually retailers; they differed from other displacees in that they were better educated (25% held college degrees) and they tended to have other sources of income. A third had been in business for over 21 years serving a predominantly Jewish population, and most were over 45 years old.

Most of these retail merchants were not displaced until the end of 1959 by the Hyde Park-Kenwood project. Despite the improvements in compensation available however, slightly more displacees liquidated during the 1959-1966 period than earlier.[1] Displacees pointed out that their ability to survive dislocation was severely reduced by loss of trade accompanying clearance of surrounding residential areas. Rent reductions by the Local Public Agency after acquisition of the stores were insufficient to compensate for these reductions in income flows (Figure 4.1 presents sample illustrative data). Though most of the rent reduction was given in the last period of displacements, only 22

---

1 Thirty four per cent as opposed to thirty per cent.

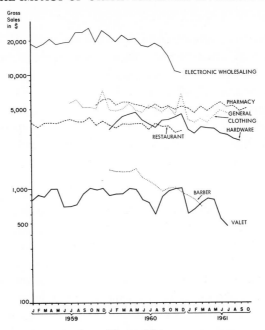

Figure 4.1
SALES VOLUMES OF SAMPLE DISPLACEES.

per cent of the displacees received any (Table 4.2) New store rents were higher than before. A real difficulty was that to obtain moving expenses they had to remain where they were until told to vacate — an entirely fortuitous event — and when ordered to move, they were provided with insufficient time to obtain alternative property, which could not be reserved until it was clear that a move would have to be made, and satisfactory financing could be arranged.[1] These provisions were liberalized by revised HUD regulations in 1961 and 1965, but these changes were essentially irrelevant for most displacees in Hyde Park-Kenwood. (See Part II of this study.) It made little difference that more than half of the displacees knew about the proposed urban renewal plan by hearing rumors before 1956. No one knew enough details to prepare themselves for what ensued.

At least 25 per cent of the relocatees unwillingly moved out of Hyde Park. Appropriate relocation space had been demol-

---

1 Half of the respondents said that claims for moving expenses were settled within 6 months after the move; an irate minority cited lags of more than a year in receiving payment.

TABLE 4.2

COMPENSATION RECEIVED

	Liquidatees	Non-H.P. Relocatees[a]	Hyde Park Relocatees	2nd/3rd Relocations[b]	Total
Rent Reduction	54	36	28	7	125
Moving Expenses	16	81	51	12	106
Property Loss	6	24	11	7	48
Other Reimbursement	23	4	6	4	37
Indirect Compensation Through Delinquent Rent	11	21	9	4	45

	Moving Expenses—Amount Received				Property Claims—Amount Received			
	Non-H.P.[a]	H.P.	Other Moves	Total	Non-H.P.	H.P.	Other Moves	Total
None	1	3	5	9				
>$100	5	4	1	10	7	6	5	18
$101-500	13	13	5	31	0	0	0	0
$501-1000	9	3	2	14	3	3	1	7
>$1000	27	11	3	41	13	2	1	16

[a] i.e., those relocating outside Hyde Park-Kenwood

[b] where multiple moves had been undertaken

ished, and only 37 of the 60 respondents who said they would have preferred to stay actually did so. Those who moved out had both a greater choice of sites and a harder decision to make. Most are satisfied with their new location. Half have been able to retain some of their old customers and most were able to attract customers similar to their former clientele. Seventy-one per cent of the businesses have regained their former business volume (fifty-seven per cent replied no decline in volumes at any time). However, they have not made up for the losses they suffered by being forced to relocate, nor are they convinced that the move will make them better off in the long run. (See Tables 4.3 and 4.6.) Over a quarter have changed merchandise lines and expanded their stores since relocation, but less than that proportion felt that their business achieved more than the old volumes. Whereas those who remained in Hyde Park (especially those in the new business centers) have already made adjustments in changing merchandise or service to suit new customers and have already invested money in upgrading their premises, those who faced adjusting and moving to a strange community are by and large still planning to improve, enlarge or change their business to suit the new market, but few have the resources yet to do so. *Most are still recovering from the extra expenditures due to relocation and moving and still are faced with regaining their own savings and paying back loans which covered dislocation costs.* Eighty per cent financed their relocation from savings and/or private bank loans, and less than ten per cent called on the Small Business Administration — only 3 of the 10 applications by businesses not in the new shopping centers were granted SBA loans.

As for the 408 businesses which liquidated, the Department of Urban Renewal kept records on 148, which were representative of the types of businesses with high failure rates described in Chapter 3. Even so, many of those who failed required licenses to be in business, and cheap space in ribbon developments or in low income neighborhoods serving a predominantly Negro population. These were precisely the kinds of businesses which the renewal plan affected most in its attempt to upgrade the community. Such businesses, despite normal turnover expectations

TABLE 4.3

BUSINESSMEN'S FEELINGS ABOUT RENEWAL

	Hyde Park Non-Displacees[a]	Hyde Park Displacees			Non-Displacees Non longer in H.P.	TOTAL
		Total	Relocated in H.P.	Relocated out of H.P.		
Better off Because of Renewal	36	31	19	12	1	68
Worse off Because of Renewal	43	71	30	41	2	116
Do Not Know	9	10	7	3	0	19
TOTAL	88	112	56	56	3	203

a i,e., Hyde Park businesses not dislocated by renewal

cited by the businessmen were varied: financial problems and the unavailability of a suitable site were the most frequent reasons offered. The majority of these displacees wanted to relocate in Hyde Park but there were seldom any appropriate sites available. Many lived in the community and were unwilling to move far away. By and large the businessmen simply did not have adequate resources with which to cover the loss in income incurred through the decline in customers, let along to cope with the expenses and hazards accompanying relocation. Twenty per cent of the respondents had no choice, because they lost the license permitting them to operate their businesses. A further twenty per cent simply took the opportunity to retire and nine died. A few merchants suffered damages through disasters such as fire, vandalism and loss of health so that they were forced to terminate their businesses, while three others were unable to renew their leases.

Little is known about the aftermath or fortunes of the many businessmen who liquidated during the thirteen year period without being displaced by urban renewal. After tracing 80 such persons, only 12 finally agreed to and completed the interview. Their feelings about going out of business were mixed. One quarter had other sources of income upon which they had relied and five were able to sell their businesses—with only one recording a profit — whereas two merchants set up new businesses elsewhere. A few clung to the belief that they would be able to start up their business again in a year or two, but like the majority of displacees they had suffered a loss in income during renewal and they were now unable to find the financial resources to start over again.

Liquidatees were critical of the urban renewal process. Half said they first learned of renewal plans for their area by rumor or from newspaper reports, and forty per cent from official notices. Although they knew that the neighborhood was to be cleared for renewal there was no warning as to when they would receive their displacement notice. Only twenty per cent recalled visits by urban renewal representatives, and half of these said that the visit was of little or no help. Barely fifteen per cent attended meetings about the renewal plan, and all but three of had a high rate of liquidation. However the actual hardships or gains made at the time of displacement can no longer be documented, for few of these businessmen can now be traced. Most left without having personal contact with the renewal officials.

Liquidatees

In confirmation of previous research, the displacees no longer in business cite acquisition of their property by the public agency as the immediate cause of liquidation — 65 per cent liquidated within 6 months of property acquisition. Otherwise, they said, they would have kept operating as long as they could. On the other hand, bankruptcy is the most frequently-cited cause of liquidation by those not displaced, usually attributed to loss of markets caused by renewal clearance.

Few thought that they might have encountered increasing business difficulties if renewal had not taken place. Nor did any of them articulate, even in hindsight, the alternatives, expressed so clearly by the representatives of chain stores of either a low-income Negro market or a "renewed" one. (This is discussed later in the chapter.) Indeed, many of them complained of a "down-grading" of the community (which they equated with more Negro residents) because of renewal or complained of the "dirty beatnik people" who visit Harper Court, without considering what the alternative to renewal might have been.

Fifteen per cent said they preferred to be out of business — these were among the twenty per cent of the businessmen who reported that their incomes were now greater — and ten per cent reported incomes to have decreased, largely the retired, those with health problems, etc.

Those liquidating were older, had less education, participated less in businessmen's organizations, were less likely to have explored alternative locations or to have attempted temporary relocations. Generally, they operated smaller businesses than those relocating. A greater proportion of service-type establishments liquidated than did retail units. Most of the barbers, laundries, places of entertainment, personal service establishments, grocery stores, eating places and taverns went out of business.

Given displacement, the contributing causes for liquidation

these said the meetings were of no help. Few risked fighting the authorities or attempted to stay beyond the six month period allowed for relocation.

Two thirds of all liquidatees interviewed felt that they had not been treated fairly, and had incurred uncompensated costs and losses of income. Almost one half of the interviewees suggested inequitable treatment permitted larger stores and chains access to Hyde Park after renewal and forbade them new locations there. The most vehement protest came from those operating businesses for which ribbon space was no longer available, and those who had lost licenses or franchises.[1]

Despite the fact that half of the liquidatees were displaced after October 1959 when compensation benefits had been improved, the rate of liquidation was greater than during the period prior to October 1956. Even after 1959 few businessmen filed claims for compensation. At the initial time of displacement due to Hyde Park *A* and *B* no benefits were available. In the later Hyde Park-Kenwood project clearance, many businesses were ineligible because they had not been tenants on the date that the official project agreement had been signed. Only 8 of the interviewees received compensation for property loss while 23 liquidatees received reimbursements for unspecified losses and 53 received partial compensation via the rent reduction scheme. In at least 11 cases of delinquent rent a follow-up was made only if a claim for compensation was also pending. This left 34 per cent of the businesses liquidating without their owners receiving any form of compensation, or only rent reduction.

Rent reductions did not significantly reduce the rate of liquidation. Merchants went out of business at about the same rate despite the extra help given by receiving rent reductions, thereby emphasizing that the critical point was not how to decrease ongoing expenses, but how to increase their decreasing income commensurate with the decline in customers. A greater percentage of the liquidated group paid rentals exceeding $200 than compared to the successful relocatees, and a greater proportion

---

1 In contrast, the Local Public Agency's officials argue that every businessman was provided with the same information equally and without prejudice. "But small merchants are a different breed" they say, and attribute the adverse opinions to communications problems and lack of receptivity by the businessmen.

therefore took advantage of the rent reduction program. Yet
only 38 per cent of the liquidatees received rent reductions as
compared to 25 per cent of the relocatees. During the period
January 1955-September 1966 when 95 premises were acquired, a total of 25 businesses received such reductions after
which 12 liquidated. In the period October 1956-October 1959
when the rate of liquidation had increased from 28 to 42 per
cent, the proportion of all businesses receiving rent reductions
also increased and by the period November 1959-December
1966 when the rate of liquidation was 33 per cent and the absolute number of liquidatees had doubled, most of the rent reductions were sought after by businesses who later liquidated.

Why did so few liquidatees file compensation claims? Besides the restraints imposed by ineligibility and changes in the
kinds of compensation that were available, few businessmen
were well enough informed or convinced that compensation
claims were worth bothering about. Although at least ten per
cent of those businessmen who went out of business said they
did not have any contact with the renewal official, neither did
those who did have contact via telephone calls, letters or personal
visits appear to have benefited from it. Many businessmen were
hard to contact and the majority of liquidatees that did have a
visit from an official only remember having one such visit and
did not find it helpful. (Table 4.8) Few merchants took the
time or trouble to contact the renewal office for further information or help. Most accepted what they had come to feel was inevitable and liquidated. Over 60 per cent of these businesses had
disappeared within six months of receiving notice of displacement. The realities of a loss in weekly income regardless of
whether or not rent reduction was eventually granted meant
that marginal businesses were adversely affected immediately
clearance began.

Some thirteen of the sample businesses liquidated after attempting to relocate, the principal cause being lower sales volume in the new market and increased costs (both of new space
and to repay funds borrowed to be able to relocate). Most said
that the critical elements in the failure was loss of the goodwill
of regular Hyde Park patrons. Four of these businesses had tried

to relocate in in Hyde Park; two of them intended relocation to be only temporary and when the time came to relocate again they simply could not afford to do it. Eight of these liquidatees had moved within six months of acquisition. The time lag did not seem to make any significant difference as to whether relocation attempts were successful or not, although, of the 44 relocatees who waited over a year before moving first four liquidated compared with one out of 41 who moved within the first month after their property was acquired. (Table 4.7).

Survivors' Changes of Sales and Income

An immediate question is what happened to sales and income levels of surviving businesses — both displacees and those not dislocated. Two "before-after" comparisons are presented in Tables 4.4 and 4.5. The businessmen were very reluctant to respond to any questions of a monetary kind, but many nonetheless answered at least one such query, so that 98 separate interviews are represented in the two tables — 64 indications of "no-change," 21 reports of decreased sales and/or income and 13 of increasing fortunes.

Focussing on the 34 businesses reporting changes, eight had Negro owners (all of whom reported decreased volumes), nine were Jewish (seven showing increases in sales and income and only two declines). Four Japanese businessmen also showed better performance after renewal, to account for all but two of those performing better. Twenty-six were displacees — seven from Hyde Park "A" and the rest from the Hyde Park-Kenwood renewal program. Only eight of the respondents had not been displaced, and these split evenly between those with increased and those with decreased fortunes. Similarly, four of the eight remained in the same premises for the entire period and four relocated, but three of the former showed decreased sales and only one an increase, exactly the converse of the relocatees. Three of those moving without displacement did so because they thought that they might be displaced, and they wanted to take no chances. One had been in Hyde Park, moved to South Shore because of racial change, and then back. Five of the earlier "A" displacees lost business as opposed to two who in-

THE BUSINESSMEN AND THE PUBLIC AGENCY 147

TABLE 4.4

MONTHLY GROSS SALES CHANGES

BEFORE	AFTER A	B	C	D	E	F	G	H
A—Under $1,000	19	2	1					
B—$1000-$2500	2	4		1	1			
C—$2500-$5000	1	3	4	1				
D—$5000-$10,000		1		5	1			
E—$10,000-$25,000				2	5			
F—$25,000-$50,000						1		
G—$50,000-$100,000							2	
H—Over $100,000								1

n = 55

TABLE 4.5

CHANGES IN ANNUAL NET TAXABLE INCOME

| | AFTER | | | | |
BEFORE	A	B	C	D	E
A—Under $3,000	12	3	1	1	1
B—$3,000-$5,000	4	6	1		
C—$5,000-$7,500		2	4	1	
D—7,500-$10,000				5	2
E—Over $10,000	1		2	3	13

n = 62

creased, which contrasts with the 12-7 split of the businesses displaced by the Hyde Park-Kenwood project.

The kinds of businesses registering declining fortunes included many service and supply type uses — paint stores, upholsterers, radio-television repair, auto supplies, printing, commercial photographers, mirror manufacturing and sales, barbers and beauty shops. On the other hand, sales and/or income increases were reported by retailers in the main — vendors of women's accessories, bicycles, books, cameras, Japanese gifts, custom furniture, jewelers, drugs and groceries.

Comparison of Those Relocating in Hyde Park and
Those Relocating Elsewhere

Hyde Park relocatees were less critical of the renewal program than those who left the community and nearly half felt that they were better off in the long run. (Table 4.3) They showed a high rate of mobility: thirty-one per cent had moved more than three times in the thirteen year period during which clearance and renewal took place. Despite this, Hyde Park relocatees did not receive a greater proportion of the compensation payments, nor were their individual claims any greater on the average than non-Hyde Park relocatees. On the other hand, they suffered a greater lag in restoring their former business volumes and on the average took longer to find relocation sites and to move there (Table 4.6).

TABLE 4.6

**TIME-LAPSE BETWEEN MOVING AND REGAINING
FORMER BUSINESS VOLUME**

Comparison Non-Hyde Park and Hyde Park Relocatees

	Non-Hyde Park	Hyde Park	TOTAL
No lag	23	23	46
6 months	1	4	5
7-12 months	—	2	2
1-2 years	2	3	5
Over 2 years	9	13	22
Total Response	35	45	80

Those who moved out in the early phases of the program had little chance of finding a relocation site in Hyde Park — they relied more on realtors and advertising than on informal ways of finding new sites. Although they had a greater choice of sites and, unlike those who stayed, most looked at several sites, almost half of each group felt they were given insufficient time to relocate. (Table 4.7) Those businessmen who finally found sites in Hyde Park showed great perseverance. Twenty-four per cent were denied sites as against fourteen per cent of those relocating outside Hyde Park, and the majority finally found their new location by hearing about it from a friend or finding it themselves. Only 44 per cent (compared with 76 per cent) of this group of relocatees looked at several sites. Most were retailers who preferred to stay and serve local customers despite the temporary upheaval that renewal brought.

Following relocation those who had moved out of Hyde Park expressed greater dissatisfaction with their new neighborhood, and were specifically concerned with problems centering around finance and their customers, whereas Hyde Parkers complained mostly about the shortage of floor space. Seventy-five per cent of those who stayed in the community were satisfied with their

TABLE 4.7

**TIME-LAPSE BETWEEN PROPERTY ACQUISITION
AND DATE OF MOVE: RELOCATEES IN
HYDE PARK AND ELSEWHERE**

A. Acquisition-Move Lag[a]   B. Acquisition-Move Lag[b]

	Non-H.P.	H.P.	Moved then Liq.	TOTAL	Non-H.P.	H.P.	TOTAL
No Lag	9	5	0	14			
1 month	18	8	1	27	122	102	224
2-6 months	63	38	7	108	36	34	70
7-12 months	39	31	1	71	4	9	13
1-2 years	17	13	3	33	8	9	2
Over 2 years	5	5	1	11	2	0	2
TOTAL CASES	151	100	13	264	172	154	326

SUFFICIENT TIME FOR RELOCATION?

	Non-H.P.	H.P.	TOTAL
Sufficient time	28	30	58
Insufficient time	24	21	45
Total responses	52	51	

[a]From Department of Urban Renewal Records
[b]From interviews

location and had no major complaints or business problems and twenty-nine per cent mentioned business problems that had emerged since relocating. By contrast the respective proportions of non-Hyde Parkers were 53 per cent and 83 per cent (Table 4.9).

Of those displacees who gave sales information, eleven out of the thirteen Hyde Park retailers showed sales increases. The four remaining service and supply stores all lost trade. The 45 per

TABLE 4.8

COMPARISONS OF HYDE PARK RELOCATEES AND THOSE RELOCATING ELSEWHERE

Date First Heard of Urban Renewal

	Non-H.P.	H.P.	TOTAL
Don't Know	2	1	3
Before 1955	15	9	24
1955-57	4	7	11
1958-60	9	5	14
Since 1961	6	5	11

How First Heard of Urban Renewal

	Non-H.P.	H.P.	TOTAL
By Rumor	25	18	63
By Newspaper	18	14	32
Other	14	17	31

Visit by D.U.R. Official

	Non-H.P.	H.P.	TOTAL
D.U.R. Official Visited	31	29	60
Helpful	11	13	24
Not Helpful	20	16	36
No Visit	25	25	50

Attended Urban Renewal Meetings

	Non-H.P.	H.P.	TOTAL
Attended Meetings	11	15	26
Helpful	3	3	6
Not Helpful	8	12	20
Did not Attend Meetings	45	39	84

TABLE 4.9

EXPERIENCE AT NEW LOCATION: HYDE PARK AND ELSEWHERE

		Non-H.P.	H.P.	TOTAL
Satisfied with Neighborhood	Yes	30	40	70
	No	26	11	37
	Total Responses	56	51	107
Business Problems Since Relocation	Yes	24	13	37
	No	29	44	73
	TOTAL	53	57	110
Changed Merchandise Or Service	Yes	15	12	27
	No	43	45	88
	TOTAL	58	57	115
Satisfied with Cost of Doing Business	Yes	33	38	71
	No	24	14	38
	TOTAL	57	52	109
Satisfied with New Location	Yes	39	43	82
	No	15	10	25
	TOTAL	54	53	107
Floor Space Adequate	Yes	46	34	80
	No	1	14	15
	TOTAL	47	48	95
Storage Space Adequate	Yes	45	33	78
	No	7	14	21
	TOTAL	52	47	99
Convenience to Old Customers	Yes	24	37	61
	No	25	12	37
	TOTAL	49	49	98
Convenience to New Customers	Yes	34	43	77
	No	14	7	21
	TOTAL	48	50	98

cent who preferred to find sites out of Hyde Park tended to be service or supply-type businesses which required cheap rentals and large premises and normally located in ribbons, e.g. auto repair and supply establishments. Eleven of these lost trade. Two of the three retailers also lost business. Twelve establishments relocated in nearby Negro communities, and only one experienced better business than before; six of the eleven businesses losing trade (ten of which were in the service or supply categories) were Negro-owned. None of the owners reestablishing their businesses in white communities outside Hyde Park were Negro. However half of the relocatees remaining in Hyde Park serve Negro customers and have regained their former business volumes.

Why did these businesses relocate in the way they did, and to what did they attribute their fates? *The prime cause of difficulty* always cited, whether by displacees or not, *was loss of customers because of clearance,* or the severance of ties to old markets and the attendant loss of goodwill. *Displacees in the supply-and-service categories also complained about the disruptions in business caused by the necessity to relocate elsewhere, because urban renewal removed the property they could afford to rent.* Generally, the new locations did not provide opportunities that compensated for goodwill lost. On the other hand, retailers who found new locations on 53rd Street and in East Hyde Park on 55th Street were generally satisfied with their fortunes. They were able to retain much of their goodwill, and benefitted from the reduction of business operating in Hyde Park and the concentration of customers on a few shopping streets.

The more financially secure the businessman, the more likely he was to stay in the community. Eight of the twelve enterprises with branch establishments outside of Hyde Park were able to relocate back into the community and prosper; nine of the twelve businessmen who had additional sources of income besides their business did likewise. Merchants who owned their own stores were less fortunate — four of the thirteen stayed in Hyde Park and none thought they were fully and fairly compensated. Only one of these purchased another store. Businesses with more than one owner were more likely to face the challenge of starting up again in another community, and less likely to put up with the uncertainties associated with the development of the renewal program.

Fortunes of other Hyde Park Businesses

In Chapter 2 we described what had happened to businesses who chose to locate in the new shopping centers in Hyde Park, but what of those businesses which were not displaced and who did not move into one of the shopping centers? In keeping with the normal turnover rate for small businesses, many of the entrants during the past thirteen years have discontinued operating in Hyde Park. Those who were present during the clearance and displacement periods complained of the long period of slack business when renewal had drastically reduced Hyde Park's population. They were adversely affected, also, by rising rents that accompanied the massive reduction in the supply of commercial space. They, too, experienced loss of certain valued markets and goodwill.

In many ways the businesses not displaced were like those who were able to relocate in the community. Most were small retail concerns which, unlike those who moved out, required little space and catered largely to the local middle-class Jewish community and university staff and students. Most had upgraded their premises and spent extra money on maintenance work in keeping with the general upgrading of physical structures in the community during the renewal period. Only a few owned the stores they occupied. Unlike those who relocated out of the community, Hyde Parkers dealt less with other businesses and depended heavily on the local residential population. This means that almost half now serve Negro customers though only fifteen of the non-displacees and ten relocatees in Hyde Park are Negro.

There were distinctive characteristics of the merchants who had not been displaced or who had come into Hyde Park after the renewal program had begun. They tended to be younger and many were not the sole owners of the business. As expected, most had a higher ratio of regular customers than did the relocated businesses, seventeen per cent as against twelve per cent had other business interests, and a slightly higher proportion had additional sources of income. Their incomes were generally better distributed — twelve exceeded $10,000 fourteen had incomes between $5,000 and $9,999 and fourteen had less than $5,000. By comparison those relocatees who reported their incomes were mostly those who were earning less than $5,000 per annum.

Many businesses moved before they were displaced and

others moved in response to the changing pattern of commercial structure in the community as 53rd Street was revitalized with the clearance of 55th and 57th Streets. Thirty-one per cent of the Hyde Park relocatees had moved more than twice in the last thirteen years and forty per cent of the other relocatees have done likewise; in contrast, only four per cent of the non-displaced had moved as often, although twenty-two per cent have moved at least twice.

Opinions of the Businessmen

The majority of businessmen felt that they were worse off now than if there had been no urban renewal in Hyde Park. Most of those who felt they were better off are located in the renewed area. This means that sixty-one per cent of the businessmen relocating in Hyde Park thought they were worse off, whereas seventy-seven per cent who relocated out of Hyde Park felt they were in a worse position than previously.

Despite these findings a large proportion of merchants said they approved of the methods that were used to renew Hyde Park-Kenwood, even though many of these same respondents now feel that they are worse off than if urban renewal had not taken place! In other words the principle of urban renewal might be right or wrong, but, given the fact of the urban renewal program, most accepted the way in which the program was carried out. But in much the same way as they would accept a tax increase, these businessmen also voiced specific grievances indicating the pervasive feeling of discontent with their particular experience. A variety of respondents expressed a general approval for urban renewal despite their individual experiences in the belief that it benefitted the community as a whole. Others were "for renewal" but also held major reservations as evidenced by the following statement from an elderly Negro displacee who relocated successfully after an initial year of hardship: "I believe in progress and urban renewal is progress, but it makes a lot of people uncomfortable while they are going through the process and it causes fear and trouble; people are pushed out by urban renewal into other places making it into a ghetto. I had a good business and a growing business, and I could have expanded. That (urban renewal) upset everthing for me, and that was bad. (Now) I am not any worse off than I was."

A general desire to forget the whole thing was frequently expressed and several displacees were still so embittered that they refused to talk about it saying, "What's the use? It's too late now!" Or, in the case of a butcher who had been in business over twenty years and observed the general trend away from small business we met with the following response — "What right have you to come here and ask such personal questions?" Those who complained referred to specific problems such as loss of customers, moving costs, too many buildings torn down, compensation not adequate or that the administration of the program was poor; but few had radical suggestions as to what could be done to improve the displacees' plight. Almost one quarter (twenty-two per cent) voiced no opinion, the remainder, and the majority, mentioned the need to increase the present forms of compensation rather than suggesting alternative kinds or methods.

Most who relocated outside Hyde Park did not approve of the urban renewal methods used in the Hyde Park program. Their chief complaint was poor administration. Fifty-five per cent (24/44) commented specifically on bad administration, uncertain programming and poor timing of the various phases of the urban renewal process as being major problems. Almost as many relocatees (nineteen) mentioned that, in their opinion, too many buildings were torn down; the remaining 27 comments focussed on compensation and relocation methods. An articulate well-informed Jewish merchant, serving Negro customers, who successfully fought urban renewal while his business has 'gone in cycles' had this to say: "There was great demolition of good property that could have been rehabilitated. They turned a deaf ear to rehabilitation. They were interested only in removing people, acting in a ruthless way, rather than joining forces with the community to solve an urban problem. They were interested solely in saving university property. This of itself is not an unreasonable goal, but they carried it out in an unethical and ruthless manner!"

By far the most complaints came from relocatees who are no longer in Hyde Park. Hyde Park relocatees on the other hand did not have as many complaints about poor administration: less than one quarter of their complaints were directed against the administration. (Table 4.10). Perhaps they are less critical simply because many of them (thirty-nine per cent) now feel better off because of urban renewal, whereas sixty-seven per cent of those relocating out of the community blame urban renewal for putting them in a worse position than before. The difficulty of finding appropriate sites in the community, and the disruptions associated with widespread commercial clearance, resulted in over thirty per cent of the Hyde Park relocatees moving three times or more during the renewal period. One third

TABLE 4.10

COMPLAINTS AGAINST RENEWAL METHODS[1]

	Non-Displacees (40 responses)	H. P. Relocatees (29 responses)	Non-H.P. Relocatees (44 responses)
Tore Down Too Many Buildings	14	12	19
Inadequate Compensation	2	10	10
Poor Administration	7	5	13
Timing Poor	18	2	8
Insufficient Time to Relocate	1	4	4
No Relocation Help	1	1	4
Uncertain Program	3	0	3
TOTAL COMPLAINTS	46	34	61

Ranking of General Categories of Complaints

Non-Displacees	H.P. Relocatees	Non-H.P. Relocatees
1. Poor Administration	Tore Down Too Many Buildings	Poor Administration
2. Tore Down Too Many Buildings	Compensation Inadequate	Tore Down Too Many Buildings
3.	Poor Administration	Compensation Inadequate
4.	Relocation Needs	Relocation Needs

[1]From question, "Do you approve of the methods by which renewal was carried out?"

of all the criticisms therefore focussed on the issue of clearance: "Too many buildings were torn down." A university graduate, now in the automatic-washer repair business, claimed that "Some buildings were torn down which were in fine condition." A fifty-two year old owner of a laundromat self-service enterprise had come into the Kenwood area during the renewal period and was reluctant to answer questions in case they might lead to further renewal plans for 47th street. From his point of view they (urban renewal agents) tear down but do not build up again to make it possible for businessmen to move back into the community. There has been a lot of tearing down, but nothing has been done — improvements appear to come too slowly; there is a lack of new facilities."

Compensation was generally felt to be inadequate. Only two of the displacees thought that adequate compensation had been given. Apart from the non-displacees, only twenty-five per cent of whom thought more compensation should be given, the general consensus was that adequate moving costs should be provided. The need for funds to maintain income and to ease the relocation process was mentioned by at least twenty-five per cent of both relocatee groups. (Table 4.12). For example, when asked how she financed her move, a beautician, dependent on retaining her regular customers and used to doing things on her own, replied: "With my own savings. I don't like borrowing!" She had not been told about compensation claims and complained that you have to "spend what money you have — or go into debt. No one takes an interest in you. Urban renewal should make up for that first year!" Non-displacees suggested that special loans be available to displacees to cover uncompensated costs. None mentioned the possibility of using Small Business Administration Loans though at least ten had tried to obtain them, seven unsuccessfully.

Loss of customers appeared as a major problem cited by a majority of the displaced merchants. (Table 4.11.) This was reinforced by general comments from seventeen merchants who complained of losing business and in some cases losing their means of livelihood. A majority felt that the Local Public Agency could and should do more to provide information on

TABLE 4.11

MAJOR BUSINESS PROBLEMS PERCEIVED TO BE ASSOCIATED WITH URBAN RENEWAL

	Non-Displacees (70 respondents)	Hyde Park Relocatees (50 respondents)	Non-H.P. Relocatees (50 respondents)
Loss of Customers	36	28	29
Moving Costs	18	21	21
Finding New Location	25	17	17
Loss of Business	21	11	13
Expense Relocation/ Remodelling	13	8	10
Loss of Livelihood	2	0	7
Trying to Relocate in Hyde Park	3	0	5
Rent	6	4	1
TOTAL PROBLEMS	124	89	103

Most Often Mentioned

    1. Loss of customers—over 50% of each group mentioned this.
    2. Moving costs—except for non-displacees 50%.
    3. Hard to find new location—⅓ mentioned this.
    4. Loss of business—¼ mentioned this.
    5. Expenses of relocating/remodelling—⅕ mentioned this.

Least Often Mentioned

    The distribution is similar for both groups of relocatees and non-displacees. The only exceptions are that fewer non-displacees cite moving expenses as a major problem, and only non-Hyde Park relocatees were concerned with trying to move back into the community.

available sites at rents they could afford. *All agreed that the relocation assistance given was inadequate.* Many reported that payments due were not made promptly, or that the LPA's renewal staff lacked experience in dealing with small business problems. For example, a printer who had been in business in the community for 22 years, and who claimed he had suffered from the renewal experience, felt that there had been a "misrepresentation of facts. Urban renewal officers do not know their business; it was a disgraceful mishandling of the situation. Urban renewal officials should give correct information about compensation, and sufficient time should be given as notice to

TABLE 4.12

PROGRAM IMPROVEMENTS SUGGESTED

	Hyde Park Non-Displacees	Hyde Park Relocatees	Non-Hyde Park Relocatees	TOTAL
More Compensation	19	28	39	86
Maintain Income Extra Finance	21	13	16	50
More Assistance and Advice to Help Businessmen Readapt	26	6	16	48
More Relocation Time	1	5	7	13
Goodwill Compensation	6	4	4	14
Help to Retain Old Customers	2	1	3	6
Less Paperwork	2	0	1	3
TOTAL Positive Responses	77	57	86	220
TOTAL Respondents	61-64	40-59	42-58	

all businessmen." By contrast, a pest exterminator who belonged to several neighborhood organizations and talked regularly with other businessmen in Hyde Park, approved of the urban renewal methods that were used even though his business has deteriorated since the program began — "I feel that considering what they had to work with they did a good job!" Several reiterated the feelings of one displacee: "They provide you with very little help, and treat you like a relief client." Most pointed out the difficulties of reestablishing themselves.

One couple who were both unable to get sufficient compensation to enable them to move their snack shop or to find a suitable relocation site, were forced to go out of business temporarily. Their losses not recovered, nor their capital sufficient to start over again, they have spent the subsequent years as restaurant employees, working extremely long hours in an effort to save enough money to go back into business for themselves. Similarly, a second respondent said that "I had to borrow from three sources and take another job to keep the business going and make ends meet." A fish merchant who has had to make a series of adjustments to successfully adapt his business to the changing neighborhood custom reported: "If I had not had another store, I would have had to go out of business." Most said that the moving expense reimbursement was inadequate, and one said that cash grants of $300.00 a month or more should be made to provide a source of income during the difficult period of reestablishing operations. Several operators of service establishments said that the Hyde Park re-use plan excluded them, and therefore deprived them of their goodwill in the community, and that this loss is the principal reason for their poorer performance after relocation. "Give displaced businessmen the chance to relocate in the area before outside businessmen are brought in; and give more financial help to offset the loss of customers. They should offer relocation at the same rent in the same area. The trouble is that urban renewal officials do not live here, they do not care about how Hyde Park is!" . . . complained a non-displacee who has been in business on the same Hyde Park site for over forty years.

Whoever the businessman, the interviewers reported a consistent undercurrent of disaffection with urban renewal as a program and with the relocation activities and representatives of the Local Public Agency. Responses varied, from suspicion that the interview might be the prelude to further renewal, to outright bigotry: "DUR did not pay a fair price for my building . . . If we didn't move things and replace them exactly as they were before, we weren't entitled to compensation. Why should some no-good-nigger in UR tell me what I could and could not do. I went above their heads — straight to city hall." Similarly, a displacee who had been unable to operate his printing business for four weeks prior to receiving the official moving notice as services had already been cut off and for which he received no compensation went to Washington to draw to the attention of his Senator the inequities in, and the lack of compensation for, business displacees. Others were quite perceptive: "Many businessmen do not have the financial resources to withstand the long period of urban renewal. Those that can stick it out and stay in the community can benefit from urban renewal in the long run, though. But the new zoning does not let valuable businesses like upholsterers remain even if they could." Or, "There

was no need to tear down so many stores so quickly and just
leave the land vacant for five years. (The stores) could have
been used for another four years." Or, from a Negro relocatee
to Woodlawn, "There just isn't the business here that there was
in Hyde Park," and, from a displacee who moved to South
Shore, "Right after I moved here my new customers started to
move away, and the Negro market just doesn't have the money."

The only wholly positive note was sounded by the Kimbark
Plaza group, which acknowledged the help and assistance provided by the Small Business Administration, and by the Chicago
Department of Urban Renewal once it looked as if the group
were going to be able to make a "go" of it. But some still felt
that their prior experiences with DUR left much to be desired.

Half of the relocatees and two-thirds of the non-displacees
wanted HUD to provide relation sites. (Table 4.13). Those
businessmen who relocated out of Hyde Park believed that the
best kind of relocation was in old space in Hyde Park or similar
space in another community; few thought that new shopping
center sites were desirable. Only one in eight recommended that
help to remain in the Hyde Park community should be offered by

TABLE 4.13

FEELINGS ABOUT PROVISION OF RELOCATION SITES[a]

	Do Not Want Site Provided	No Opinion	Want Site Provided	Older Space	Other Space	New Shopping Center	Total
Relocated Out of Hyde Park	29	—	29	66% 23	20% 7	14% 5	100% 35
Relocated In Hyde Park	27	3	22	29% 6	48% 9	29% 6	100% 21
Non-Displacees in Hyde Park	24	13	43	32% 15	25% 11	43% 20	100% 46

[a]The discrepancy between the total number of respondents answering the
question whether sites should be provided or not, and the number answering the questions about specific kinds of sites is explained by a few
respondents replying negatively to the first question but still specifying
what kind of site they would prefer given that provision.

HUD. By contrast the 22 merchants who did relocate in Hyde Park and favored relocation sites being provided preferred other kinds of sites than in new shopping centers or space in old structures. The remaining fifty-five per cent of the Hyde Park relocatees preferred that no relocation sites be provided. On the other hand non-displacees operating in Hyde Park were overwhelmingly in favor of the provision of relocation sites for displacees—43 out of 67 approved, 13 did not know—and the majority of these respondents recommended a new shopping center location.

THE CHAIN STORES[1]

(Draft of this section prepared by David M. Solzman)

Because of the ability of small businesses to compete in renewal neighborhoods is in part dependent upon the actions and opinions of chain stores, we decided also to elicit the feelings of chain store executives about renewal. Many of the chains considered the choice in Hyde Park to be a simple one—between a low-income Negro market and a racially-mixed middle-income one. If urban renewal had not taken place, they would have had to contend with the former; because of renewal, the context is now the latter. Both, they argue, can be adequate chain-store markets, and the processes producing each have the same salutory effect on chain store operations. Racial transition and urban renewal both, they feel, reduce the number of small competi-

---

1 This section is based on interviews with executives and operatives of nine major chain store operations and a number of smaller but important multistore firms in the Chicago area. The firms included represent the drug, food, general merchandise and variety segments of the retail industry. Firms contacted include: *Drugs;* Walgreen Co., Rexall Co., Ford-Hopkins-Steinway, Steinway System and Osco. *Foods;* Hi-Lo, Kroger, National Tea, Jewel, Del Farms, and Market Basket. *General Merchandise and Variety;* Sears, Carson Pirie, Scott and Co., Woolworth. Discussions also included: Key Rexall Stores, Shopper's World, Kinney Shoes, Woolco (currently planning entry into Chicago), Worth Mart Stores, Pretty Penny Stores.

The interviews obtained information on the way in which major retailers view the processes of racial change and urban redevelopment and on the responses which such companies make within the city to such changes. Of primary interest were those responses which affect store locations, sizes, means and modes of contruction, staffing and lines of merchandise handled and changes in territory served or size of market required for a given location to be chosen. Also of general interest was internal company planning on the several levels of corporate organization as it relates to the way in which major chain operations perceive and accommodate renewal.

The presentation of this material, must of necessity, be general rather than specific in order to protect confidences of the interviewees. Therefore any specific situations described will be presented without direct reference to the organization from which the information originally came.

tors[1] and permit greater concentration of sales in larger stores and more complete market penetration by the chains, for only multi-store operations have the resources to be able to overcome either kind of stress.

In Hyde Park, a variety of older chain store outlets which existed before renewal were displaced by urban renewal. Some of these have been replaced by newer more modern stores serving larger areas. Some previously profitable operations in the area were closed due to uncertainty and the drop in volume and profit which accompanied racial change or because of extensive clearance of residential areas by the renewal agency. New operations owned by firms which successfully weathered the storms of neighborhood change have replaced the earlier units. Additionally, some firms that fled the area are now seeking new locations to tap the market which renewal has created, a positive effect of the renewal program worthy of note. Intense inter-firm warfare has thus become a feature of Hyde Park as new chain operators (primarily food chains) seek access to the market and cross legal and political swords with vested interests. A key combatant in this present struggle is the Hyde Park Coop, which is fighting attempts by supermarket chains to gain access to the community, and simultaneously is itself diversifying into durable goods, thereby challenging other large chains in the competition for the consumer's dollar.

Of course, Hyde Park is by no means typical of renewal neighborhoods, and situations of the kind described above are rare. The income level and the high level of education that characterizes most of the Negro residents of Hyde Park cannot be compared, most chain executives argue, with most renewal areas in Chicago. One repeated the charge that, "Hyde Park is an area in which black and white stand shoulder to shoulder against the poor," and added that, "this is why we find it such an attractive opportunity." "Although both renewal and racial change lead to greater concentration of trade, profits are greater in a renewal area like Hyde Park because of the middle-income community created!"

---

[1] This is consistent with what we now know about Negro buying habits. See Real Estate Research Corporation, *Retail Location Analysis Manual: Small Business in Low Income Areas, op. cit.*

The Impact of Racial Change

If the alternatives perceived in Hyde Park were a low-income market, or one reconstructed by urban renewal, the chain store executives clearly preferred the latter. Problems exist during the period of transition, usually from middle-income white to low-income Negro, when sales volumes can drop anywhere from 15-40 per cent in a period of 2-3 years as a community is ghettoized. Thereafter, there are continuing problems of merchandising, staffing and safety, all of which impair profitability. They require extreme solutions, such as redesign of stores, or the creation of wholly-owned subsidiaries under new names directed at the low-income market. If renewal is the alternative that helps avoid such problems, it is preferred.

The Effects of Urban Renewal

The attitudes of chain executives vary with the nature of the retail operations, however.

All agree, with resignation, that they have been able to exercise little role in renewal planning, but instead have had to accept the crude facts of store displacement (generally, "we are large enough to withstand the effects on our system operations of closing one or two stores"), change in market conditions for stores remaining on shopping streets not scheduled for reconstruction ("hard times when many of the homes are torn down can be borne by the chain, and are compensated by better profits later"), and limited availability of land for commercial redevelopment. All agree that politics as well as economics are important in obtaining redevelopment opportunities.

Greatest interest in redevelopment opportunities was shown by grocery chains, which can create a profitable operation on a yearly volume of a million dollars and about 12,500 square feet of floor space. But chain drugstores require a larger proportion of the consumer's drug dollar than supermarkets require of his food expenditures, and so there is greater caution about seeking new locations—in a small community shopping center at the very minimum. General merchandise chains only begin serious exploration if there is a chance of redevelopment by a large community center or a regional shopping center.

Scale of store and degree of market penetration are reiterated as prime locational considerations. Renewal is welcomed because the executives feel, "There's no question about it—the little guy is out," and urban renewal "gets rid of the little guys." Thus, as one food chain executive put it, "as soon as we hear of an urban renewal project we get busy."

But despite the utility to food operations of more scattered sites, executives of drug companies express considerable interest in and approval for renewal projects. As one representative stated: "I personally feel that urban renewal is good for business and residential functions." This man was thinking in terms of large regional centers, but two drug firms also expressed interest in smaller shopping centers.[1] This interest was provoked by specialized sales arrangements devised by both companies. In one case, nearly all stores are independent operations participating in the distribution of a special brand name product group which is nevertheless a house name. In the other case, some small drug stores can participate in the chain operation as far as buying and advertising are concerned but are not actually owned by the chain itself. Such specialized arrangements are also of interest in a review of the financing of small centers.

Finally, the major department store and general merchandise operations are only interested in the largest centers. But even then renewal districts are of value. As stated by a real estate executive from the largest firm investigated: "it really isn't possible to develop land in city centers without massive (government) intervention." And he added the additional observation that "without political pressure we would elect to locate and spend money (only) where we could anticipate the greatest return." Politics and the politics of renewal in particular create, on occasion, a constraint on the purely economic factors which otherwise might singly determine store locations.

The differences in services provided and in the character of goods offered by different types of chain stores obviously lead to different views of the availability of suitable sites. Food chains

---

1 Aside from this one type of specialized operation, all attention is riveted on larger centers: "Chains go more for larger stores in larger centers. The day of the neighborhood drugstore is about done. We are going to the larger centers."

often "build (their) operations to what they can get." Some have four or five standard plans to suit whatever is available. To be sure, good practice sets lower limits on floor space, but floor space considerations are more flexible than are the buying power of the surrounding populations. Even in large centers some drug stores develop only moderate sized sites since they feel that smaller floor areas allow for greater merchandise control and security. One food chain "began with smaller stores, moved to larger stores, and then dropped back from gigantic stores (to accommodate) older people (and others) who complain about enormous stores."

One high quality department store has oriented its operations almost exclusively toward middle class customers and "they gravitate to areas where present customers live." This informant "doubts that effort will be expended within the city limits of Chicago." He noted further that renewal in downtown Rockford, Illinois is making it "more difficult to obtain land (there)."

If differences in scale and type of operation create different views on site availability, there is little disagreement that site acquisition costs in renewal areas are seldom cheap. Most of those interviewed complained about relatively high site costs that restrain their participation in many renewal plans.

With the single exception of the largest firm consulted, all other chains prefer to rent stores either in or out of renewal areas. This reduces the sunk investment, allows for plant to be written off as business expense for tax purposes, and frees working capital. "We'd rather put our money into merchandise and fixtures." There is also the feeling that rental allows more freedom of movement as a hedge against unforeseen changes in the neighborhood of operation. Thus, there is general approval of renewal by private developers from whom stores in new large centers can be rented.

One interesting variant on this approach was developed by one of the chain drug companies which, on some occasions, enters into partnership with a private individual who invests no less than ten thousand dollars and then buys out the parent firm over a period of from seven to twelve years. This allows a small business man to negotiate under favorable interest rates for a long term (15 year) lease and offers an opportunity to get started in business for himself. This interesting approach may be useful if applied in the future to small businessmen displaced by renewal plans, in for example the context of a redevelopment corporation like Kimbark Plaza.

The single case in which ownership was found to be preferable was related to the scale of operation of the parent company and to the internal financing capabilities of that firm. In this case, depreciation and control overrides other considerations.

But aside from this rather straightforward view of tenurial arrangements, long term leases from established chain store operators give shopping center developers many advantages. It cannot be concluded, on the basis of the interviews, to what extent other types of assistance are provided to contractors and developers by chains. But the impression was given that assistance to developers can, on some occasions, secure a position in a key market for knowledgeable firms, and so such arrangements must occur frequently. In Hyde Park, for instance, a site was bid-on and secured by a third party in order to gain re-entrance to the north Hyde Park market by a major chain store.

It is noteworthy that not a single firm investigated found it necessary to organize a special department to handle renewal locations. All such development was handled by their regular real estate and location staffs, or under the guidance of already available and organized real estate divisions of the parent company. In one drug and one variety chain there were indications that company policy favored seeking renewal locations, but for all other firms, criteria of density, traffic and buying power were applied to locational analysis of both renewal and non-renewal sites.[1] As a representative of the largest firm insisted; "we're not dealing with a new market, we're already there." The regional approach to location employed by his company removed the necessity for considering renewal districts as special cases.

The redevelopment of obsolete or blighted districts frequently

---

1 For a review of the procedures commonly used see Chapter 7 of Brian J. L. Berry, *Geography of Market Centers and Retail Distribution.* Englewood Cliffs, N. J.: Prentice-Hall Inc., 1967.

elicits praise, but problems arising from the displacement of older and often smaller businesses also may arise. It was the feeling of every firm interrogated however, that displeasure was usually vented at the renewal authority itself and, since there is frequently a time lapse of five years for the completion of renewal projects there seemed no concern on the part of chain operations that they would be blamed for the demise or displacement of smaller firms. Indeed, the partnership arrangement mentioned above for drug store development might well draw favorable comment since it presents an avenue by which a small businessman may participate in shopping center development. In any case, the large firms perceived their "image" unblemished by taking advantage of renewal opportunities.

Despite the general interest in renewal locations expressed by large chain operations, however, certain constraints were felt to operate within the renewal process, to confound and confuse the general intent. Chief among the problems stated is uncertainty and lack of information arising from inadequate communication between governmental authorities and potential site developers. Interviewees unanimously felt that information on plans for renewal is either *unavailable* much of the time or that such information is *selectively distributed*.

As might be expected, such opinions are difficult to verify empirically, but overtones of favoritism were encountered a number of times under different circumstances with executives from different types of operations. An interesting case in point was provided by a food chain which has been displaced in the Hyde Park renewal and which has failed to gain re-entry to this market. "I do think they were wrong. They should have contacted people who were to be put out. That wasn't done! Speaking frankly, the whole bidding that was done after the demolition was done very wrong. A private bidder got it for ("X" company). We did bid on this site but were outbid some way or another. "X" took this site. They had to guarantee they would finish by a certain time but they haven't done it. Uncertainty is harmful—we depend upon them (the renewal authority)." Favoritism cannot be ignored in descriptions and analyses of the ways in which major chain operators plan for renewal and in consideration of factors which complicate the process. Uncertainty, in the minds of many executives, is worse than definite bad news. Such uncertainty not only restrains plans for new operations in renewal neighborhoods; it has, on occasion, been responsible for vacating existing operations. Another national chain food operation was involved in the general uncertainty which surrounded the renewal of the north section of Hyde Park along Hyde Park Boulevard. "We pulled the store before the plan was finalized because the lack of information was so great."

Of course, it must be remembered that such a store would probably not close if it continued as a very profitable operation, but because of racial change, stores in changing areas undergo a trying period of declining sales and profits until community equilibrium is reestablished. Under such protean circumstances, uncertainty and lack of firm renewal plans often constitute the last straw. One respondent reflected: "One cannot help feeling that if major corporations operating chain stores throughout the nation have trouble getting information that small businessmen must be completely out of luck and information."

SUMMARY OF ATTITUDES

Whether valid or not, the prevalent feelings among both small businessmen who remained in Hyde Park and those who had been displaced from the community was that they were worse off following renewal—that it would have been better for them if urban renewal had not taken place. And although relocatees fortunate enough to be able to reestablish themselves in Hyde Park are more satisfied with their new locations and have fewer business problems than businessmen who relocated out of the community and now express a high level of dissatisfaction, there is clearly no perception on the part of the small businessmen that conditions might have been worse if urban renewal had not taken place.

To be sure, displacement is a major crisis to the small businessman, emotionally and financially, and he cannot be as detached as the chain store executives, who articulate the alternatives more dispassionately. Whatever the reasons, and all the aggregate analyses of the previous chapter notwithstanding, however, the great majority of the *individual* businessmen now *feel* that urban renewal hurt them.

Part of the problem is that *the very conception of Hyde Park-Kenwood's urban renewal plans introduced inequities into relocation possibilities.* More retail than service, supply or manufacturing establishments were able to relocate in Hyde Park, while the liquidation rate for grocery stores, eating places and drinking places was especially high. The chain store executives also note that re-use plans generally favor larger stores, especially chains with sound credit ratings and easy access to credit. Further, in more than one-third of the cases of displacement no compensation was received by displacees and only 160 moving expense claims were received and 85 other kinds of reimbursements were made amongst the remaining two-thirds. Rent reductions were granted to less than one-third of the displacees, with liquidatees receiving the most. In spite of this, only 44 per cent of the relocatees stressed that compensation was inadequate. Fifty per cent had to use their own savings to help finance their move; one-quarter also relied on bank or private loans.

Despite the inadequacies of the compensation program a majority of the respondents (with the exception of those who relocated out of Hyde Park) said that they approved of the methods used to carry out the renewal program. Many of the respondents did not dispute the principle of urban renewal, nor did they speak out against the program, especially those who were still in business in the community.

The most frequent criticisms of the program were instead that too many buildings were torn down, compensation was inadequate and the program had been badly administered. Both small businessmen and chain store executives talked frequently about communication problems and informational inadequacies.

When asked about specific major problems that they confronted, comments from both relocatees and non-displacees centered on the following issues:

1. loss of customers and/or business
2. moving costs
3. finding a new location
4. other expenses of relocating

Finally, displaced merchants did not favor provision of relocation sites by the renewal authority. Most relocatees who had left the community favored sites in old space while displacees in Hyde Park overwhelmingly supported the idea of providing new shopping center locations.

In one sense, the businessmen in Hyde Park-Kenwood were unfortunate. Many of the problems they cite have since been taken care of by new legislation or by revised HUD regulations. Some of the problems they faced remain: inequities among different types of business and between establishments in the same line and loss of sales during the renewal process. The legislative changes already made and the problems still outstanding are the topic of Part II.

PART II

NATIONAL EXPERIENCE

. . . displacement problems reviewed
. . . new benefits for displaced businesses
. . . inequities requiring resolution

CHAPTER FIVE

Displacement Problems: Other Literature Reviewed

THE MOUNTING EVIDENCE OF DISPLACEMENT PROBLEMS

Urban renewal is undertaken by public agencies in what they perceive to be the general community good because private decisions and actions are held to be incapable of achieving the ends desired and because the benefits exceed the costs by a greater margin than they would in some alternative use of public funds. Eminent domain proceedings are required to assemble the tracts of land desired for redevelopment and to prevent individuals from extracting artificially high prices for the last "hold out" piece(s) of real property.[1] But use of eminent domain introduces the complex question of exactly what constitutes "just compensation."

This question can be addressed at least in part by surveying the mounting evidence of small business problems created or brought to a head by displacement. As we will show in Chapter 6, some of these problems have already been corrected by new legislation or changed administrative regulations However, at this point a general overview of the range and complexity of issues involved in small business displacement is warranted, as they have been revealed by other studies of the subject, to see what in the Hyde Park experience may be general, and what may be peculiar to the community.

---

1 Even then, individual property owners can oppose the renewal plan, but their right to retain their site is always superseded by the right to government to use the site for a public purpose. Once the renewal plan has been approved by the federal government it is unlikely that subsequent local objections will materially affect it, although owners of small businesses have opposed and delayed effectuation of urban renewal proposals. For example, in Philadelphia six small firms employing 24 persons held up one $100 million project for over eight months. Kinnard, *op. cit.*, p. 6. Several factors work against property owners opposing renewal plans. The opposition has to be well organized. There is only a limited time in which opposition is effective. Conflicting interests exist amongst the opposition. The need to phrase the issue in terms of loss to the community rather than to the individual, and lack of information as to how, when, and where the stages of renewal will be implemented are additional factors inhibiting effective opposition to the plan.

Improving the Economic Base

Local public agencies view displacement problems and commercial renewal quite differently from the small businessman. Emphasis is placed on the contributions of the program to the entire community. The problem is seen as one of upgrading the *area*. Private developers implement a re-use plan that assures a rise in property values and therefore in property taxes. Higher income residents and/or an increase in jobs are seen as the means to improve the base. The agency therefore tries to create an economically and physically attractive plan to gather both financial and public support. But re-use plans that imply change in community character are of critical concern to the displaced business, just as they are to the residents to be relocated. A business displaced by urban renewal must relocate in order to survive. The primary question therefore facing the displaced merchant who aims to stay in business is where to relocate, and, to begin with, whether to stay in the same community or to move elsewhere. Relocation in the same neighborhood is likely to be advantageous both to the small businessman and to the community, the businessmen are likely to argue. By remaining in the area, the merchant may salvage much of the goodwill that must otherwise be sacrificed without compensation. In some cases the retrieval of this asset may enable a man to stay in business when an uncertain start elsewhere might be beyond his capacities.

The neighborhood itself, in the eyes of the businessman, benefits from the retention of locally established merchants, whose services are likely to be replaced by outside chain operations, if at all. The inconvenience caused by the loss of handy, walk-in stores, as well as the intangible damage to the neighborhood identity, if such exists or persists, make it incumbent upon the community to encourage and facilitate the local relocation of at least a portion of its displaced small businesses.

However, this view is questioned by the public agency. Most urban renewal projects, from the public stance, are undertaken because the area is blighted. In many cases, the area has undergone ethnic transition which in itself has caused a radical disturbance in the retailing balance in the community. Many retailers relocate out of the area during the changing period. By the time the neighborhood has completed transition and gone through the urban renewal process, chances are that the old merchants will not be able to meet the competitive demands of the new market, much less survive the time and financial demands of relocation and redevelopment. The public agency's attitude is thus that the neighborhood benefits from merchants who understand the wants and desires of the consumers who reside in the area and organize their merchandise-mix to meet this demand. In effect, renewal disbands the neighborhood to which the displacee had formerly been oriented, to achieve broader community objectives.

The re-use plan that is put into effect therefore favors allocation of commercial sites to businesses that will meet the demands of the new residential community that is created, and thus relocation needs of displacees are of secondary consideration, if a consideration at all, in mapping re-use. The result is that only a handful, if any, of the small business displacees are able to relocate in the area from which they are displaced. Many are considered unsuitable, others cannot withstand a period out of business or even the unreimbursed costs of a temporary move. Less than 4 per cent of 1,142 displaced businesses in four cities moved back into renewal areas.[1] Commercial uses in renewal areas generally occupy a smaller percentage of land than prior to renewal. Chicago's experience up to 1964 is that 21 out of 32 projects recorded a decrease in acreage occupied by commercial and industrial uses. This amounted to a total of 322 acres before renewal and 312 acres after.[2] From 27 projects in Chicago, 2,282 businesses were dislocated and only 1.81 per cent remained in the project areas. In 12 schemes no provision was made for commercial re-use and in all but 10 of the 27 projects no businesses relocated in the renewed area; five of the projects involved clearing land for "public" use, that is institutional uses available to the public.

1 Hearings, Chicago, op. cit., p. 183.
2 Jack Meltzer et al., *Selected Aspects of Urban Renewal in Chicago; an Annotaed Statistical Summary*. Chicago: Center for Urban Studies, The University of Chicago, 1965, p. 6.

Combatting the Spread of Blight

Most projects involving small business displacement are located in older parts of central cities where dilapidated buildings and mixed land uses dominate. Residents are predominantly of low income, often belonging to some ethnic or racial minority. Slum conditions such as overcrowding, unsanitary and unsafe buildings and inadequate local public services (e.g., garbage collection, police protection, fire prevention, street cleaning and repair of public facilities) are common, and indeed are the central elements in the justification of the renewal project by the local public agency—"for the community good." Commercial blight is clearly evidenced in such areas by the number of store vacancies and low rents, by the deterioration of store fronts and business premises and by obsolete facilities.[1] However, the renewal of one district to combat blight may put pressure on other areas offering low rentals.[2] Businesses that are most likely to succeed and contribute to the local economy move to the suburbs.[3]

Costs of Renewal

To achieve the desired goal, the community is willing to incur

---

1 Berry, *Commercial Structure and Commercial Blight.* Department of Geography Research Paper No. 85, University of Chicago, 1961. Also Kinnard and Malinowski, *op. cit.* and Zimmer, *op. cit.* who report that the displacement-liquidation problem is compounded by characteristics of displaced businesses in the residential areas selected for renewal. Retail and service establishments predominate, wholesale firms are of secondary importance, while manufacturing and institutional uses account for less than ten per cent of the business establishments. Licensed drinking and eating places, liquor stores and a high proportion of food stores are typical unless proximity to downtown attracts clothing stores, professional firms and high value specialty manufacturing, eg. jewelry, engravers and printers. Tenancy rates are high. Kinnard and Zimmer cite the ratio of owner-occupiers to tenants as being 1 to 3 and both agree that there is no particular relationship between property ownership and size of business. Small businesses make up the bulk of the displacees. Few are incorporated or associated with larger firms or with chain store operations. Most firms employ less than 10 persons. There are marked variations in number of employees by type of business, however. Ubiquitous service and food-related retail establishments consistently rank low in number of employees and provide only a small annual income for their owners. Sales volume and profits from service and food-related firms are characteristically small. In Zimmer's study, seventy per cent of the businesses reported either losses, or profits below $5,000 (Zimmer, *op. cit.,* p. 9.)

These small scale business operations in blighted areas reflect the general lack of economic financial power that characterizes such districts. A significant proportion of all establishments are owner-operated. This means that the typical businessman is deeply and personally dependent on the success of his business for his own livelihood. Less than 10 per cent of the businesses are likely to be operated by managers. A large proportion of the owner-operators are elderly, and few have alternative skills or sources of income.

2 Herbert Gans, "Human Implications of the Redevelopment and Relocation," *Journal of the American Institute of Planners,* February 1959, pp. 18-20.

3 Zimmer, *op. cit.,* p. 344.

substantial costs in the belief that the long-run benefits to the community at large will provide adequate rewards. Some of the financial costs are shared by local, state and federal governments. Other costs involve loss of tax revenue during the time between demolition and reconstruction. Less obvious is the amount of land lying unused during the renewal process and the costs in terms of time and money to the local community leaders. But even counting these elements, individual costs possibly borne by displacees are not included by the Local Public Agency in its accounting, although these individual costs are the ones that obviously are central to the concern of the displacees.

Opposition

In the eyes of the public agencies, in many instances, businessmen have fought the idea of redevelopment, to their own detriment and possibly to that of the program as well. "Antagonisms built up through lack of understanding have manifested themselves in delaying tactics."[1] Many small and medium sized business establishments, especially those that are part of an ethnic community, are owned by people who are unable to accept the fact that their moving is inevitable, despite several years knowledge of the project and constant interpretation on the part of agency staff.[2]

Decline in Sales

One of the many problems facing the businessmen in an urban renewal area (displacees and those not to be dislocated alike) is a decline in sales. Neighborhood merchants suffer a rapid decline in customers and sales once residents are forced to move from the community (the exception being in Central Business District projects). In many instances shops have been left until the last to be displaced; meanwhile the value of the businesses drops substantially. A decline in sales also accompanies demolition activity in an area. Various inconveniences such as noise, traffic diversions and dust accompany this activity. And as more

---

1 Kinnard, *op. cit.* p. 72.
2 This is well illustrated by a West End displacee in Boston.—"I don't believe it; I won't believe it till it happens. I'll wait till I get my notice . . . You'll see they'll start at the lower end, and they'll never come up here." Gans, *The Urban Villagers*, p. 290.

homes and stores become vacant, vandalism increases. These problems can cause real hardship to small businesses whose owners cannot or will not move immediately.

Time Lags

Most small businesses have very limited resources with which to cover additional and unforeseen expenses or losses. Therefor delays in carrying out the dislocation-relocation process put an additional strain on the business and cause some to go out of business. Such delays include:

(a) Time lags before compensation payments are received following dislocation (payments are supposed to be prompt, but few businessmen feel they are prompt enough).

(b) Extra delays due to the multiple estimates required for each claim submitted.

(c) Lag between preliminary planning and discussion of the project and final announcement that the plan is proposed. During this time the area tends to deteriorate, possibly at a faster rate due to a "wait and see" attitude on the part of the owners of property, or to some merchants taking the initiative and vacating their premises on the assumption that by the time the acquisition process begins their property will have decreased in value, and compensation will be inadequate.[1]

(d) Time lag in acquiring real properties. This may carry on over 5 or 6 years and have an adverse effect on property values. An accelerated rate of decline in property worth in the area and the policy of appraising property value for purposes of compensation *at the time* of acquisition, means that businesses that remain the longest may suffer the most. Moreover, valuation can be made under many state laws as of the date of the original "taking" when blanket condemnation is possible at the outset of the acquisition process.

(e) Once property acquisition begins, clearance may proceed rapidly or take several years. Attendant unpredictability may have drastic consequences for those displacees who do not prepare for dislocation.

(f) The time lag between first announcement and actual acquisition

---

[1] As compensation for real property loss is based on a valuation made at the time of acquisition and not when urban renewal is first announced, many businessmen suffer a loss in business and income that is no fault of their own. This loss is measurable and characterizes almost all displaced businesses. For marginal and small businesses it is often the greatest expense incurred as it depletes capital reserves or current earnings that could be used to cover uncompensated moving expenses. Devaluation of business and property between the time of the formal announcement of redevelopment plans and actual acquisition of property was cited as the "real cause" of many of the other difficulties experienced. Kinnard, *op. cit.*, p. 66. Losses of $20,000 or $30,000 on small businesses worth $60-85,000 do not appear unusual judging from the *Chicago Hearings*.

may also have the effect of reassuring the community that nothing is ever really going to happen.[1]

(g) The period between clearance and rebuilding in the area seldom
affects small business displacees except for the few who hang on,
hoping to be able to relocate back into the area. Few small enterprises can survive the temporary relocation followed by a second
uprooting or period out of business for an uncertain length of
time. If there is to be relocation of firms within the project area
in the re-use segment, this point is especially critical, underscoring
the importance and the problems of staging of displacement and
relocation.

Interruption in Income

A period out of business constitutes a very real loss to the displacee. It is not subject to compensation[2] and causes particular
hardship at a time when extra capital is needed to start up
business again.

Tenancy

Business tenants fare worse than owners of buildings. The
latter have close contact with the public agencies and generally
receive better relocation service and compensation. It is up to
the owner of the building to arrange specific details with the
agency, which may not be in the interest of the tenant. Tenants
were until 1965 forced to remain according to the terms of their
lease if they were to be eligible for relocation assistance and
compensation. If their lease expired at or during the time of
renewal, but before the rented property was acquired, they
received no compensation.

Relocatees find that rents are on the average nearly double
those paid in the blighted area.[3] If tenants relocate their business
in the suburbs they usually move to better premises.[4] However,
most seek a location not too far from their old one and in an
area of lower property values, yet the rents are also always
higher. This is because property owners in nearby areas raise

---

1 Herbert Gans, Harriet Saperstein and Kinnard have noted this attitude in cases where
the time lag has been between 10 and 15 years.
2 Except as it may be subsumed under the Small Business Displacement Payment that is
now available. See Chapter 6.
3 Kinnard, *op cit.*, p. 67. Other sources cite increases of only 25 per cent; Zimmer,
op cit., p. 134. This, of course, depends on where the businesses relocate. The finding
is substantiated in William N. Kinnard, Jr., *Current Issues in Business Dislocation from
Public Improvement Project Areas.* University of Connecticut, 1967.
4 Zimmer notes that these relocatees generally live in the suburbs and seek a site closer
to their place of residence.

rents in response to the increased demand for space caused by the temporary flood of displacees, and because adequate alternative space is not plentiful.[1]

Those tenants who are unable to terminate their leases prior to property acquisition must often pay double rents for a period of time in order to reserve a desirable new location until property acquisition takes place. The tenant will not always be kept informed as to when this is going to happen, and in general is given less time to prepare and plan his move. Only if the leasehold interest has market value are the tenants eligible for a portion of the condemnation award. Landlords often insert a release clause in the lease, eliminating this type of claim against the award.

Marginal Business

Some small businesses are considered marginal because they are illegal, substandard or a nuisance.[2] More commonly, marginal business describes those firms who are barely making enough profit to keep in business, and for whom there is a high probability of going out of business.[3] Little distinction has been

---

1 The point can also be made that owners face the same rising prices as tenants do, and if they wish to relocate by using the proceeds of their old property, they will probably face as much of an increase as did the tenants.

2 The small business may also be marginal in its dependence on a single person. This brings particular problems when business decreases, as the small businessman must cut down on running expenses and perhaps stay open longer in the hope of catching extra business. Furthermore, owners of small businesses cannot afford the time required to search out new locations.

3 Many may in fact be sub-marginal in that they cannot survive *except* in substandard quarters with lower-than-market rentals. This means that they are below the margin or threshold of survival if even enforcement of codes and standards is undertaken without demolition and clearance. Service and food-related enterprises serving a local market area may provide a means of livelihood in a slum neighborhood, but seldom do they meet competitive standards in other than slum areas. Such businesses require little capital investment and will spring up almost overnight in those areas where vacancy rates are high and rentals low. Examples are shoe-shine parlors, confectionary stores, beauty and barber shops and pawn shops. Many function less as profit-making enterprises than they do as social gathering places. When the small scale of business in terms of sales volume, employment and profits is considered, and when it is noted that most businesses in blighted areas serve low-income minority groups, it is hardly surprising that the majority of these ephemeral establishments provide neighborhood services or retail functions which reflect a different set of values and standards from those of middle class areas. Their owners see the business environment as economically viable without necessarily recognizing the physical blight apparent to "outsiders" (Gans, p. 315; Saperstein, pp. 30-31). Few of these displaced small businessmen find sites in renewed areas. Businesses with AAA credit ratings are preferred by private redevelopers as the prime tenants of new retail centers. Renewal plans for commercial re-use favor enterprises that are clean, noiseless and cater to the tastes of middle income residents. An individual business applicant succeeds in obtaining a redeveloped site only after considerable screening and on the condition that specified standards and regulations are met. Some of the latter are to the merchant's benefit, but initially it is both a costly and time-consuming process for the applicant, so that larger organizations with fiscal strength are at a considerable advantage in competing for redeveloped sites.

made as to which businesses were marginal and/or were declining *before* urban renewal affected them and which businesses were marginal and/or declining *as a result of* the specific redevelopment project. Certainly, compensation measures and relocation assistance in the present urban renewal program do not adequately deal with this issue, nor has an assessment been made as to the value of encouraging certain kinds of marginal enterprises that depend on cheap space in inner city areas.[1]

Disadvantaged Groups

The special problems of the elderly and ethnic or racial minority groups must again be noted.[2] General welfare issues are involved, and it is not surprising that the urban renewal program has done little specifically to help these groups. The hardships for these groups are especially pronounced when they involve small one-man businesses that are the sole source of livelihood.[3] Such businessmen often see their business environment as economically viable without necessarily recognizing the physical blight apparent to outsiders. Zimmer mentions that "nearly 90 per cent of the units in the renewal areas would have remained in the original areas indefinitely." This high proportion clearly indicates that there is a rather marked indifference about the physical deterioration on the part of businessmen in these areas. It is also quite evident that the pressure for renewal would not come from the businesses in the slum neighborhoods. "On the contrary, such areas appear to be attractive business locations for certain kinds of units."[4] Often the purchasing power of the ethnic or racial minority served is considerably below that of most Americans,[5] and the businesses that serve them make

---

1 Some blighted areas act as incubators for new businesses. Relatively little is known about this process, which is now being studied by Kinnard and Messner. The issue is raised, in particular, in connection with conflicts between renewal and economic development in the ghetto.

2 For example, The Front Market area of Hartford served an Italian-American population. The West End area of Boston contained mainly Italian, Russian Jewish, Polish and Irish second generation immigrants. Herbert J. Gans, *The Urban Villagers*, New York: The Free Press, 1965, p. 3. Out of 33 Chicago urban renewal projects at least 22 projects contained predominantly minority group populations, 18 of which were "all Negro" areas. Eleven of the 33 projects (i.e. the remainder) may also have been minority group communities but this information was not available. Hearings, Chicago, *op. cit.*, pp. A116-A129.

3 William N. Kinnard, "Business Relocation Problems of the Elderly Caused by Forced Dislocation under Public Improvement Programs," *Essays on the Problems Faced in the Relocation of Elderly Persons*, Chester Rapkin ed., Philadelphia: University of Pennsylvania, 1964, p. 82.

4 Zimmer, *op. cit.*, p. 39.

5 *Ibid.*

smaller profits. For example, 45,000 Negro enterprises in blighted areas have annual profits under $3,300 (43 per cent lower than the white average).[1]

Licensing, Franchising and Zoning

Licensing, franchising, and zoning restrictions result in special difficulties for liquor stores, taverns, junkyards, currency exchanges, automobile and other dealerships, and the like. The present program does not ensure that the displaced business can obtain another license or a franchise in a new location, and that licensed or franchised businesses that do obtain them will be able to meet zoning and building standards regarded as essential to an improved neighborhood.

Locational Requirements

Most small businesses have special requirements if they are to continue to operate in the old way at new locations. Examples include proximity to particular clientele, retaining trading and delivery patterns and sources of supply, and premises suitable for the installation of old equipment and fixtures if new ones cannot be afforded. Is it the responsibility of the LPA to ensure that there is an acceptable alternative location or to offer special services enabling businessmen to adapt themselves to the new situation forced upon them? At present the program offers neither alternative.

Financial Limitations

The majority of small businesses have very limited capital reserves, are poor credit risks to private lending companies, and

---

1 U. S., Congress, Subcommittee No. 4 on Distribution Problems Affecting Small Business, *Hearings, Small Business Problems in Urban Areas.* 88th Cong. 2nd Sess., 1965, p. 48. Cited hereafter as Hearings, Baltimore. Few studies deal with the question of ethnicity as a variable affecting small business in urban renewal areas. Simmons finds that ethnicity is a factor correlating with types of businesses. James W. Simmons, *Toronto's Changing Retail Complex; A Study in Growth and Blight.* Department of Geography Research Paper No. 104, Chicago: The University of Chicago, 1966, pp. 54-55. There are smaller demands for specialized commodities at lower income levels. Growth of the Negro population in Chicago has meant declining retail markets throughout the city, according to Berry, *op. cit.* Zimmer does not give any figures on the racial or ethnic composition of the areas he studied and only refers in passing to ethnicity in relation to consumers and not to businessmen. Saperstein's comments on Elmwood's Negro merchants are also pertinent. Negro businessmen operated 50 per cent of the businesses (many of which were neighborhood convenience stores) in the Elmwood district of Detroit. These, in contrast to other minority groups (Puerto Ricans, Italians and Greeks), served relatively low income, but otherwise standard markets. Many were involved in small service businesses like beauty shops and barber shops.

cannot afford high interest rates. Most displaced businesses incurred a greater expense than the amount of reimbursement in the early phases of the program,[1] so that loans available to merchants over the dislocation and relocation period (and probably for at least 6 months following relocation) are of critical importance in the success or failure of the business. The Small Business Displacement Loan is a step toward solving this problem. An attempt has been made in several cities to get the cooperation of private lending institutions to extend low interest long-term loans, but there is no effective way to ensure that small businessmen, especially Negro merchants, will be granted loans. The onus therefore tends to fall on the Small Business Administration and its ties with the HUD.

Relocation Assistance

The extent to which relocation assistance and payments are provided for displaced businesses varies substantially from city to city, and even from project to project within the same community. Kinnard's findings indicate that most local public agencies have followed federal advice and provided at least financial aid to dislocated business establishments. Yet only 67 per cent of these establishments in the Church Street, New Haven project, 77 per cent in Santa Cruz, 52 per cent in the District of Columbia, 66 per cent in Providence, 83 per cent in Worcester and 33 per cent in Cleveland received relocation payments.

Kinnard's conclusion is that ignorance or misinformation is the basic reason that many dislocated firms do not receive payment. This is exemplified in Hartford and New Haven where the relocation offices exerted efforts far above the average found among U.S. cities. Only 10 per cent out of a sample of 195 LPAs offered services or conducted preacquisition activities of consequence. Less than 5 per cent could possibly have rendered a professional-type service in view of the personnel and organization presently employed in almost every agency involved in business relocation. Thus, many small businessmen

---

1 Although substantial changes in reimbursement procedures have now been made. See Chapter 6.

are completely unaware of the services or technical assistance available to them when they move in the context of renewal. In large projects each relocation assistant handles a greater number of relocatees than in small projects. Therefore, the chance that relocatees from large projects will be informed is reduced to half that of relocatees from small projects. A test case study indicates the critical variable to be the number of persons available at all times to perform the relocation assistance function; this has an immediate effect on the casualty rate of displaced businesses.[1]

When businesses are allowed more time to relocate, liquidations and disappearances are reduced.[2] However, the liquidation rate remains higher for larger projects because (a) a greater demand for space results when there are many firms being relocated; (b) there is less time to render relocation service on an individual, personalized basis; and (c) the supply of business enterprises seeking a location in the same community exceeds the remaining demand.

In renewal agencies where personnel perform business relocation exclusive of other duties, the business failure rate is dramatically improved over those that combine business relocation with other activities.[3]

Information

Despite public notices, letters and personal visits, renewal officials find that some business dislocatees neither know nor understand what is going to happen. Rumors prevail and adequate information is lacking; for example: How can new locations be found? What are the market conditions in various locations? What forms of assistance are available? There is a great need for improved informational procedures for the benefit of firms affected by these programs. Many small businesses are almost synonymous with the merchant's way of life. He may refuse to believe what is going to happen, and later may be totally unable to cope with the situation when it comes about.

1 Massachusetts Department of Commerce and the Bureau of the Public Affairs of Boston College. *An Effective Program for the Relocation of Business from Urban Renewal Areas.* Boston: Massachusetts Department of Commerce, 1963, pp. 10-11.
2 *Ibid.*
3 *Ibid.*

Compensation

Moving and property loss allowances have been held to be inadequate. Others complain that rules for submitting claims are too rigid for the businessman. Payments are especially inadequate where the movement of machinery, equipment and special fixtures are involved and when the owner is forced to spend a large portion of time and money adapting these to the new premises. Payments are seldom prompt. And no compensation for loss of goodwill or going-concern value is paid despite such expenses being incurred when a new premises is taken.

Coordination of Services and Agencies

Ineffective or non-existent coordination between governments and agencies account for a large number of the local discrepancies in the urban renewal program. Neither a standard definition of "blight" nor an equal treatment clause in renewal practices has been achieved, due to the intervention of particular state and local laws.

Lack of coordination between the SBA and the Urban Renewal Administration initially hindered the provision of relocation advice and guidance to displaced small businessmen. The SBA was not authorized to use the mail to insure that every small merchant about to be displaced was notified of the assistance available to him through SBA. Staff limitations meant that a significant number of the premises could not be visited. The news media and local agencies were deficient in passing on information about SBA programs to potential urban renewal displacees. This limitation, however, was corrected after 1964.[1]

Non-monetary forms of assistance and advice may be more crucial to the continued life of the displaced business than reimbursement of moving expenses. Few relocation offices of redevelopment agencies have professional real estate or business location personnel at their disposal. They are not usually equipped to advise displaced businessmen about the availability or desirability of potential locations. They cannot give unbiased

---

1 *Hearings, Baltimore*, p. 166.

advice on whether the businessman should relocate quickly or stay put until the agency acquires the building.[1]

PRINCIPAL CONCLUSIONS OF OTHER STUDIES

The companion studies of the impact of dislocation on small business therefore conclude that certain kinds of small business are more likely to benefit from urban renewal than others.[2] Zimmer found that "medium" and "large" small businesses fared better than the very small.[3] The former tended to move to the suburbs following dislocation; most of them were in the non-food-related retail, manufacturing, wholesale or construction categories. Rentals are much higher than in the inner city but average monthly sales are much greater.[4]

Businesses moving into the suburbs occupy larger and more attractive sites than businesses that relocate in the city. Parking facilities, age and condition of business premises are also better.[5] This does not mean that there were clear-cut reasons for businesses being attracted to the suburbs. One quarter of suburban relocatees in Zimmer's sample moved there because there were no alternative locations in the city.

The National Federation of Independent Business conducted a similar survey of relocation due to government construction projects. They found that despite the difficulties encountered by those who had completed their moves, and despite the difficulties anticipated by those facing the need to move: (a) a significant number of firms which had completed their moves (60 per cent) reported incomes as great or greater than that in their old locations, as against 40 per cent of those left behind; (b) only three of the 79 firms in these categories reported having to close down their operations.[6]

---

1 In one charge, which is probably somewhat unfair, the typical business relocation officer is said to be a "desk jobber" of clearance timetables and "G.I. regulations," cloaked under a veneer of concern and interest in the welfare of displaced businessmen. Massachusetts Department of Commerce, *op. cit.*, p. 19. On the other hand Kinnard and Messner report that their experience in at least 15 cities would indicate that there is not only concern but actual personal participation in the relocation process by the business relocation officer.
2 Kinnard, *op. cit.*, pp. 43-44.
3 Medium businesses are those who have a workforce of between 4 and 10 persons.
4 The rent-to-sales ratio in the suburbs declined by 20 per cent following the move, but increased by 49 per cent among the businesses that remained in the city.
5 Zimmer, *op. cit.*
6 Statement of George J. Burger, Assistant to the President, National Federation of Independent Business, to U. S. Subcommittee on Housing Senate Committee on Banking and Currency, March 1964.

But on the other hand, very high rates of liquidation have been observed for:

1. Retail or service establishments dependent upon a particular neighborhood clientele dispersed as a result of urban renewal, especially in the case of neighborhoods with dominant ethnic or racial groups.
2. Marginal businesses which may or may not have been profitable.
3. Businesses whose owners retired, usually because of their age or lack of commercial enthusiasm.
4. Businesss for which no technical or specialized skills or knowledge were required.
5. Businesses with special licensing or franchise problems, such as liquor stores or automobile dealers.
6. Illegal businesses. No information is available about these, despite their significance during the pre-clearance stage and following the initial urban renewal announcements.

Relocation has far less serious implications for businesses serving wide markets than it does for local neighborhood stores. For example, in the Elmwood area of Detroit only 57 per cent of the local businesses survived, but almost all of the non-locally oriented establishments relocated.[1] In Providence the types of units least likely to survive displacement were those that had close and frequent relationship with their customers, serving neighborhoods in which a particular ethnic or racial group was dominant.[2]

Further, since race of owner is usually correlated with a variety of other variables such as level of education, skills, capital resources, general business know-how, site preference, type of business, income, profit and attitude toward business as a profit-making enterprise or as a way of life, and since Negroes make up the largest percentage of persons in the low-income levels, Negro-owned businesses in Negro communities undergoing urban renewal generally have high liquidation rates.[3]

---

1 Saperstein, *op. cit.*
2 Zimmer, *op. cit.*
3 Saperstein records that in the Elmwood area of Detroit 57 per cent of the negro-owned businesses failed to survive urban renewal, whereas only 35 per cent of the white-owned businesses met the same fate (*op. cit.*, p. 12).

CHAPTER SIX

Evolving Legislative Provision

LEGAL BACKGROUND

The legitimacy of urban renewal as a device for assembling land for redevelopment relies upon the "eminent domain" clause of the Fifth Amendment to the U.S. Constitution:

> ". . . nor shall private property be taken for public use, without just compensation."

This clause and its analogues in the constitutions or statutes of every state are consulted by the courts in any litigation regarding acquisition of private property by a public authority. Generally speaking, two inquiries are required. First, the constitutionality of the "taking" itself is tested by deciding whether it is for a "public use," as that phrase is currently interpreted. Secondly, if the acquisition so qualifies, the court with the aid of a jury must determine "just compensation" to be paid to the owner.[1]

Both concepts, public use and just compensation, were originally applied very narrowly by courts during the era of "rugged individualism" in the Nineteenth Century. Public use meant literally that private property could only be acquired for use by the Public, as a street, park, railroad right of way, or the like.[2] Similarly, just compensation was strictly construed to mean the "fair market value" of property actually "taken," with no indemnity for "incidental losses," such as lost profits or goodwill.[3] While tangible enough to the business condemnee, such financial burdens were considered not compensable because they did

---

1 If, however, a "regulation" of land, rather than a "taking" is in issue, the owner is not entitled to compensation unless he can show that the regulation is not reasonably related to protection of public health, morals, safety or welfare.

2 Philip Nichols, Jr., "The Meaning of Public Use in the Law of Eminent Domain," *Boston University Law Review*, Vol. 20 (Nov., 1940), p. 615.

3 Most courts restrict compensation to a "voluntary sale" cash price, with no allowance for goodwill, loss of income through business interruption, damages and loss of rentals. And as of 1965, no federal guidelines for implementing the guarantee of "just compensation" on a consistent basis had been made. U.S. Advisory Commission, *op. cit.*, p. 4. One major problem is that the businessman is often a renter, and the property *owner* is the one entitled to compensation for the property demolished.

not represent "property taken" and because they were "too speculative."[1]

Since the end of World War II, the concept of public use has undergone a drastic transformation.[2] According to Haar, the process began with the late Nineteenth Century cases upholding the Mill Acts[3] which he suggests "in more than a poetic way were forerunners of the urban renewal statutes."[4]

In 1946, the Supreme Court in *United States ex rel. T.V.A. v. Welch*[5] sustained the theory that a congressional determination of public use, demonstrated by a grant of federal power, would not be reviewed by the courts. The import of this decision inspired a *Comment* in the Yale Law Journal entitled "The Public Use Limitation of Eminent Domain: An Advance Requiem."[6]

Finally, the famous case of *Berman v. Parker*[7] held that the benefit to be derived from an area-wide redevelopment scheme was a sufficient public use to justify the acquisition of a concededly non-blighted and profitable department store which happened to be located inside the project area. The Court so held despite the fact that the plan provided that upon demolition of the department store, the land would be resold to a private developer, who would be permitted to build his own store on the site. The taking being justified, all that the owner of the original store could demand was just compensation.

Unfortunately for the displaced businessman, however, while expansion of the meaning of public use has permitted increasingly massive programs of acquisition and displacement, the just compensation requirement is still interpreted much as it was

---

1 See generally, Comment, "Eminent Domain Valuations in an Age of Redevelopment: Incidental Losses," *Yale Law Journal*, Vol. 67 (1957), p. 61. On "just compensation" in federal acquisition programs generally, see Select Subcommittee on Real Property Acquisition, House Comm. on Public Works, 88th Cong., 2d Sess., "Study of Compensation and Assistance for Persons Affected by Real Property Acquisition in Federal and Federally Assisted Programs," (Comm. Print 31, 1964).

2 Eugene J. Morris, "The Quiet Legal Revolution: Eminent Domain and Urban Redevelopment," *American Bar Association Journal*, Vol. 52 (April, 1966), p. 355.

3 E.g. *Head v. Amoskeag Manufacturing Co.* 113 U.S. 9, 5 S Ct. 441, 28 L. Ed 889 (1885), which sustained a New Hampshire Act which authorized "any person or any corporation" to erect a mill and dam on non-navigable streams upon payment of damages to upland owners, as determined by a jury.

4 Charles M. Haar, *Land-Use Planning*. Boston: Little Brown and Co., 1959, p. 444.

5 327 U.S. 546 (1946).

6 *Yale Law Journal*, Vol. 58 (March, 1949), p. 599.

7 348 U.S. 26, 75 S. Ct. 98, 99 L. Ed. 27 (1954).

in 1893.[1] The displaced operator is constitutionally entitled only to the value of his interest in real property which is acquired by the public. If he owns his premises, he is entitled to receive the fair market value of the property, as determined by a jury. If he rents the acquired premises, he is theoretically entitled to the value of his leasehold, measured by the difference between the fair market value of the lease minus the rent which would be payable if the term were completed. In other words, to use a legal cliche, the lessee is entitled to the "benefit of his bargain" with his landlord.[2]

In the most frequent case, however, a small business displaced by an urban renewal program rents his place of business on a short term lease, probably three years or less. The value of such a leasehold, measured by the above formula, is minimal. And to add to his problem, the typical commercial lease contains a condemnation clause which terminates the lease upon condemnation of the premises by eminent domain and precludes the tenant from claiming any share in the award made to his landlord on the total value of the property.[3]

Finally, in the typical case of displacement the courts adhere to the traditional rule on incidental or consequential injury to the condemnee:

> "Where the sovereign takes the "fee," "compensation" does not include future loss of profits, expenses of moving removable fixtures and personalty from the premises, loss of goodwill, or other like consequential losses..."[4]

The result is that the small businessman, whose damage may largely consist of such losses, can be displaced from his place

---

1 The origin of the restrictive meaning of "just compensation" is ascribed to *Monogehela Navigation Co. v. U.S.*, 148 U.S. 312 (1893). Of this doctrine, the *Yale Law Journal* Comment, supra, note 1, p. 60, says: "*Monongehela* remains an outdated common-law concept of property developed in the absence of conditions revealing its harshness." Henry H. Krevor, "A Congressional Study of Just Compensation," *Manual of the American Society of Appraisers*, 1963. Hon. John Kyl, "Government Land Acquisition—Equity or Compensation for Small Businesses," *Congressional Record*, Feb. 17, 1964, 88th Congress, Second Session.

2 Lewis Orgel, *Valuation Under the Law of Eminent Domain*. Charlottesville: The Michie Co., 1953 (2nd edition), §124.

3 Philip Nichols, *The Law of Eminent Domain*. Albany: Matthew Bender and Co., Inc., 1963 (Rev. 3rd Ed.), §5.23 [2].

4 *United States v. General Motors Corp.* 323 U.S. 373, 65 S. Ct. 357, 89 L. Ed. 311, 156 A.L.R. 390 (1945). Also seen generally, 27 *American Jurisprudence* 2d §§ Sp 287, 353, 434 (1967).

of business empty handed. It is to this problem that increasing public and congressional attention has been directed, since one conclusion drawn by many authorities is that this very fact is responsible for the high liquidation rates among displacees.

Early Congressional View: "Predominantly Residential"

Satisfactory relocation of individuals and families displaced by urban renewal has been established as a requirement of the program since the inception of federal urban renewal legislation. In fact, the success of relocation activities has been recognized as a substantial constraint upon the progress of the program itself:

> ". . . If the relocation phase is not managed successfully, urban renewal can do enough damage to families and businesses to create a wave of reaction that might be sufficient to stop the momentum of the urban renewal process itself."[1]

The Housing Act of 1949 required as one condition precedent to approval of a local plan by the Housing and Home Finance Agency (now HUD—the Department of Housing and Urban Development) "a feasible method for the temporary relocation of families displaced from the project area."[2] This requirement was expanded in 1964 to include "individuals"[3] in addition to "families," thereby covering all non-commercial displacees.

The protection provided in 1949 was further strengthened as of August 10, 1965, by addition of the following clause:

> ". . . the Administrator [of HUD] shall require, within a reasonable time prior to actual displacement, satisfactory assurance by the local public agency that decent, safe, and sanitary dwellings . . . *are available* for the relocation of each individual or family."[4] [Emphasis added]

Previous legislation had only required that "there are, or are being provided . . . [relocation facilities"][5] which contrasts with

---

1 Martin Millspaugh, "Problems and Opportunities of Relocations," *Law and Contemporary Problems*, Vol. 26 (Winter, 1961), p. 6.
2 § 105(c), 63 Stat. 417, 42 U.S.C. 1455(c) (1949).
3 Housing Act of 1964 § 305(a)1, 78 Stat. 786 (1964); 42 U.S.C. § 1455(c).
4 Housing Act of 1965 § 305(a), 79 Stat. 475, 42 U.S.C.A. § 1455(c).
5 Housing Act of 1949 § 105(c), 63 Stat. 417, 42 U.S.C. 1455(c).

the positive phrase "are available" of the latest formulation. This stringent requirement, creating virtually a legal right in families and individuals to be relocated, significantly *does not extend to businesses*. The variety of statutory payments and services made available to businessmen by recent legislation[1] reveals that Congress has not failed to consider the plight of the commercial displacees, by compensating businesses for expenses other than those associated with profit. But the omission of "businesses" from the mandatory relocation requirement, despite the deliberate addition of "individuals," clearly indicates a legislative purpose that the relocation of commercial enterprises and the implication of guaranteed profitability shall *not* be treated as a *sine qua non* of urban renewal programs.

The lack of positive relocation protection for displaced businesses undoubtedly stems from the original Congressional intent to avoid the necessity for relocating businesses by limiting redevelopment to "predominantly residential" areas. As embodied in the first Housing Act, the "predominantly residential" requirement[2] represented a compromise between the proponents of city-wide redevelopment and the viewpoint of Senator Robert Taft, endorsing redevelopment only of housing.[3]

But dislocation of businesses, in contrast to residences, involves peculiar economic and constitutional side-effects. Dislocation-relocation is at worst an inconvenience many times for families. For businesses, on the other hand, it necessarily tampers with the "natural" laws of economic survival of presenting "artificial" difficulties and opportunities that may be critical to survival. Indeed it may destroy the livelihood of persons affected. Furthermore, issues of "equal protection" may arise, where the public authority is left in the position of selecting among competing businesses located within and without an urban renewal project area. And a "successful" relocation re-

---

1 These are discussed in chapter 6.
2 " 'Project' may include (1) acquisition of (i) a slum area or a deteriorated or deteriorating area which is predominantly residential in character . . ." Housing Act of 1949 § 110 (c), 63 Stat. 420 (1949), as amended 42 U.S.C. 1460 (c), (Supp. II, 1959-60).
3 Henry Strand, "Urban Renewal of Business Property—The Predominantly Residential Requirement," *Dicta*, Vol. 39 (Sept.-Oct., 1962), p. 308.

quirement might carry with it the implication of guaranteeing future operations at the same profit level as in the past.

Despite the obvious difficulties afflicting commercial displacement, the philosophy reflected by the "predominantly residential" clause has not prevailed. From its inception the broadest possible meaning was ascribed to the qualifier "predominantly" by HUD. Liberal interpretation resulted in an annual average of 3700 business displacements during the first decade of the program.[1]

The requirement itself has been steadily eroded by Congressional enactments. The first change came in a 1954 Amendment to the Housing Act which provided that the Housing Administrator could devote up to 10 per cent of available federal urban renewal funds to projects having a non-residential purpose, if the area "is substantially occupied by slums."[2] This discretionary quota was increased in 1959 to 20 per cent, and the slum restriction removed.[3] It was further raised in 1961 to 30 per cent[4] and in 1965 to its present level of 35 per cent.[5]

Ambiguity concerning the applicability of the quota to projects having no residential aspect whatsoever has been raised at least once in a legal attack upon a project involving a central business district. The Court of Appeals for the Sixth Circuit in *Blachman v. Erieview Corp.*[6] held the disputed phraseology to mean that the discretionary quota could be used to redevelop a "predominantly nonresidential" area for a "predominantly nonresidential" purpose.

Obviously scant vitality remains in the "predominantly residential" requirement. Occupants of business districts are no less likely now to be displaced than their counterparts in "predominantly residential" areas. Indeed, as *Berman v. Parker* demonstrates, even a thriving department store may be condemned if such is deemed to be necessary to an area-wide redevelopment scheme.

1 Note: "Citizen Participation in Urban Renewal," *Columbia Law Review*, Vol. 66 (March, 1966), p. 485.
2 68 Stat. 626 (1954), 42 U.S.C. § 1460 (1958), as amended, 42 U.S.C. § 1460 (b)-(e), (g), and (k) (Supp. II, 1959-60).
3 73 Stat. 675 (1959), 42 U.S.C. § 1460 (Supp. II, 1959-60).
4 75 Stat. 149, 168 (1961), 42 U.S.C. § 1460.
5 79 Stat. 477, 42 U.S.C.A. § 1460 (Supp. 1965).
6 311 F. 2d 85 (6th Cir. 1962).

NEW BENEFITS FOR DISPLACED BUSINESSES: RELOCATION ASSISTANCE BY HUD

Congressional efforts to make adequate provisions for commercial displacees, given the changing character of renewal plans, originated in the Housing Act of 1956, which attempted to correct many of the inadequacies and inequities reported in Chapter 5.[1] Congress therein authorized reimbursement of moving expenses and/or direct property losses up to a maximum of $2,000. That amount was increased in successive years (Table 6.1). Additional benefits and services were introduced by Congress in 1964 and 1965. These included reimbursement for "miscellaneous other expenses" and a direct displacement payment to small businesses meeting certain criteria. Other benefits authorized in recent legislation include Small Business Administration "Disaster Loans" (in 1966, significantly, the title was changed to *Displacement* Loans), lease suretyship, and counselling services to acquaint businessmen with the foregoing and assist them in finding a new location.

The predominant characteristic of all federal relocation efforts is the contract relationship between the federal government and a local public agency (LPA). The latter may be either an existing political entity, such as a city or county, or it may be an "ad hoc" body empowered by state law to enter into contract with the federal government. The LPA is charged with direct administration of its project. Formal approval of a local plan by the LPA is prerequisite to application for federal assistance from the Department of Housing and Urban Development (HUD). Approval by HUD is evidenced by the signing of a "Loan and Grant" contract, in which the Government undertakes to pay either ⅔ or ¾ of the cost of the project.[2]

One of the many respects in which the local plan must conform to national standards is in its provisions for relocation of

---

1 70 Stat. 1101, 42 U.S.C. 1465 (b) (1956). See also Henry H. Krevor, "A Congressional Study of Just Compensation, *"Manual of the American Society of Appraisers,* 1963.

2 The federal share of local urban renewal projects is normally *two-thirds* of the "net project cost," as determined by statutory formula, unless the LPA contracts to absorb all administrative expenses, in which case the federal share is *three-quarters.* Housing Act of 1949, § 103 (a) (2), 63 Stat. 416, as amended, 42 U.S.C.A. § 1453 (a) (2) (Supp. 1965).

displacees. Proper notification and opportunity to attend a public hearing must have been provided to all site occupants.[1] Full information on available payments and services, including counselling, must have been supplied to each occupant prior to the date of LPA approval of the plan.[2] Unlike other costs of the urban renewal plan, relocation payments are paid in their entirety with federal funds through the "Loan and Grant Contract":

". . . The primary reason for the one-hundred per cent federal grant was the concern that many LPA's would be unable to expend money for relocation payments because of various state constitutional prohibitions against gifts to privàte persons, or the more general public purpose limitation on public spending."[3]

This policy incidentally removes any constraint which the LPA might experience in processing claims if a share of each payment were to come from its own budget.

LPA determinations on individual claims are usually final but must be consistent with regulations issued by HUD.[4] National uniformity is thereby intended, although there remain significant differences locally in the administration of the relocation program, and local and regional interpretations and treatment vary.

Moving Expenses and Loss of Property

Subject to numerous qualifications, a business occupant displaced from an urban renewal area since 1956 may claim reimbursement for his "reasonable and necessary moving expenses" and/or his "actual direct loss of property."[5] (Tables 6.1 and 6.2.)

Eligibility for these payments, generally speaking, requires actual occupancy of a site in the urban renewal project area at the time of execution of the "Contract for Loan and Grant," or at the time of public acquisition of the property occupied.

1 Housing Act of 1949 §105 (d), 63 Stat. 417, 42 U.S.C. §1455 (d).
2 See HUD, Local Public Agency Letter No. 322, Jan. 13, 1965.
3 David E. Pinsky, "Relocation Payments in Urban Renewal: More Just Compensation," *New York Law Forum,* Vol. 11 (Spring, 1965), pp. 80, 84.
4 25 Fed. Reg. 9874 (1960), as amended.
5 Housing Act of 1956 §305, 70 Stat. 1101, 42 U.S.C. 1465 (b). The responsibility for filing a claim for reimbursement rests with the businessman.

TABLE 6.1

CHRONOLOGICAL DEVELOPMENT OF COMPENSATION

Major Housing Acts	Percent of U.R. Budget Authorized for Non-Residential Projects	Moving Expenses (M) and/or Property Losses (P)	Small Business Displacement Payment	SBA Loans	Counselling
1949	—				
1954	10 Per cent				
1956		$2,000 (M + P)			
1957		$2,500 (M + P)			
1959	20 Per cent	$3,000 (M + P)			
1961	30 Per cent	No Limit (M only) $3,000 (M + P)		20 year term disaster	
1962		$25,000 (M only) $3,000 (M + P)			
1964			$1,500	New Construction	LPA must establish program
1965	35 Per cent	$25,000 (M only)* $3,000 (M + P)	$2,500	30 year term	Must supply Real Estate Information

*See Table 6.2 for 1965 provision

TABLE 6.2

MAXIMUM PAYMENTS PERMITTED

Moving Expenses (M) and Direct Losses of Property (P)

For Moves Completed Between:	Maximum Reimbursement Is:
Aug. 7, 1956-July 12, 1957	$2.000 M + P
July 13, 1957-Sept. 22, 1959	$2,500 M + P
Sept. 23, 1959-June 29, 1961	$3,000 M + P
June 30, 1961-Oct. 1, 1962	No Limit on Moving Expenses*
Oct. 2, 1962-Aug. 11, 1965	$25,000*
Aug. 12, 1965-	$25,000* (plus ⅔ or ¾ of excess **if** LPA pays remaining fraction)

Small Business Displacement Payment

Jan. 27, 1964-Aug. 9, 1965	$1,500
Aug. 10, 1965-	$2,500

*If claim for "direct loss of property" is also filed, the maximum payment is limited to $3,000.

Occupants at the time of an Early Land Acquisition Loan from HUD also are eligible, as are those under certain other infrequent situations. Occupants who leave prior to these points in time are disqualified from reimbursement even if urban renewal is the motivation for the move.

Originally only one payment was authorized to be made for each premise. It would go to the site occupant on the date of the Loan and Grant Contract. However, the 1965 Regulations amended this policy by permitting a claim for moving expenses to one who moves into the site *after* the date of the Contract and remains through the date of acquisition of the premises by the LPA, which may be considerably later. In this situation, two payments may be made pertaining to the same premises if the preceding occupant was present on the date of the Contract.[1]

---

1 Authorization was provided in 1959 to acquire and clear slum land *prior* to the signing of a "Loan and Grant Contract," provided (1) local law permits such early acquisition and clearance, (2) land acquired under this procedure shall not be disposed of until the urban renewal plan is approved by the local community, or the community has consented to the disposal, and (c) the loan made to finance acquisition and clearance is secured in a manner satisfactory to the Administrator. Housing Act of 1959 § 404, 73 Stat. 671, as amended, 42 U.S.C. 1452 (a) (1964).

In 1965 eligibility was extended to code enforcement or re-habilitation projects, such that either direct dislocation by the project, or relocation caused by a 25 per cent increase in rent, would render a business eligible for relocation payments.[1]

In all cases, relocation must appear to the LPA to be perma-nent. Also the occupant must provide the LPA with written notice of his plans "at least 30 but not more than 90 days prior to the moving date."[2] And when amounts above $500 are to be claimed as moving expenses, the applicant must also submit three bids from "reputable" moving firms, the lowest of which will determine his payment.[3]

As defined by HUD regulations, "moving expenses" means:

". . . Costs of dismantling, crating, storing (for a period of one year or less), transporting (less than 100 miles), insuring, reassembling, reconnecting, and reinstalling of property (including goods or other inventory kept for sale), exclusive of the cost of any additions, im-provements, alterations, or other physical changes in or to any struc-ture in connection with effecting such reassembly, reconnection, or reinstallation."[4]

"Actual direct loss of property" means:

". . . Actual loss in the value of the property (exclusive of goods or other inventory kept for sale) sustained by the site occupant by reason of the disposition or abandonment of the property resulting from the site occupant's displacement. A loss resulting from damage to the property while being moved is not included."[5]

In other words, the two categories are approximately com-plementary. The first covers the costs of moving property; the second represents the cost of leaving personal property behind, either by abandoning it or by selling it at a loss.[6] It is clearly

---

1 See HUD Local Public Agency Letter No. 320, Jan. 13, 1965. Regulations published in the *Federal Register* as of October 23, 1959 predicated eligibility for relocation pay-ments upon the business having been a site occupant *both* on the date of execution of the project contract (or approval by HUD of the Project Expenditures Budget) and at the time the real property occupied was acquired or slated for acquisition by the LPA. In the *Federal Register* for June 27, 1961, the latter requirement was removed, although a second occupant could only obtain relocation payments if the former occupant disclaimed them. Finally, in the *Federal Register* of January 13, 1965, provisions were liberalized to permit two payments.

2 HUD Reg. 24 C.F.R. (Subtitle A) §3.103(d) (1965).

3 HUD Reg.. 24 C.F.R. (Subtitle A) §3.106 (1965).

4 HUD Reg. 24 C.F.R. (Subtitle A) §3.101(m)(2) (1965).

5 HUD Reg. 24 C.F.R. (Subtitle A) §3.101(a) (1965).

6 "Direct loss of property" however is considered not to include the value of property *stolen* from the acquired premises. The displacee is therefore not protected against the very real threat of vandalism which attacks most buildings scheduled for demolition, under conditions when adequate insurance is hardest to obtain.

appropriate therefore, to place a ceiling on the two claims combined.

For the ten years of its existence, however, the wording of the provision has been inscrutable. A statutory limit of $3000 is imposed upon combined claims of moving expenses and direct property losses.[1] But if the actual moving expenses exceed $3000 in themselves, the total payment that may be made or recognized shall be:

"1) The total actual moving expenses or $25,000, whichever is less," [plus a fraction of moving expenses in excess of . . . $25,000 as shown in Table 3.][2]

This means that if moving expenses exceed $3000, the total payment shall be measured only by such moving expenses; the claim for direct losses cannot then be asserted. It has been suggested that this regulation is "unnecessarily stringent."[3] Indeed it is quite illogical since high moving expenses do not necessarily signify an absence of losses on property left behind.

Even greater difficulty to the displaced businessman is presented by the requirement that moving expenses be "actual and certified."[4] Designed to prevent inflated claims, this provision allows only limited payment for expenses if, instead of transporting his old equipment to the new premises, the applicant purchases new fixtures or machinery:

"He is forced to elect between moving his equipment and obtaining reimbursement for moving expenses up to $25,000 or disposing of it and asserting a direct property loss claim limited to $3000."[5]

The unique opportunity to modernize afforded by relocation is therefore discouraged by the wording of the statute. A possible solution might be to pay in any event the "imputed cost of moving," determined by the lowest of three bids submitted

1 73 Stat. 675 (1959), 42 U.S.C. 1465(b), as amended (Supp. 1965).
2 HUD Reg. 24 C.F.R. (Subtitle A) § 3.109(a)(2) (1965).
3 David E. Pinsky, "Relocation Payments in Urban Renewal," op. cit.
4 70 Stat. 1101 (1956), 342 U.S.C. 1465 (6)(1), as amended (Supp. 1965).
5 Pinsky, op. cit. Actually, Pinsky was not completely correct. A displaced business may desire to modernize at the time of the move by purchasing substitute equipment. By substitute equipment is meant new equipment which replaces old equipment similar in type, purpose and function and which does not represent additional equipment. The costs of installation of the substitute (new) equipment may not exceed what it would have cost to reinstall the old equipment. Naturally, no property loss payment may be made for the discarded old equipment, nor may any payment be made for the costs of cartage of the old equipment.

according to the procedure followed when the move is actually to be made. To prevent "unjust enrichment," the LPA might take title to the old equipment or reduce the "imputed" payment by the amount of profit, if any, realized by the displacee. Another solution, however, might be an outright payment to all displacees, regardless of whether or not they move their property. Such a payment would be determined according to some legislative formula based on the size and nature of the business. The first example of an outright payment in federal urban renewal law is the Small Business Displacement Payment.

Small Business Displacement Payment

The Housing Act of 1964[1] implemented various measures requested by President Johnson in his message to Congress on housing, January 27, 1964. Among these was a direct payment to small independent businessmen displaced by urban renewal, unconnected with actual out-of-pocket expenses of any kind. The original amount of the payment was $1500.[2] For moves completed after August 10, 1965, this amount was raised to $2500.[3]

Eligibility for the Small Business Displacement Payment under the original 1964 legislation required the following:[4]

1. The concern was doing business in the urban renewal area on the date the local governing body approved the urban renewal plan or the acquisition under an Early Land Acquisition Loan of property occupied by the concern.
2. The concern completed its move from the urban renewal area on or after January 27, 1964.
3. The concern is not part of an enterprise having establishments outside the urban renewal area.
4. The concern had average gross receipts or sales exceeding $1500.
5. The concern has filed an income tax return with the Internal Revenue Service for 2 years preceding displacement, or if not in business that long, for 1 year preceding displacement.
6, 7, and 8 [Detailed provisions requiring the concern to have had an average annual net income before taxes, including wages and salaries, of less than $10,000.]

1 78 Stat. 769, 42 U.S.C. 1441, *et. seq.*
2 § 114(b)(2), 78 Stat. 788, 42 U.S.C. 1465(b)(2) (1964).
3 79 Stat. 480, 42 U.S.C.A. 1465(b)(2) (Supp. 1965).
4 HUD Local Public Agency Letter No. 321, p. 16, Jan. 13, 1965.

Provision One of the foregoing has been changed by recent regulations. The concern must not only show that it was "doing business" on the date of LPA approval of the plan, but must additionally have been an "occupant" of the site on the date of the execution of the Loan-Grant Contract between the LPA and HUD.[1]

Provision Three now reads: "The concern is not part of an enterprise having *two or more* establishments outside the urban renewal area."[2] (Emphasis added)

The date of displacement in the case of a "continuous move" is administratively considered to be the date the move is completed.[3] Careful LPA determinations are required on this matter to rule out unnecessarily prolonged moves from eligibility for the $2500 grant effective after August 10, 1965.

However, an important aspect of the payment is that relocation is not required. Payment is contingent upon displacement, not relocation in a new place of business. Elderly persons may therefore retire upon displacement without forfeiting their claim to this payment.

The requirement that a business concern furnish the LPA with written notice of intention to move or dispose of property in order to qualify for a relocation payment covering moving expenses or direct loss of property has been expanded to apply to the Small Business Displacement Payment.[4]

However, the purpose of the Small Business Displacement Payment is in part defeated by a HUD policy requiring that it "shall not be made until the business has been displaced."[5] Requiring actual vacating of the premises before payment can be made thus prevents the $2500 from reaching the businessman when he most needs it, at the time he is seeking a lease on a new premises. Securing of a lease requires the lessee to pay at least a month's rent in advance, plus an amount to be held as security which may be an additional two months rent. The merchant for whom the SBDP is designed is in no position to

1 HUD Local Public Agency Letter No. 363, Feb. 10, 1966.
2 *Ibid.*
3 HUD Local Public Agency Letter No. 362, p. 9, Feb. 10, 1966.
4 *Ibid.*
5 HUD, LPA Letter No. 321, Jan. 13, 1965, p. 20.

pay three months rent, especially at a time when trade is falling, and other expenses of moving must be paid.

Although a "letter of eligibility" for the $2500 may be issued by the LPA prior to the occupant's vacating, such a letter is not regarded by banks to be valid collateral: it appears to be a "hedge" by the LPA against a change of plans and not an irrevocable commitment. Besides Congress did not intend for the payment to be reduced by amounts paid in bank interest.

Clearly, the intention of Congress requires that the $2500 payment be made as soon as it becomes ascertainable that the occupant *will be* displaced. Assuming that his financial eligibility for the payment is otherwise established, the obligation to make the payment becomes fixed at the earliest time at which the occupant may move in reliance on the LPA's promise of assistance, namely at the time the premises is acquired.

"Rootedness"

The rationale underlying the Small Business Displacement Payment was explained by the House Committee on Banking and Currency as follows:

". . . This payment would be available only to small businesses because they are far less able than large businesses to adjust to a new environment and compete with established or more modern enterprises. Often there is a period of time required for them to reestablish operations, and often the cost of doing business is substantially higher in the new location. For some time after their displacement, small businesses suffer a loss in volume of sales while their operating expenses are greater than they were in the location in the urban renewal area."[1]

The Internal Revenue Service requires the Small Business Displacement Payment to be included in the recipient's gross taxable income because it "is considered to be in the nature of lost profits."[2] This characterization, if justified, contributes great importance to the payment. Heretofore, compensation for lost profits has never been authorized in government condemnation programs. In fact, as mentioned earlier, urban renewal law explicitly denies reimbursement for losses of "goodwill or

1 1964 *U.S. Code Congressional and Administrative News*, p. 3431.
2 HUD Local Public Agency Letter No. 350, Sept. 27, 1965.

profits," at least under the provision entitled "Relocation Payment."[1]

Even if the Small Business Displacement Payment is not considered as compensation for lost profits *per se,* the Committee Report cited above reveals that the payment is an attempt to offset damage to the intangible and unmeasurable interest which David E. Pinsky calls "rootedness,"[2] otherwise termed goodwill or going concern value. Traditionally this interest could be ignored by public authorities in accordance with the usual interpretation of the constitutional requirement of "just compensation":

> ". . . The market value of just compensation firmly denies that the occupant has any legally protected right qua occupant . . . in 'rootedness.' "[3]

But according to the same writer:

> The relocation payments program of urban renewal has played a pioneering role in the development . . . of a limited protection [for] 'rootedness'."[4]

The State of Pennsylvania has carried such experimentation a step further in its new Eminent Domain Code of 1964.[5] Applicable to all "takings" under the state power of eminent domain (including urban renewal), the new law authorizes payments to displaced businesses "where it is shown that the business cannot be relocated without substantial loss of patronage.[6] The payment is to be determined by a rough formula:

> ". . . Compensation for such dislocation shall be the actual monthly rental paid for the business premises, or if there is no lease the value of the business premises, multiplied by the number of months remaining in the lease . . . not to exceed 24 months . . . The payment shall not exceed $5000 and shall not be less than $250. A tenant shall be entitled to recover for such business dislocation even though not entitled to any of the proceeds of the condemnation."[7]

---

1 HUD Reg. 24 C.F.R. Subtitle A) §3.101(p)(2) (1965).
2 David E. Pinsky, "Relocation Payments in Urban Renewal," *op. cit.*
3 *Ibid.*
4 *Ibid.*
5 Purdon's *Pennsylvania Statutes Annotated,* Title 26 §§1-601-614 (1964).
6 *Idem,* §1-609.
7 *Ibid.*

This section provides a workable method for compensating the intangible losses to displaced businesses. Hopefully it may stimulate further development in both the federal law and the laws of the other states.[1]

A different problem, not yet remedied in any jurisdiction, is the injury caused by urban renewal to businesses not physically displaced. "Rootedness," of course, may be as severely damaged by removal of the neighborhood from the business as by the reverse. Yet under the current law, a business physically located outside the project area, say across the street, may not claim any remuneration for loss of customers.

In one situation, however, payment has been authorized to a business located outside the urban renewal area. According to a 1964 provision, the expense of removing an "outdoor advertising display" will be repaid to its owner, wherever his business may be located.[2] While the display may be regarded as a physical extension of the business into the project area, nevertheless this represents the first departure from strict observance of the boundaries of the project as the geographical locus of persons entitled to compensation. The next step might logically be the recognition of *intangible* effects upon businesses located physically outside the project area.

Miscellaneous Expenses of Property Transfer

Although accruing to owners rather than business tenants, mention should be made of another example of the tendency of recent urban renewal legislation to expand the customary boundaries of "just compensation." 1965 legislation authorized reimbursement of real property owners (business and residential) for the incidental costs of transferring title to the LPA.[3] These include documentary stamps, transfer taxes, recording expenses, penalty charges for prepayment of mortgages, and a pro rata share of property taxes payable after transfer.

---

1 However, evidence from HUD Region II relocation personnel indicates that this compensation is extremely difficult to qualify for, so operational effectiveness remains to be demonstrated.
2 78 Stat. 770, 42 U.S.C.A. 1465(b)(1) (1964).
3 Housing and Urban Development Act of 1965 §404(d), 79 Stat. 486, 42 U.S.C.A. 1465(d).

SMALL BUSINESS ADMINISTRATION ASSISTANCE

The Small Business Administration (SBA) has been directed to supplement the local public agencies in rendering assistance to displaced small businesses.[1] Upon approval of a Loan and Grant Contract, the LPA is required to furnish the local SBA office with the name, address, and type of business of all firms to be affected by the project. SBA will then send each firm a letter describing the assistance available.[2]

In addition to its regular loan programs, SBA may assist urban renewal displacees through displacement loans, lease guarantees, and general counseling services.

Displaced Business Loans[3]

A 1961 amendment to the Small Business Act empowered SBA to make loans to "small business concerns" which are deemed to have suffered "substantial economic injury as a result of displacement by a federally aided urban renewal or highway construction program or by any other construction conducted by or with funds provided by the Federal Government."[4]

A "small business concern" is defined as one which is "independently owned and operated and which is not dominant in its field of operation."[5]

The maximum term of loans allowed by the 1961 statute was 20 years;[6] this was increased to 30 years by a 1965 amendment.[7]

---

1 75 Stat. 149, 15 U.S.C. 631 (1961).
2 HUD Local Public Agency Letter No. 322, Jan. 13, 1965.
3 At the time of writing (April, 1968), SBA has indicated that it plans to curtail its 4¼% loan program and direct applicants towards private sources at market interest rates (as high as 8%), or to continue DBIs with commercial bank participation and minimize SBA 100% direct loans. The effectiveness of SBA assistance has long been hampered by extreme delays in processing applications and by the stringency of its requirements. According to an SBA letter (March 27, 1968) to the Chicago Department of Urban Renewal, the applicant must show:
  "First, . . . that the business suffered an economic injury by being displaced; secondly, . . . that the condemnation awards and their own resources of the business entity have been used, and the principal owners thereof have used their own resources to the maximum feasible extent; and third, . . . that private financing is not available on normal acceptable terms."
  Thus a business must be virtually "wiped out" before SBA will consider extending assistance. Moreover, the recipient of an SBA loan must commit his assets as collateral and thus has nothing to pledge to obtain any additional loans from private sources.
4 75 Stat. 167, 15 U.S.C. 636 (1961).
5 75 Stat. 149, U.S.C. 631 (1961). However, through June 30, 1967 only 914 Displaced Business Loans had been approved by SBA to business concerns displaced by urban renewal anywhere in the U.S. During the 4½ years ended June 30, 1966, less than 2 per cent of the businesses displaced were granted DBLs.
6 75 Stat. 155, 15 U.S.C. 636 (7)(b)(3) (1961).
7 79 Stat. 482, 15 U.S.C.A. 7(b)(3) (Supp. 1965).

Interest as determined by a statutory formula is below market rates, except where a private institution participates in extending the loan.[1]

The amount of a loan is determined by SBA's estimate of "the applicant's need for working capital during the period of readjustment, replacement costs of realty, and purchase of machinery and equipment for upgrading the business in the new location."[2] However, there is a 25 per cent expansion limitation to qualify for the loan.

Application of the loan to the purchase or construction of a new premises, even when the displacee did not previously own his own place of business, was authorized in a 1964 amendment.[3]

Lease Guarantees

The policy of helping displacees to modernize in the process of relocating is further implemented by a 1965 provision authorizing SBA to guarantee rental payments of small business concerns who are otherwise eligible for "disaster loans," or for loans under the Economic Opportunity Act of 1964.[4] As with SBA's other loan programs, acceptance of an application is discretionary:

> ". . . No lease insurance could be granted by SBA unless it found that the small concern was financially sound and efficiently managed and that there was a reasonable expectation that it would be able to perform its obligations under the lease."[5]

The applicant must be able to pay twenty-five per cent of his annual rental to be held in escrow by SBA and must pay an administrative fee averaging about one per cent of the annual rental.[6]

The function of this device was described as follows:

> ". . . The Committee believes that such lease guarantees will be a

---

1 *Ibid.*
2 Small Business Administration Notice "SBA Loans for Displaced Business Concerns under Section 7(b) of the Small Business Act," July, 1961. One problem emerging is that businesses with their collateral tied up in DBL's have found it extremely difficult to obtain supplementary loans on the conventional market.
3 75 Stat. 167, 15 U.S.C. 636(7)(b)(3) (1964).
4 79 Stat. 482, 15 U.S.C. 661 (Supp. 1965).
5 1965 *U.S. Code Congressional and Administrative News*, p 2643.
6 *Ibid.*

significant aid to small concerns displaced by urban renewal to enable them to reestablish their business operations in desirable locations. At present, such concerns are often forced to relocate their operations in unsatisfactory premises due to their inability to obtain leases of modern or well-situated property."[1]

More recently, the lease-guarantee program and concept has been extended to non-displacees.[2]

Counselling Services

In order to overcome a lack of communication with displacees concerning relocation benefits and opportunities, Congress in 1964 required a "relocation assistance program" to be established for each urban renewal project "at the earliest possible time."[3] The program must include "measures, facilities, and services" to:[4]

1) Determine the needs of such displaced families, individuals, and business concerns for relocation assistance;
2) Provide information and assistance and otherwise minimize the hardships of displacement; and
3) Assure the necessary coordination of relocation actions with other project activities and other planned or proposed governmental actions in the community which may affect the carrying out of the relocation program.

A 1965 amendment added to item (2) above:

". . . including information as to real estate agencies, brokers, and boards in or near the urban renewal area which deal in residential or business property that might be appropriate for the relocating of displaced individuals, families, and business concerns."[5]

More recently, SBA has created a Service Corps of Retired Executives (SCORE) to further assist small businessmen in general and displacees in particular.

---

1 *Ibid.*
2 As of January 9, 1967 the lease-guarantee program became generally effective and program eligibility was extended to any small business desiring to relocate, rather than merely those displaced by urban renewal. In November, 1967, it was being applied in three pilot projects in Chicago, Miami and Mobile.
3 78 Stat. 786, 42 U.S.C. 1455(c) (1964).
4 *Ibid.*
5 79 Stat. 480, 42 U.S.C.A. 1455 (c) (Supp. 1965).

GROWTH OF CHICAGO'S COMMERCIAL
RELOCATION STAFF

To build up some capacity to meet the needs of small business displacees, responding to the framework of changing legislation, commercial relocation staffs have been established by many cities. This move is,
in part, an attempt to offset the complaints of the displacees and to
attempt to reduce the liquidation problem. The City of Chicago, for
example, has now developed a substantial organization to deal with
commercial relocation problems, and its character may serve as a guide
to what is now possible, and an index of what remains to be done. The
sequence of development was as follows:[1]

1956—"Commercial Relocation Staff established, after the Housing Act provided the first
relocation benefits for profit and non-profit establishments. Field representatives were
supposed to assist businessmen in determining possible relocation sites, maintain a file
on current commercial real estate listings and brokers dealing in commercial properties, and assist businesmen in preparing claim for relocation benefits to insure they
receive full reimbursement. Rent reductions were provided in buildings acquired by
the public agency prior to displacement if sales losses could be shown to be correlated with surrounding clearance activity.

1962—"Arrangements were made to refer to the Mayor's Commission on Economic and
Cultural Development those displacees facing difficult zoning and technical problems
in finding suitable relocation space. Also, at about the same time, an SBA liaison
staff was established and began working with businessmen to be displaced, to band
together in forming corporations and cooperatively developing new shopping centers
with SBA financing on urban renewal land so designated for re-use in the area from
which they were to be displaced. (Most notable are 53rd-Kimbark Shopping Center
in Hyde Park-Kenwood and Jeffro Shopping Plaza at Roosevelt Road and Jefferson
Avenue.) Staff assigned to this unit explain the benefits and eligibility requirements
for SBA loans and assist the businessmen in assembling necessary information for
submittal of preliminary and final applications to SBA. They arrange meetings
between the businessmen and SBA, and assist in finding ways to meet eligibility
requirements, and help secure short-term loans where necessary.

1965—"Arrangements were made with SBA to provide professional management counselling
seminars in order to provide information on current business practices which would
ease the problems of re-establishment.

1967—"Arrangements were made with the Small Business Opportunity Corporation (established under the Anti-Poverty Program and now called the Chicago Economic
Development Corporation) for referring interested small marginal businessmen for
intensive management counselling. Also, during the past two years, the Department of
Urban Renewal has become the principal agency providing relocation assistance to
all displacees caused by governmental action. The Chicago Board of Education and
the Medical Center Commission are the only agencies excepted. The agencies included
are: Chicago Housing Authority, Chicago Dwellings Association, Neighborhood
Service Program, Department of Public Works, Highway Department, and code
enforcement. To further this role, current real estate listings, for rental and sale,
are obtained from the various industrial and commercial realtors in the city. Searches
are made by field representatives for specialized needs.

"As of 1967, there are 15 persons working full-time on commercial
relocation in Chicago's Department of Urban Renewal—1 appraiser,
3 to review all commercial relocation claims, 2 SBA liaisons, and 9 field
representatives. Most of the personnel have had some business background prior to employment by the Department. Civil Service exam-
inations are given for these positions.

"This staff attempts to inform the businessman about renewal proposals in meetings in the community prior to final development of plan,

---

1 Description provided by Chicago LPA staff. See Appendix A for an outline of the
renewal process as currently undertaken in Chicago.

212 THE IMPACT OF URBAN RENEWAL ON SMALL BUSINESS

public hearings before submission of plans for approval, public announcement of plans through various news media. Likewise, the potential displacee is informed about his future as soon as possible after the approval of the plan, when a preacquisition survey is conducted at which time each displacee is interviewed and is given information regarding procedures, services and benefits available.[1] The appraisals of the value of commercial property are made after acceptance of the project plan by the federal Department of Housing and Urban Development (HUD) and the acceptance of the offer by DUR and City Council. Immediately upon acquisition of the property by the city, information is given once again. A special attempt is now made to give help to non-English speaking displacees, to elderly or sick persons and to members of minority groups. For non-English speaking displacees, interpreters on the staff (Spanish, Greek, Italian, Polish) or from the community are used. For all four categories, assistance in previously-mentioned services is intensified. The Chicago Economic Development Corporation is the only service group that emphasizes assistance to minority and marginal businessmen."

---

1 The reader will note the differences between the LPA staffs' perceptions of what they do and the Hyde Park businessmen's statements about what was provided to them. Part of the difference is due to difference in time—many services were not available in the early stages of the Hyde Park-Kenwood prjects, and many of the program improvements resulted from the early experiences, as we have already noted. The commercial relocation staff now does hand each displacee a 16-page brochure entitled *Commercial Relocation Payments. A Guide for Businessmen in Preparation of their Relocation Claims.* This describes eligibility requirements, claim limits, moving expense provisions, storage costs, claims for direct property losses, and the Small Business Displacement Payment. Required forms are identified by DUR numbers.

CHAPTER SEVEN

Unresolved Problems: Lessons From The Hyde Park Experience

Much of the small business dislocation in Hyde Park-Kenwood came too late for the displacees to benefit from the new legislation and the elaborate Chicago Commercial Relocation Staff now in existence. (Table 7.1) Indeed, perhaps the most direct contribution of Hyde Park to the nation's urban renewal program stemmed from the unhappy experiences of its businessmen and led to the concept of commercial relocation payments and the gradual translation of these concepts, through actions of its Congressman and Senator, into federal law.[1] In addition, new ground was broken in the Kimbark Plaza and Harper Court experiments,[2] types of redevelopment that will undoubtedly find more extensive expression elsewhere, to complement the "conventional" work of private redevelopers.

Many of the specific problems reported by Hyde Park businessmen[3] have already been corrected, but the Hyde Park ex-

TABLE 7.1

HYDE PARK-KENWOOD RENEWAL CHRONOLOGY

Year: 1951
Compensation available to small business displacees: none
June   Hyde Park-Kenwood Community Conference Report

Years: 1952, 1953
Compensation available: none
March 19. 1952   S.E.C.C. Organized

Year: 1954
Compensation available: none
March   Field Foundation Planning Grant to U. of C.
June 30   "Hyde Park A and B" published (SECC Renewal Project No. 1)
Dec. 12   Redevelopment Plan passed by City Council.

1 See Chapters 2 and 6.
2 See Chapter 2.
3 See Chapter 4.

TABLE 7.1 (continued)

Year: 1955

Compensation available: none

Jan. 17   Redevelopment Plan passed by Illinois Housing Board
Feb. 15, 18 Federal approval of Hyde Park "A" and "B."
Dec.   Business displacement begun in Hyde Park *B*

Year: 1956

Compensation available. $2,000 Moving Expenses and Property Losses)

Jan.   Business displacement begun in Hyde Park *A*

Years: 1957, 1958

Compensation available: $2,500 (Moving Expenses and Property Losses)

Nov. 7   "Final Plan" for Hyde Park-Kenwood Urban Renewal passed by
             City Council.

Year: 1959

Compensation available: $3,000 (Moving Expenses and Property Losses)

March 18   Acquisition Plan announced; 53rd-Woodlawn site designated for
             convenience shopping center
April-July Announcement of tenants for 55th St. Center by Webb and
             Knapp
Oct.   Business displacement completed in Hyde Park A and B
Dec.   Business displacement begun in Hyde Park-Kenwood Project

Year: 1960

Compensation available: $3,000 (Moving Expenses and Property Losses)

Jan. 20   Preliminary design for Kimbark Plaza revealed

Year: 1961

Compensation available: No Limit on Moving Expenses; $3,000 (Moving
             Expenses and Property Losses); 20 year term
             SBA disaster loans.

Nov. 1   Special disposition plan for Kimbark Plaza approved by City
             Council.

Year: 1962

Compensation available: $25,000 (Moving Expenses Only); $3,000 (Moving
             Expenses and Property Losses); 20 year term
             SBA loans

June-March, 1963   Organization of Harper Court Foundation
Oct. 30   Sites conveyed to Kimbark Plaza merchants

Year: 1964

Compensation available: Same as 1963, plus $1,500 Small Business Dis-
             placement Payment; SBA New Construction
             Loans; LPA Must Establish Counselling Program.

Dec. 1   Harper Court, Bricklaying Ceremony

Year: 1965

Compensation available: Same as 1964. plus $2,500 Small Business Dis-
             placement Payment, 10 year SBA loans. Must
             supply Real Estate Information

August-Feb., 1966   Harper Court Tenants move in.

perience also furnishes a variety of insights and lessons pointing to the improvement of commercial redevelopment techniques and plans. For example, the relocation process might be smoothed through careful timing and deliberate staging of dislocation. Likewise, alternatives might be found to the "classical" planning concepts currently in vogue (separation of land uses, complete clearance of ribbons, and provision of new business opportunities only in new shopping centers). Such alternatives might reduce some of the current inequity of displacement and provide opportunity for new small business enterprise, particularly in the lower-echelon communities of the metropolitan area.

SMOOTHING THE RELOCATION PROCESS

An obvious lesson of Hyde Park "A and B" is that relocation of those concerns which intend to stay in business should be accomplished at the earliest appropriate time after execution of an urban renewal plan becomes certain, according to a definite staging plan.

Early moves were discouraged in Hyde Park-Kenwood under the original "moving expenses" regulations which required a claimant to stay in the premises until it was acquired by the renewal authority. The Hyde Park experience clearly shows that large-scale acquisition is haphazard and unpredictable, however. To require businessmen to predicate their moving plans upon such a fortuitous event is to compound the difficulty already presented by displacement. Current HUD regulations are more liberal. Relocation payments are authorized to be made to: "A site occupant of the property on the date of execution of a Federal financial assistance contract . . . which contemplates acquisition of the property, *regardless of when or if such acquisition takes place* . . . " (emphasis added).[1] But for a business that tries to "hang on" as long as possible, the ultimate date of dislocation still remains unpredictable.

Importance of Staging

One justification for discouraging early moves is that a prema-

---

1 HUD Reg. 24 C.F.R. (Subtitle A) § 3.103 (b) (1965).

ture emptying of stores leaves the neighborhood without shopping facilities before the project is actually underway. The solution to this problem is really the same as for the problem of furnishing adequate commercial space to the community once renewal is completed. In either case it is necessary to anticipate the needs of the community and of the displaced merchants for commercial space and to provide for such needs in the urban renewal plan. The original Hyde Park renewal plan provided for the interim relocation of businesses between the time of their displacement and the completion of the shopping center, in a careful sequence of staging. These provisions were, however, not implemented by the Land Clearance Commission, which sacrificed staging of commercial redevelopment to a more immediate need for rapid provision of new housing.

Of course, it probably cannot be required that a new shopping center be completed before a single business is displaced; usually, as in Hyde Park "A", businesses will have to be moved in order to clear land for the center itself. However the Hyde Park experience does indicate that where necessary, a well-established enterprise can move twice in a comparatively short time, and wipe out losses thereby incurred by expanding in the process. Such was the experience of the Hyde Park Co-op, Cohn and Stern, and Anderson's Hardware. The essential factors in such successful double moves are interim premises located very close to both the previous and the future places of business, thereby protecting that uncompensable asset, goodwill, plus a firm financial base from which to make the initial relocation.

Where interim space is available nearby, liquidation rates are evidently somewhat lower, at least in the short-run. To cite one current example, the 60th Street-Cottage Grove Avenue project in Woodlawn is currently in the process of dislocating twenty-one businesses, and present plans call for them to be replaced by a new supermarket and a small shopping center to house "indigeneous" businessmen, preferably displacees, under the management of The Woodlawn Organization (TWO). Four of the displacees have liquidated—a ladies' apparel shop, a cigar store, a donut shop and a record shop. Seventeen have relocated or at the time of writing are in process of moving. Twelve businessmen, seven of them Negro, have moved to previously vacant stores located on 63rd Street within three blocks of their previous stores. Because space was available so close, a currency exchange and tavern also were able to relocate and retain their licenses, an unusual circumstance. Nearby space was available, and most of the displacees have found satisfactory new locations and preserved their goodwill. From this interim base they are prime candidates to occupy a new shopping center planned by the local community organization with the best interests of the Woodlawn community in mind.

Staging is not without its difficulties. Chicago's Commercial Relocation Staff point out that they have tried to stage relocation in several instances. For example, in the case of Jeffro Plaza they purchased the old Central National Bank on Roosevelt Road and rented it to the merchants at a loss pending completion of their new structure. And they have cooperated many times in facilitating temporary quarters for individual businessmen both in Hyde Park and elsewhere while they were waiting for their new sites to be readied. For these businesses they point out that two moves are as problematic as just one, and the re-use plan may prevent them being left where they are.

But staging, to be accomplished properly, they argue, requires simultaneous phasing of business clearance and of residential development, and even empathy toward the particular seasonal and other requirements of the mix of business firms in existence on the renewal site. The difficulties are evident, but they are compounded by the likelihood of certain businesses in the stage one clearance area filing a suit in court and delaying the program, while property owners in areas designated for later stages of clearance beg the local agency to purchase their property early. Such delays and pressures, the Chicago staff feel, confound the entire staging notion.

Need for Cooperation

The need for cooperation between merchants facing displacement and the city officials responsible for executing the project is obvious, whether the renewal plan is staged or not. During the period of acquisition and demolition, the city becomes the major owner and operator of real estate in the area affected. Moreover the renewal officials often are vested with discretion in the timing of demolition after property has been acquired, and provision of adequate information is their responsibility. This means that instead of immediately reducing each property to a vacant lot, the old structures may be left intact until a redeveloper is actually selected and ready to begin. Subject, of course, to building code standards and city licensing restrictions, these structures can be made available to displaced businesses on a temporary basis. In this way merchants already installed in a building may be allowed to continue until new permanent quarters are ready. Likewise shop space which becomes vacant may be filled by other businesses turned out of demolished buildings who also await new construction. It will be recalled that among the three displacees who entered Harper Court, the Acasa was a beneficiary of the former arrangement, and the Fret Shop and Van Tellingen's Bookstore of the latter.

Custom-made arrangements such as those just described, or the deliberate postponement of demolition which saved the Hyde Park Co-op, are obviously the result of close communication between the renewal officials and the individual merchants. This phenomenon occurred in only a handful of cases during the earlier renewal years in Hyde Park. Correspondingly, only a handful of displacees are still in business in Hyde Park today. The lesson is that cooperation between the displacees and the urban renewal officials is not only desirable to promote harmony, but is absolutely essential when the renewal authority controls virtually all of the vacant commercial space in the community.

UNEQUAL BURDENS OF DISPLACEMENT

Another lesson to be learned from the Hyde Park experience is that displacement presents vastly different opportunities and hardships to different businesses. For the sake of analysis businesses may be differentiated from one another in two planes: (1) the comparative economic vitality of businesses *in the same line,* and (2) the comparative effects of displacement on *different lines of business.*

The first of these refers to the normal "free enterprise" inequalities of bargaining position, managerial efficiency, and general profitability which always exist amongst small business competitors. Even the most sophisticated system of compensation could scarcely be expected or even desired to counteract the effects of such inherent inequalities. Inevitably marginal businesses are more likely to disappear upon displacement than financially stronger enterprises; such is the philosophy of free enterprise. Business displacees as a class still are not vested with any legal right to be relocated. Nor is it likely that they will be; whereas families and individuals *must* have a place to live, it is quite another matter for the government to undertake to insure the profitable survival of small businesses, regardless of their status prior to renewal.

The premise underlying commercial efforts remain that the initiative in relocating must come from the businessman himself. Public assistance is designed to facilitate his move, and to minimize the impact of dislocation upon his business. But prospects for survival, as in any other crisis, must ultimately depend upon the determination and initiative of the individual businessman.

On the other hand, the economic inequalities among businesses may be reinforced when relocation opportunities in a given community are limited to shopping centers in which a one-of-a-kind philosophy prevails, so that a large-scale store in effect replaces several smaller shops providing similar goods and services to the communities. To enter a development like the New Hyde Park Shopping Center, a displacee is required to compete with outside chains for admission.[1] An all-displacee center such as Kimbark Plaza accepts only the strongest representative of each line of business that it wants. Even the Harper

---

1 The attitude of the developers is understandable. The difficulty of financing independents, and the time required to put the deals together are usually deterrents to the developer. In most cases, the land costs of urban renewal projects are relatively high. Hence, the time delays which occur through both the result of delays on the part of the developer, and those on the part of the local urban renewal authority, tend to raise the cost of the project. Attractiveness of independents may have been increased somewhat to developers by the SBA lease guarantee program, but industry representatives suggest the need for stronger incentives to encourage developers to work with local merchants.

Court model provides no refuge to the displacee unless he happens to be in some way exotic or unique.

In the absence of any private market in low rent commercial space, therefore, most small businessmen, whether marginal or otherwise, must either leave the area or leave the business or both: their weak bargaining position is acutely worsened by displacement.

The second plane in which the effects of displacement may be analyzed is amongst *different kinds of businesses*. Commercial displacement and redevelopment work unequal hardship due to impediments peculiar to different kinds of businesses which restrict their ability to relocate.

Such impediments may be classified as follows:

1) Special moving problems, such as immovable capital fixtures.
2) Administrative obstacles, such as:
   a) Liquor licenses—valid only for particular premises
   b) Franchises—valid only for particular area
3) Redevelopment zoning criteria—uses deemed incompatible with the character of the neighborhood.

The effect of each of these impediments upon a specific line of business is illustrated by the drastic reduction of automobile-related enterprises in Hyde Park-Kenwood as a result of urban renewal.

In 1956, for instance, there were four new-car agencies in the community, dealing respectively in Chevrolet, Lincoln-Mercury, Ford, and DeSoto-Plymouth. Today only Chevrolets may be bought in Hyde Park-Kenwood. The owners of Lake Park Motors (Lincoln-Mercury) were advised by letter from the Land Clearance Commission:

". . . As you know from examining the tentative redevelopment plan for both project areas Hyde Park A and B, there will not be in either area land available for the operation of a garage business or an automobile salesroom. We hope, of course, that you will not have difficulty in locating another location as satisfactory as your present one."[1]

Subsequently, however, Hyde Park Chevrolet was permitted to continue in its premises at 5506 Lake Park, in the heart of the Hyde Park "A" project area.

---

1 Chicago Land Clearance Commission letter to Messrs. Stewart Tauber and Eli Kaplan of February 14, 1955.

The Lincoln-Mercury business successfully relocated itself at 6035 S. Cottage Grove Avenue, in neighboring Woodlawn. At this writing the owners face displacement a second time due to the execution of the new urban renewal project in Woodlawn. Again, the redevelopment proposal for the 60th Street-Cottage Grove Avenue project will not permit automobile dealers.

The two other new car dealerships in Hyde Park did not survive. One of them, Ritz-Central Ford, had recently installed $50,000 worth of new fixtures and could not afford to relocate.

In the same vein, a concentration of repair shops and garages located along Harper Avenue between 55th and 57th Streets was entirely removed by Hyde Park "A" and replaced by Webb and Knapp's townhouses. Altogether, the 1956 RERC study reported 45 automobile-related businesses in Hyde Park-Kenwood, including new and used car dealers, repair shops, gas stations, and private parking facilities.[1] Today such businesses number eight.[2]

Another striking example of the curtailment of a particular type of business through the operation of licensing restrictions and redevelopment criteria is the reduction of the tavern population of Hyde Park-Kenwood. Of twenty-three taverns formerly located on eastern 55th Street, only the students' tavern ("Jimmy's") survives, enjoying a monopoly as the only tavern between 53rd Street and the Midway.

The policy which regards automobile facilities, taverns, and miscellaneous heavy services as uses incompatible with the residential character of Hyde Park-Kenwood is perhaps comprehensible in view of the proliferation of such uses before urban renewal. The wisdom of that policy is not questioned. Rather, it bears pointing out that numerous owners of displaced automobile facilities, taverns, and other businesses were prevented from relocation by factors unrelated to their economic sound-

---

1 RERC Report, *op. cit.*, p. 36.
2 Hyde Park Chevrolet, 5506 S. Lake Park Avenue
  Foreign Car Hospital and Clinic, 5424 S. Kimbark Avenue
  Hyde Park Car Wash and Mobil Station, 1330 E. 53rd Street
  Sam Bell Shell Station, 5200 S. Lake Park (next to Harper Court)
  Bulk Petroleum, 5701 S. Cottage Grove Avenue
  Moore's Standard Station, 5601 S. Cottage Grove Avenue
  Chicago Beach Service Station, 5042 S. Cornell Avenue
  Lakeside Garage, 5140 S. Lake Park Avenue

ness. Stated more generally, a re-use plan that has no provision for low-rent "ribbon" business premises immediately denies location opportunities in a community to the service trades and all space-consuming or other retail uses which have no need to relocate in shopping centers and which, in any case, cannot afford centers' rents. In the long-run, too, their exclusion may turn out to be inconsistent with the needs of neighborhood residents, as well as residents of nearby areas served by shopping facilities in the neighborhood.[1]

Need for Broader Commercial Redevelopment Concepts

There is evidently need for a broader concept of commercial redevelopment, in keeping with the entire range of community retail and service needs. Not all low-rent business ribbons necessarily need clearance; single-standing retail stores with residential communities are not always detriments. Careful selection and retention of some of both could do much to provide alternative locations that retain goodwill and ensure availability of space for new business enterprises.

For the most significant impact of renewal upon business revealed in Chapter 3 was not displacement and liquidation: it was removal of store buildings that normally house new entrants and the drastic reduction of the entry-rate of new merchants into the community. This was confirmed by interviews with businessmen, who repeatedly complained that too many buildings had been torn down (Chapter 4). In part clearance furthered on-going trends, but it also removed opportunity for new enterprises and initiative. Figure 7.1 shows the resulting commercial pattern of Hyde Park-Kenwood in 1967.

The redevelopment concept that recognizes only neighborhood and community shopping centers—and where the community is a center of more specialized department store and specialty trade, centers of regional level—automatically denies relocation opportunities to the service trades, the large single-standing space-consuming stores, to wholesalers and light man-

---

1 One of the consistent complaints of the residents of Hyde Park-Kenwood today is of the absence of many kinds of retail and service uses in the neighborhood and the shortage of others.

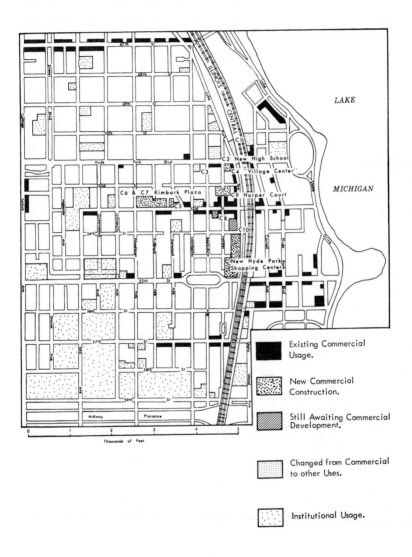

Figure 7.1
COMMERCIAL PATTERN OF HYDE PARK-KENWOOD IN 1967.

ufacturers. That a relatively limited concept of commercial redevelopment should have characterized much urban renewal is perhaps understandable, given the housing orientation of the program and the ready attribution to business ribbons of the causes of many kinds of residential and community blight.[1] But it is now time to generalize the concept, by recognizing the parallel need for neighborhood, community and regional "service districts." Provided they have good highway accessibility they can, otherwise, be peripheral and may indeed be of real value in providing sensible re-use of areas where residential or other forms of redevelopment are most difficult.

It is little wonder then that Hyde Park-Kenwood's chief planner, Jack Meltzer, argues that two principles must be adhered to strictly if small merchants are to have adequate protection:

1) Small businesses must be evaluated on bases other than simply the structural soundness of their premises—for example, the best interests of the community and the special needs of the merchants; and

2) Staging of demolition and relocation must be conducted in accordance with the pre-determined plan, despite the penalties of delay and cost which they may entail to the renewal authority.

THE LOCAL PUBLIC AGENCY AND ITS PROCEDURES

The discrepancy between local government practices and goals appears to be the most critical factor in assessing the impact of urban renewal on businesses that are not the most efficient or competitive. Too often to be coincidental, the businessmen interviewed complained of lack of information, peremptory methods, and undue delays. On its part, the local public agency complained about too much work and too few staff, although its representatives insisted that every businessman was treated equally, provided with all the information available and required.

With all of the assistance now provided by elaborate reloca-

---

1 Ironically, the concept combines to reappear. The Chicago *Sun-Times* of Thursday, April 11, 1968 reports in a story on rebuilding plans of retailers hit by the west side riots, that F. Adrian Robson, executive director of the Midwest Community Council urged Thomas Gause, regional director of SBA that: "We are opposed to rebuilding Madison St. in toto as a ribbon shopping development. It's been a symbol of blight. We want to erase this with shopping malls and plazas."

tion staffs such as have been created in Chicago (Chapter 6) one might ask what can now go wrong? Surely, the businessman will now get adequate information and help. But whenever intentions and achievements of the Commercial Relocation Staff differ, so long as there are built-in inequities in the displacement process, problems will emerge. One is reminded of the way relocation staff members attribute failure to file claims to illegal or sub-rosa elements in the business operation that would lead to difficulties with the Internal Revenue Service, or to ignorance on the part of the businessmen. But failure to communicate also stems from the businessmen themselves. Many of our interviewers were repulsed and some were berated by respondents, and one can understand the feeling: "Get out of my shop. Three times in my life I have been interviewed by people from The University of Chicago, and three times I have been moved." Wherever information is provided or received imperfectly or selectively—wherever communications break down—the relocation process runs into difficulties. The most apparent difficulties occur among the oldest, least-educated, ethnic businessmen to whom administrative forms and procedures are threats and mysteries. These people are more likely to be given a "standard bureaucratic treatment" by public officials who have already decided that they are destined to liquidate in any case—too often, a self-fulfilling prophecy.

LOSS OF PATRONAGE AND GOODWILL

Whether among displaced merchants or those who were not forced to relocate, liquidatees or survivors, whether now in Hyde Park or elsewhere, whether in one of the new business centers or not, a substantial undercurrent of disaffection with urban renewal remains. The source of some of it is clear—when once in business and forced to liquidate by dislocation, a businessman cannot be expected to view the urban renewal process in a kindly fashion, even if compensated. But the fundamental reason cited by all is loss of patronage and goodwill.

Most businesses suffered substantial losses of income simply because residential areas around them were cleared and then remained vacant for several years; renewal removed their established market and its attendant goodwill. Those relocating had even more of the ties to their markets cut.

This fact has, to be sure, already been partially recognized in the Small Business Displacement Payment and the Internal Revenue Service has already interpreted the grant as a payment for lost profits. An extension of the idea is already part of the Eminent Domain Code of 1964 of the State of Pennsylvania, and this is not restricted to "small" businesses (see Chapter 5 above). However, experience in Pennsylvania suggests that few businesses can qualify for reimbursement under the code as presently written.

Undoubtedly, availability of such provisions at the time of displacement in Hyde Park-Kenwood would have diminished the businessmen's disaffection today. But those not displaced would still have been forced to bear the losses caused by clearance and some would still have gone bankrupt as a result. Documentation and reimbursement of such losses would present many problems, but an accompaniment of socially responsible public intervention must always be the recognition of the areas of indirect as well as direct impact, and adequate compensation for the social costs that are imposed.

Recommendations

. . . improved claim processing
. . . income losses require compensation
. . . new commercial redevelopment
  guidelines

CHAPTER EIGHT

Towards Greater Justice In Compensation

The continuing problem is that of compensating businessmen adequately for the losses they incur as a direct result of renewal activity—of loss of patronage among community businesses not displaced, of both loss of patronage and expenses of relocating on the part of displacees who wish to continue in business, and loss of income among displacees who decide to discontinue their businesses.

In most cases today, there is adequate moving expense provision, although more attention has to be given to the actual replacement cost of irremovable fixtures, and to such issues as the timing of displacement. The Small Business Displacement Payment may adequately cover losses for the smallest displacees. But businesses not dislocated and the larger displacees are still not adequately compensated, if at all, for losses of patronage which they would have enjoyed in the absence of renewal clearance and for income losses during periods out of business. And for all displacees, the informational and emotional barriers are so great that there is no adequate assurance that they will be aware of all the claims they can make, and when, as well as other assistance available.

Claim processing can be speeded up. Although now required, payments of claims still could be made more promptly, and in particular, if payments are due they could be made when they are needed most—before and during relocation rather than some time thereafter.[1]

But more significantly, the principle established *de facto* in the Small Business Displacement Payment of reimbursement for losses of patronage needs to be extended to all displacees, and

---

1 Eric Mayer comes to similar conclusions in his study of The Lindsay Park Urban Renewal Area in New York City, *op. cit.*

to all businesses located in a "project impact area" but not displaced that can demonstrate declines in income due to clearance of markets. To be sure, there are obvious difficulties in defining a "project impact area," in developing an equitable compensation schedule and a proper measurement procedure for income losses, and in setting up adequate administrative procedures and safeguards. But these are researchable questions to which precise answers can be given.

The extension of reimbursements is essential because burdens of displacement fall unequally on different kinds of businesses and upon individuals within a given line of business. Certain types, such as funeral parlors, veterinarians, or machine shops, may be totally banned from a neighborhood as incompatible uses, despite the fact that they have long been operating there. Urban renewal is likely to be accompanied by changes in zoning classifications, against which a displacee has no cause for complaint. He must relocate elsewhere, if at all, despite the almost certain loss of trade reputation and goodwill, and the frequent additional necessity of moving his home as well.

Within a given line of business, even if not banned from the community, it is tautological that the stronger businesses are inherently better equipped to look after themselves. Kimbark Plaza is the perfect example where the most solvent members of the 55th Street business community banded together to build their own center. Small businesses that lack the resources to build their own premises, who cannot afford to enter a standard shopping center, and who are not exotic enough for a Harper Court must find cheap space in existing commercial buildings. In Hyde Park the supply of such space was drastically reduced by elimination of the "commercial rectangle." It was the community's alarm at the consequent loss of so many small but convenient shops and services that led to development of Harper Court to house the arts and crafts. However, that center was no substitute for an open market in standard rentable commercial space for small businesses of other kinds.

And even given an adequate compensation schedule, it is essential to institute a procedure for anticipating the demand for alternative premises that should be available at the time of displacement. The promise to provide relocation space in a center not yet built is useless to the displaced merchant: in order to survive he must move directly with a minimum disruption of trade. This means that the space requirements of those site occupants desiring to relocate must be included in the original urban renewal plan, or in the detailed planning of the commercial relocation staff if relocation is outside the project area.

Moreover, once the plan goes into execution, for those merchants who actually move into the quarters set aside by the published plan, it is essential that the renewal authorities adhere to that plan. Far too often, Hyde Park businesses were forced to make a second or even a third move because the building to which they moved was later acquired under a subsequent plan or amendment. The agency must designate *at the outset* which buildings will be safe, at least for period of ten years or so, and thereafter be subject to injunction issued by a court of equity against changing its plan to the detriment of anyone who relied on its original program. If this designation proves impractical for unforeseen reasons, it is doubly necessary to ensure that adequate compensation for displacement and help in further relocation be provided.

Staging of acquisition, relocation, and demolition was not successfully followed in Hyde Park-Kenwood. The inclusion of staging in the plan merely raised undue expectations, encouraged complacency, and obscured the need to secure "off-site" relocation space. Staging therefore is not to be recommended as a relocation technique unless the agency honors the expectations raised thereby, and accepts the penalties of time and cost implied.

In Hyde Park-Kenwood, too, in part because the commercial rectangle was perceived as the source of creeping blight, and in part because conventional planning doctrine so prescribed, commercial re-use in the community was conceived entirely in terms of shopping plazas. Careful prior thinking about a community's total array of retail and service needs after renewal would perhaps suggest broader commercial redevelopment concepts that would be less likely to introduce inequities between different lines of business. Here, there is an opportunity for HUD to develop a creative set of standards and policy guidelines for commercial redevelopment sensitive to the needs of the redeveloped community.

Above all, a community contemplating urban renewal should consider the welfare and just compensation of displaced merchants to be just as important as the relocation of families and individual residents. Continuing attempts to further improve consultation and cooperation between planners and site occupants will not only facilitate relocation with the least possible hardship, but will also ensure the availability of convenience goods and services in the renewed area and bring about support and respect of the Local Public Agency by the business community.

The Renewal Process in Chicago, 1968

The renewal process that involves business displacements is an elaborate one, and many of the problems that emerge for business displacees can be related to its very complexity. As of January 1, 1966, Chicago's Department of Urban Renewal[1] identified the following procedures in carrying through urban renewal projects:

A. *Steps in Proceeding with Slum and Blighted Area Projects*
(some can be taken concurrently)

1. Designation
   a. Authorization by the Department of Urban Renewal (DUR) for staff to study area.
   b. Survey of Structural Condition and Population.
   c. Designation by DUR of the area as a slum and blighted redevelopment project as defined in the State Statute.
   d. Local Approvals.
      1) Chicago Plan Commission (Report by Department of Development and Planning)
      2) City Council—Public Hearing by the City Council Committee on Planning and Housing

2. Authorization by the federal Department of Housing and Urban Development (HUD) for DUR to proceed with survey and planning activities.

3. Redevelopment Plan.
   a. Analysis of community and preparation of plan—in cooperation with:
   Department of Development and Planning, Board of Education, Park District, Department of Streets and Sanitation and other city Departments.

4. Part I of the Application for Loan and Grant Contract to the HUD.
   a. DUR resolution authorizing the filing of application.
   b. Application submittal to HUD.
   c. Approval by HUD.

5. Redevelopment Plan and Part II of Application for Loan and Grant Contract.
   a. Local approvals.
      1) DUR approves plan
      2) Chicago Plan Commission (report by Department of Development and Planning)
      3) City Council approval of the plan and authorization for

---

1 The outline was provided by DUR staff.

DUR to apply for a loan and grant contract, after hearing
by the Committee on Planning and Housing
b. Other
1) Application submitted to HUD
2) Approval by HUD and offer received from HUD for loan
and grant
3) Acceptance of offer by DUR resolution and City Council
4) Supporting acceptance papers submitted to HUD
6. Project Execution
a. Land Acquisition
b. Relocation and Management
c. Demolition
d. Land Disposition
1) Land Disposition Plan—approved by DUR, City Council
and Council Committees on Planning and Housing and
HUD
2) Land Sale
a. Offer for sale
b. Evaluate offers
c. Award
d. Approvals of sale
1) DUR
2) City Council and Council Committee on Planning
and Housing
3) HUD
e. Improvement
1) Construction by Redevelopers.
2) Construction in public right-of-ways and other public improvements by DUR and other public agencies.
3) Field check by DUR staff to assure completion in accord
with approved plans and completion certificate given to
developer.
B. *Steps in Proceeding with*
Conservation Projects
(some can be taken concurrently)
1. The Department of Urban Renewal (DUR) authorizes staff study.
2. Study determines area eligibility under State Statute requirements
report submitted to DUR Board members.
3. Authorization by the federal Department of Housing and Urban
Development (in the following outline referred to as HUD) for
DUR to proceed with survey and planning activities:
a. Approval of the application by DUR
b. City Council ordinance authorizing submittal
c. Transmittal to HUD
4. DUR designates the study area as a conservation area.
5. The Mayor appoints members of the Conservation Community
Council upon nomination by DUR.
6. Survey and Planning
a. Survey and analysis of conditions:

    1) Structures
    2) Population
    3) Housing Market
    4) Community Facilities
    5) Circulation
  b. Urban Renewal Plan analysis of community and preparation of Plan in cooperation with Department of Development and Planning, Board of Education, Park District, Department of Street and Sanitation and other City Departments, Community Conservation Council (CCC) and Community Groups.

7. Part I of the Application for Loan and Grant contract to HUD.
  a. CCC resolution authorizing filing of application
  b. DUR resolution authorizing filing of application
  c. Application to HUD
  d. Approval by HUD

8. Urban Renewal Plan and Part II of application for Loan and Grant contract.
  a. Local approvals:
    1) Community Conservation Council
    2) DUR approves Plan and authorizes submittal of application for loan and grant
    3) Chicago Plan Commission (Report by Department of Development and Planning)
    4) City Council approval of the plan and authorization for DUR to apply for a loan and grant contract after public hearing by City Council Committee on Planning and Housing.
  b. Other:
    1) After approval by City Council, DUR certifies the Urban Renewal Plan as the plan for the designation conservation area
    2) Application to HUD
    3) Approval by HUD and offer received from HUD for loan and grant
    4) Acceptance of offer by DUR Resolution
    5) City Council ordinance authorizing DUR to enter into loan and grant contract
    6) Supporting acceptance papers to HUD

9. Project Execution:
  a. Community Organization Assistance
  b. Rehabilitation Assistance
    1) Structural standards and design
    2) Financial
  c. Clearance areas
    1) Land acquisition
    2) Relocation and management
    3) Demolition
    4) Land Disposition
  d. Land Disposition Plan approved by DUR, City Council and

Council Committee on Planning and Housing, and HUD.
- e. Land sale
  - 1) Offer for sale
  - 2) Evaluate offers
  - 3) Award
  - 4) Approvals
    - a. DUR
    - b. City Council and Council Committee on Planning and Housing
    - c. HUD
- f. Improvement
  - 1) Construction by redevelopers
  - 2) Construction in Public right-of-ways and other public improvements by DUR and other Public Agencies
  - 3) Field check by DUR staff to assure completion in accord with approved plans and completion certificate given to developer

APPENDIX B

Questionnaire and Related Data

Records kept by the Chicago Department of Urban Renewal and personal interviews with businessmen provided the information on small business used in Chapter 4 of this study. This information originally appeared in several forms—numerical values, positive and negative responses, verbal descriptions, and personal opinions. The annotated list below describes how the data were categorized and coded into the 262 variables which were analyzed. Two or more possible responses were assigned to each variable. The following coding symbols are alternative answers to all variables:

X = question not applicable to respondent or to his business

D = respondent answered that he "did not know" when a question was posed

blank = no response

Other coding symbols which are not self-explanatory will be tabulated individually as they occur in the list below. The choice between negative or positive responses is indicated by the symbols 0-1.

Variable Number	Description of Variable	Possible Responses
1	Type of Business	1-42

All businesses were classified according to the following 42 types

1	groceries
2	other food
3	drugs
4	eating places
5	drinking places
6	general merchandise
7	apparel, etc.
8	furniture, etc.
9	beauty
10	barber
11	laundry, dry cleaning
12	physicians
13	dentists
14	real estate
15	insurance
16	other retail
17	other personal services
18	other professional services

    19   other finance
    20   entertainment, etc.
    21   motor vehicles
    22   auto accessories
    23   auto repair
    24   radio-TV repair
    25   business services
    26   other repair services
    27   printing, etc.
    28   building materials, hardware
    29   veterinary
    30   utilities
    31   transport
    32   education services
    33   contract constructs
    34   miscellaneous services
    35   wholesalers
    36   manufacturing
    37   mining offices
    38   residential uses (hotels, etc.)
    39   Business NEC
    40   gift shop
    41   artists, artisans, etc.
    42   liquor stores

2	Age of businessman	no. of yrs.
3	Years at location	no. of yrs.
4	Rent	no. of $ in 10's

Variables 5 through 31 correspond to information provided on DUR forms, for each business displaced by the Local Public Agency.

5	Official contact (with urban renewal officials)	0-1
6	Acquisition date—date at which business premises were acquired by Department of Urban Renewal	no. of months after Jan. 1955
7	Rent reduction from DUR after acquisition of premises	0-1
8	Date rent reduction received	no. of months after Jan. 1955
9	Loss of business—rent reduction granted for a documented loss of business	0-1
10	Claim filed with the DUR for expenses	0-1
11	Claim filed for moving expenses	0-1
12	Claim filed for storage expenses	0-1
13	Claim filed for property loss	0-1
14	Other reimbursements received	0-1
15	Delinquent rent owed by respondent to DUR	0-1
16	Temporary move	0-1
17	Date of the temporary move	no. of months after Jan. 1955

18	Temporary move to Hyde Park	0-1
19	Permanent move	0-1
20	Date of move	no. of months
21	Move to Hyde Park	0-1
22	Liquidated	0-1
23	Date of liquidation	no. of months after Jan. 1955
24	Liquidation due to financial problems	0-1
25	Liquidation due to health problems	0-1
26	Liquidation due to loss of license	0-1
27	Liquidation due to retirement	0-1
28	Liquidation due to disaster	0-1
29	Liquidation due to lack of suitable location	0-1
30	Lag between acquisition and liquidation	no. of months
31	Lag between acquisition and move	no. of months

The remaining variables correspond to questions asked during personal interviews with businessmen. In the list below, questions and variables will be juxtaposed in order to show how translation from one form to another was accomplished.

The first section of the interview concerned the structure and operation of the respondent's business. Wherever applicable the blanks following each question provide space for two separate answers, one on the right and one on the left. The questionnaire sought to bring out differences between pre- and post-urban renewal conditions. The space on the left was for information on the present situation, and that on the right was for the past situation. Where "before" and "after" responses were recorded, two sets of cards were punched for the business.

Could you tell me all the locations of your business since 1953? And the reason why you moved?

Dates   Place   Reason (by whom moved)

_____
_____
_____
_____
_____

| 32 | Number of locations since 1953 | no. of locations |
| 33 | Number of locations in Hyde Park | no. of locations |

Do you feel that you offer any special goods or services that are unique in the community?

_____

| 34 | Special goods or services | 0-1 |

Do you own this business alone?

_____

35 Owns alone   0-1
    Is this store part of a larger organization?
    Yes _____ No _____   _____
    What is the connection? (Franchise, branch,
    chain) _____   _____
    How large is the organization?
    Citywide? _____
    Statewide? _____
    Nationwide? _____
36 Corporation   0-1
37 Partnership   0-1
38 Part of larger organization   0-1
39 City organization   0-1
    Do you own the store or rent it?

    _____

    (If you own it) How much property tax did
    you pay last year on this property?

    _____

    Do you recall the original purchase price of
    the property?

    _____

40 Owns store   0-1
41 Amount of rent $ in $10's
42 Length of lease   no. of months
    Have you made any capital improvements on
    this building in the last, say, two years?
    (Probe) (What and How much cost?)

    _____

    _____

43 Capital improvements   0-1
    Could you tell me what kinds of maintenance
    services you find necessary? (e.g. repainting,
    anything for the upkeep)

    _____

44 Maintenance necessary   0-1
    What kinds of advertising do you use? (Probe:
    How often and how much?)

    _____

45 Informal advertising   0-1
46 Local advertising   0-1
47 Other advertising   0-1
    Can you tell me which letter on this card
    corresponds to average monthly state sales
    tax payments? (Card will be coded accord-
    ingly)

    _____

48 Sales tax
    A. Under $5.00   A = 1
    B. $5.00 to $15.00   B = 2
    C. $15.00 to $30.00   C = 3
    D. $30.00 to $150.00   D = 4
    E. $150.00 to $300.00   E = 5
    F. Over $300.00   F = 6

49 Floor space   1, 2, 3
    1 (small) = 200 sq. ft.
    2 (medium) = 800 sq. ft.
    3 (large) = 2000 sq. ft.
    Roughly what proportion of your total floor
    area is used for selling space?

---

50 Selling space   0, . . . 3
    0 = none
    1 = less than ⅓
    2 = ⅓ to ⅔
    3 = ⅔ to all
    What is the total amount of land owned
    and/or rented here?

---

51 Owns or rents land not built up for business   0-1
    How old (approximately) is this building?

---

52 Age of building   no. of yrs.
    How many parking spaces do you provide
    for customers?

---

53 Parking space provided   0-1
    Has the building or store been specially modi-
    fied for your business? Or built for it?
    Yes _____ No _____

54 Building modified   0-1
    Who are your major competitors?

---

55 Numbers of major competitors   No.
    How many workers do you have?
    Yourself _____
    Members of family _____
    Male employees _____ Part time _____
    Female employees_____ Part time _____

56 Number of workers   No.
57 Number of family members employed   No.
    Approximately how many hours a week are
    you open for business?

---

58 Number of hours open   No.
    Would you select the letter on this card which
    corresponds to your annual net taxable in-
    come from this business?

    Which letter corresponds to your average
    annual net taxable income for the three years
    prior to relocation?

    A. Less than $3,000.00   A = 1
    B. $3,000.00 to $5,000.00   B = 2
    C. $5,000.00 to $7,500.00   C = 3
    D. $7,500.00 to $10,000.00   D = 4
    E. Over $10,000.00   E = 5
59 Net income   1, 2 ... 5
60 Previous net income   1, 2 ... 5
    How much of your business is on a credit
    basis?

61 Credit given to customers   0-1
    How much of your business is to charge
    account customers?

62 Charge accounts offered   0-1
    What proportion of your customers are
    "regulars"?

63 Proportion regular customers   1, 2, 3, 4
    0 = none
    1 = few (25)
    2 = some (50)
    3 = most (75)
    4 = all
    About what percentage of your customers
    come from:
    a. The nearest 5 or 10 blocks?_____   a._____
    b. The community? _____   b._____
    c. The south side?_____   c._____
    d. Chicago? _____   d._____
    e. Outside Chicago? _____   e._____
64 All local customers (nearest 5 or 10 blocks)   0-1
65 Mostly local customers   0-1
66 Mostly from the community   0-1
67 Mostly from the south side   0-1
68 Mostly from Chicago   0-1
69 Customers from outside Chicago   0-1
    Does any one group patronize you more
    than other groups? If so, who?

70	Particular group	0-1
71	Particularly university customers	0-1
72	Particularly Jewish customers	0-1
73	Particularly Negro customers	0-1

Roughly what proportion of your business results from customers coming to your shop?

| 74 | Proportion of customers visiting premises | 0, 1, 2, 3, 4 |

0 = none
1 = few
2 = some
3 = most
4 = all

| 75 | Proportion of customers coming by car | 0, 1, 2, 3, 4 |

0 = none
1 = few
2 = some
3 = most
4 = all

| 76 | Proportion coming by foot | 0, 1, 2, 3, 4 |
| 77 | Proportion coming by public transportation | 0, 1, 2, 3, 4 |

Do you take orders by telephone?
Yes _____ No _____   _____
By mail? Yes _____ No _____   _____

| 78 | Telephone orders | 0-1 |
| 79 | Mail orders | 0-1 |

Do you provide delivery service?
Yes _____ No _____   _____

| 80 | Delivery service | 0-1 |

What proportion of your sales or services went directly to other businesses in the neighborhood? What kind of businesses?

_____   _____

| 81 | Sells to other businesses | 0-1 |

Could you tell me which letter on this card corresponds to your average monthly gross sales? (Code card)

A. Under $1,000.00	A = 1
B. $1,000.00 to $2,500.00	B = 2
C. $2,500.00 to $5,000.00	C = 3
D. $5,000.00 to $10,000.00	D = 4
E. $10,000.00 to $25,000.00	E = 5
F. $25,000.00 to $50,000.00	F = 6
G. $50,000.00 to $100,000.00	G = 7
H. $100,000.00 and over	

| 82 | Average gross sales | 1, 2 ... 8 |

Do you plan to make any capital improvements in the future? (Expansion, renovation)

83	Future improvements rare Do you expect to change your merchandise or services in any way? (Probe)	0-1
84	Expect to change merchandise Do you expect to enlarge the business?	0-1
85	Expect to enlarge business On the average, how many hours weekly do you spend on matters connected with this business?	0-1
86	Hours spent on business matters What interest do you own in other businesses?	No. of hrs.
87	Has other business interest Do you have another paid job? Yes _____ No _____ How many hours a week do you work at it?	0-1
88	Other job Approximately what proportion of your per- sonal income is derived from your (this) business?	0-1
89	Proportion of income derived from this business 1 = less than ⅓ 2 = ⅓ to ⅔ 3 = over ⅔ 4 = all	1, 2, 3, 4

Section 2 of the questionnaire provided information on the respondent and his business activities. The first set of questions in this section drew a brief profile of the respondent's background.

90	Sex	0 = female 1 = male
91	White	0-1
92	Negro	0-1
93	Oriental	0-1
94	Other race	0-1
95	Age	no. of years
96	No religion	0-1
97	Jewish	0-1
98	Protestant	0-1
99	Roman Catholic	0-1

100	Other religion	0-1
101	Number of dependents	0-1
102	Born in the United States	0-1
103	Date of immigration if not born in U.S.	no. of yrs. after 1860
104	No education	0-1
105	Elementary school education	0-1
106	High school education	0-1
107	Some college education	0-1
108	College degree	0-1
109	Higher degree	0-1

In addition to providing a personal sketch of the businessman, this section sought to clarify his social involvement in the community.

| 110 | No. of years in business | no. of yrs. |

What neighborhood organizations do you belong to?

_____

_____

_____

Do you talk regularly with other businessmen in the neighborhood or in your line of business? (Probe)

_____

Do you use a foreign language in conducting business? If so, what?

_____

Where have you and your family lived since 1953, or, since you first started this business?

Address	Dates	Reason for Move

111	Member of neighborhood organizations	0-1
112	Talks with other businessmen	0-1
113	Uses foreign language in business	0-1
114	Number of residences since 1953	1, . . . 9
115	Number of Hyde Park residences since 1953	1, . . . 9

Section 6 of the interview applied only to former Hyde Park businessmen who were no longer in business.

What is your present address?_____

| 116 | South Side residence | 0-1 |
| 117 | Hyde Park residence | 0-1 |

What is your present occupation?_____

Could you tell me why you went out of
business?

Retirement _____
Reasons of health_____
Offered better opportunity in different busi-
ness_____
Business losing too much money_____
Forced to relocate by public agency (if so,
specify which)_____

118   Business terminated due to retirement   0-1
119   Business terminated due to health   0-1
120   Business terminated due to better opportunity   0-1
121   Business terminated due to business failure   0-1
122   Business terminated due to public acquisition   0-1
      of premises
123   Business terminated due to loss of license   0-1
124   Business terminated due to family reasons   0-1
125   Business terminated due to disaster   0-1
126   Business terminated due to expiration of lease   0-1
127   Business terminated due to financial prob-   0-1
      lems
      Could you tell me how your Hyde Park busi-
      ness terminated?

Thru liquidation _____
Sale of business_____ to whom?_____
Was the sale profitable? Yes____ No____

Bankruptcy_____
128   Business terminated through liquidation   0-1
129   Business sold   0-1
130   Business sold at profit   0-1
131   Business terminated through bankruptcy   0-1
132   Business only temporarily discontinued   0-1
      When you went out of business, did you have
      any other sources of income? (Probe)

Did you hold any other jobs?

---

133   Other income   0-1
134   Other job   0-1
      Generally speaking, has your personal in-
      come increased, decreased or stayed the same
      since going out of business?

135	Change in income	0-1
136	Income increased	0-1
137	Income decreased	0-1

Do you prefer to no longer be in business?
(Probe)_____

138	Prefers not to be in business	0-1
139	Now in another business	0-1

All relocatees were asked to respond to the question in Section 4. This section explored the logistics of relocation. On instances where a business relocated more than once, the respondent was asked to distinguish between the experiences connected with each move. On the final coding, a complete set of variables was prepared for each separate move.

140 Moved to Hyde Park   0-1
    Approximately how long before you moved
    did you begin looking for a new location?
    _____

141 Time spent looking for site   no. of months
    How many possible sites did you investigate?
    _____

142	Looked at sites	0-1
143	Looked at few sites	0-1
144	Several sites investigated	0-1

    What kinds of considerations did you use to
    evaluate the sites?
    _____
    _____

145	Preferred to stay in Hyde Park	0-1
146	Required specific location	0-1

    Were you denied any available sites? Why?
    _____
    _____

147 Site denied   0-1
    Can you tell me how long a period there was
    between closing your old business and open-
    ing at the new location?
    _____

148 Time lag between closing at old location and
    opening at new location   no. of months
149 Both sites operating at same time   0-1
    Can you estimate the total expenses of
    making this move?

150	Cost of move	$ in $100's
151	Extra expenses of relocation	$ in $100's

    How did you finance the move?
    _____

152	Small Business Administration loan	0-1
153	Savings used	0-1
154	Urban renewal financing	0-1
155	Private loan	0-1
156	Loan from friend or relative	0-1
157	University loan	0-1

After moving, how long did it take for the volume of business to reach what it had been at the old location?

158	Lag in business volume	0-1
159	Old volume reached	0-1

Of your former customers, did most _____ few_____ some_____ or none_____ patronize you?

160	Retained former customers	0 = none
		1 = few
		2 = some
		3 = most

Were your new customers of a different type than your customers in the old location? (Probe)

161	New customers same type	0-1

Did you make any changes in merchandise or services when you relocated?

162	Change in merchandise or services	0-1

What advertising did you use to publicize your new location? (Probe)

163	Used formal advertising	0-1
164	Used local advertising	0-1
165	Used other advertising	0-1

Have you had any business problems since you relocated?

166	Business problems since relocation	0-1
167	Site problems	0-1
168	Customer problems	0-1
169	Crime problems	0-1
170	Financial problems	0-1
171	Rental problems	0-1

Please indicate your general feelings of satisfaction with these aspects of your new location, as compared with your old (pre-urban renewal) location.

	Very Satisfactory	Satisfactory	Unsatis.	Not Applicable
Character of neighborhood				
Condition of building				
Design or appearance of building				
Cost of doing business				
Location in neighborhood				
Adequacy of: selling floor space				
storage space				
office space				
display window space				
parking space				
loading, shipping, handling facilities				
public services (police, fire, etc.)				
Convenience to: old customers				
new customers				
public transportation				
truck routes				
your home residence				
residences of your employees				

172	Character of neighborhood	1 = Satisfactory
		0 = Unsatisfactory
		X = Not applicable
173	Building condition	1-0-X
174	Building design	1-0-X
175	Cost of doing business	1-0-X
176	Location	1-0-X
177	Floor space	1-0-X
178	Storage	1-0-X
179	Office space	1-0-X
180	Display space	1-0-X
181	Parking	1-0-X
182	Loading facilities	1-0-X
183	Public services	1-0-X
184	Convenience to old customers	1-0-X
185	Convenience to new customers	1-0-X
186	Public transportation	1-0-X
187	Truck routes	1-0-X
188	Convenience to home residence	1-0-X

189   Convenience to home residences of employees   1-0-X
When and how did you first learn of urban
renewal plans for your area? (Probe)

_____

190   First heard of urban renewal   no. of yrs. after 1950
191   Heard rumors   0-1
192   Read plans in newspaper   0-1
193   Other information source   0-1
Do you recall when you received an official
notice that you would have to move out?
(Probe for approx. date)

_____

194   Received a notice to move   0-1
195   Date notice received   no. of months
after Jan. 1955

When did you actually move out?

_____

196   Date moved   no. of months
after Jan. 1955
197   Lag between date of notice and date of move   no. of months
Were you planning to move, sell or end your
business anyway?

_____

198   Planned to move or liquidate   0-1
Did any public officials visit your business
premises in connection with urban renewal?
Yes _____   No _____
From what agency?
Were they helpful to you? How?

_____

199   Visited by official   0-1
200   Visit helpful   0-1
Did you attend any organized meetings concerning relocation? Yes_____ No_____
Which meetings?

_____

Were they helpful? (How)

_____

201   Attended urban renewal meetings   0-1
202   Meetings helpful   0-1
Did you apply for assistance from the Small
Business Administration? Yes_____ No_____
What assistance did they give you?

_____

Did you have any problems in dealing with SBA? (Probe)

_____

Did you apply for a bank loan or other private financial assistance? Yes_____ No_____
What kind of assistance did you receive? (Probe)

203	Applied for Small Business Admin. assistance	0-1
204	SBA assistance received	0-1
205	Applied for bank loan	0-1
206	Bank loan received	0-1

Did you try to relocate as a group with other businessmen? Yes_____ No_____
What was the group?

_____

What were the results?

_____

207	Attempted group relocation	0-1
208	Group relocation successful	0-1

How did you go about looking for a new site? (Probe)

_____

209	Agent helped find site	0-1
210	Looked by self for site	0-1
211	Urban Renewal agency helped find site	0-1
212	Friends helped find site	0-1
213	Advertised for new site	0-1
214	Site found by other means	0-1

Do you feel you had sufficient time to carry out an orderly relocation? Yes_____ No_____
If not, in what way were you rushed?

_____

215	Sufficient time for relocation	0-1

Did you file a claim for:
Moving expenses? _____ How long after you made the claim were you compensated

_____

Losses on sale or abandonment of property? How long after you made the claim were you compensated? _____

_____

Other items? How long after you made the claim were you compensated?_____

216	Moving expenses claim filed	0-1
217	Moving expenses compensation received	no. of $ in $10's
218	Date compensation received	no. of months after application
219	Property loss claim filed	0-1
220	Property loss compensation received	no. of $ in $10's
221	Date property compensation received	no. of months after application

Did you receive a rent reduction for documented loss of business? _____
How much?_____ For how long?_____

222	Rent reduction	0-1
223	Amount of rent reduction	no. of $
224	Rent reduction period	no. of months

Do you think you were treated fairly as to the claim?_____

225	Fairly treated	0-1

Did you have any other losses or expenses for which you were *not* compensated?

_____

226	Not fully compensated	0-1

Section 6 allowed the respondent to express his personal opinions on urban renewal as it affected him, his family, his business, and his community.

Do you think your business is better off now than it would have been if there had been no urban renewal in Hyde Park?

_____

227	Business better off now	0-1

Do you approve of the methods in which Urban Renewal has been carried out in Hyde Park? Yes_____ No_____ (Probe)

_____

228	Approve of methods	0-1

Reasons for disapproval (if 228 = 0)

229	Inadequate compensation	0-1
230	Not enough time for relocation	0-1
231	Poor administration	0-1
232	Poor timing	0-1
233	Too many buildings torn down	0-1
234	Uncertain program	0-1
235	No relocation help	0-1

What do you see as the main problems of a businessman affected by Urban Renewal?

(e.g. loss of sales, loss of customer goodwill, cost of moving business, etc.) (Probe)

_____

_____

236	Moving costs	0-1
237	Customers lost	0-1
238	Difficulty in finding new location	0-1
239	Loss of business	0-1
240	Loss of livelihood	0-1
241	Expense of relocating or remodeling	0-1
242	Difficulty of moving back into the community	0-1
243	Rents increase	0-1

What kinds of assistance or compensation beyond what is now provided ought to be supplied to the small business which gets displaced by Urban Renewal? (Probe)

_____

244	No opinion	0-1
245	Advice and assistance in readapting	0-1
246	Too much paperwork	0-1
247	More compensation	0-1
248	More time for relocation	0-1
249	Financial help to maintain income	0-1
250	Compensation for loss of customer goodwill	0-1
251	Help to retain old customers	0-1
252	Present compensation satisfactory	0-1

Should a renewal agency provide a new location for every business it relocates? Yes_____ No_____. If yes, what kind of space should be provided?
New shopping center _____
Older space within the community _____
Space of a similar kind in another community_____
Other (Specify) _____

253	New location should be provided	0-1
254	Shopping center	0-1
255	Older space within the community	0-1
256	Similar space in another community	0-1
257	Other space	0-1

Variables 258 to 261 were established in order to distinguish between the major categories of businesses.

258	Urban renewal displacees	0-1
259	Business now in Hyde Park	0-1
260	Business formerly but no longer in Hyde Park	0-1
261	Whether or not before-after responses were made, for comparative purposes	0-1

APPENDIX C

A Recent Case History

During the preparation of this study, it was the privilege of the authors to become personally acquainted with several of the Hyde Park-Kenwood merchants who have undergone urban renewal displacement. In the case of one such businessman who was displaced while the study was going on, it was possible for one author to share in the process vicariously and occasionally even to participate in the events. The following is a distillation of this particular case history, obtained directly from the participants involved and from their correspondence. While this example hopefully is not typical, in that it illustrates nearly every pitfall, disappointment, and frustration that could imaginably enter the dislocation process, it nevertheless demonstrates what a small businessman determined to relocate may face, even under the present statutory compensation scheme and with a sympathetic, if overworked relocation staff.

The business in question is engaged in the selling of used books and the framing of pictures, both of which lines are appropriate and amenable to a university community. Mr. X started in the book business in 1926 and since then has occupied eight different premises in the Hyde Park-Kenwood neighborhood, including for nine years a space in the legendary Art Colony.

In 1959 when the Hyde Park-Kenwood Urban Renewal Plan was passed into law, scheduling his 55th Street store for demolition, Mr. X moved immediately, without applying for any of the relocation assistance available, to space on Hyde Park Boulevard which was at that time designated to remain untouched under the Urban Renewal Plan.

The "Final Plan" enacted in 1958 has been subsequently changed by amendment several times, however. In 1967, Amendment Five to the Urban Renewal Plan of 1958 changed the use of the Hyde Park Boulevard site from "commercial" to "school" and called for acquisition and demolition of the structures to make room for a new Hyde Park High School. Tenants of the buildings affected included, in addition to the book store, a tropical restaurant (now in East Hyde Park), a leather crafts shop (now in Harper Court), a small theater group (now looking for a home), and several others.

The property was duly acquired and on September 1, 1967 the book and framing business became a tenant of the City. The store rental was not changed. On September 8 Mr. X received from the City a "letter of eligibility" for the $2500 Small Business Displacement Payment (for which Mr. X had applied after first learning of its existence from an earlier draft of this study!). Under HUD regulations, however, that sum was payable only after actual vacating of the premises.

Community pressure was urging prompt action in starting the new school; the City on October 27 sent notices to each site occupant giving them thirty days in which to vacate. However an official in the Department of Urban Renewal made oral assurances that demolition would await relocation of each tenant. That promise was kept.

About a week after receiving the 30-day notice, Mr. X wrote the managing agents of Harper Court to apply for admission to that center. This was followed by a longer letter two weeks later defining the scope of the business and contending that it would be compatible with the spirit and present composition of the center to admit him.

Assuming that he would qualify for a vacancy in the center, Mr. X filed on November 29 a "Notice of Intent to Vacate," required by urban renewal regulations to be filed between 30 and 90 days before moving, and listed Harper Court as his future location. However, at the December Board meeting of Harper Court his application was rejected, apparently due to the policy of "non-competition" between tenants, there already being a used book store and a picture framer in the Court.

The private market in commercial space, whose drastic reduction by urban renewal Harper Court was intended to alleviate, afforded only one suitable, vacant alternative space, approximately one-third the size and at 150 per cent the rental of the premises on Hyde Park Boulevard. Despite cheaper space being available in South Shore, Mr. X wanted to stay in business in Hyde Park and decided on this premises.

In order to enter a lease, the landlord required two months' rent to be held on deposit and a month's rent in advance, a total of $675. Lacking available cash, Mr. X attempted to obtain a bank loan, offering the City's "letter of eligibility" for the $2500 as collateral. He was refused successively by the local Hyde Park Bank and Trust Co., by his own bank, Harris Trust, and by a north side institution which reputedly had accepted such collateral in the case of another displacee (apparently a special favor for a customer). Out of desperation, he and his wife cashed in an annuity life insurance policy to obtain cash for the lease deposit.

The foregoing efforts consumed the month of January, 1968. By February most of the other tenants had moved out, leaving an inviting situation for vandalism. The *Hyde Park Herald* described the ensuing events as "beyond belief"—part of the building was flooded, equipment was stolen, plumbing and telephones were removed. During the last week on Hyde Park Boulevard, the electrical cables were stolen and the books had to be packed by the light of a kerosene lamp!

Finally on March 15, the move was accomplished and within a week the old building fell under the wrecker's ball.

Mr. X informed the City that the move had been "financially disastrous" and appealed for fast action in making the $2500 Small Business Displacement Payment. The City assured him that payment of the $2500 as well as his moving expenses would be "prompt," in accordance with the law. Mr. X received his check on May 28, 1968.

INDEX